CW01574911

ONE GOOD TURN DESERVES AN ENCORE

My Journey Through 53 Years in Showbusiness

by

Jim Kennedy

First published in 2001 by
Showbiz Publications
P O Box 692A
Surbiton
Surrey
KT5 8DZ

Tel: 020 8399 6080

E-mail: MJ48ALPHA@AOL.com

Copyright © Jim Kennedy 2001

The right of Jim Kennedy to be identified as the author of this work has been asserted by him in accordance with the Copyright, Designs and Patents Act 1988

All rights reserved. No part of this publication may be reproduced, stored in a retrieval system, or transmitted, in any form or by any means, without the prior permission in writing of the author nor be otherwise circulated in any form of binding or cover other than that in which it is published and without a similar condition including this condition being imposed on the subsequent purchaser.

ISBN 0 9540587 0 4

Designed and produced by
The Short Run Book Company Limited
St Stephen's House
Arthur Road
Windsor
Berkshire SL4 1RY

FOREWORD

by

Shane Richie

Who would have thought it, eh? Shane Richie stuck for something to say.... This is doing my head in!!!!!

I have written musicals, game shows, comedy routines and the odd pop tune which will probably pop up at your local petrol station in the bargain bucket for 99p. But can I write a foreword for Jim Kennedy's book....???

As I sit in my office rocking back and forth in my squeaky leather chair, it's there right in front of my eyes. Pinned to the wall, in big, bold, black letters *'Always remember where you've come from for, that way, you'll always know where you're going – Jim Kennedy'*

I firmly believe showbiz is made up from those who **think** they know and those who really know. Thankfully, for myself and countless others, Jim falls into the latter. Whether it's a reassuring handshake, a fatherly hug or merely a wink in your direction, you know that Jim really does know. His knowledge of showbusiness is unparalleled and his understanding of those who work in it for a living is unequalled.

I first met Jim in the early eighties when I first applied for, and was awarded, the famous Pontin bluecoat and, throughout my career, he has been a constant support – both professionally and personally. He is a true gentleman in every sense of the word and, that, my friends – believe me, is a rare commodity in this business.

Jim has that unique quality of making people special in his presence – the unknown act who opens the show, to the 'name' act that tops the bill at the London Palladium – he really does have time for everyone.

So many artistes and musicians today have cause to thank Jim for giving them their first step on the ladder of success, whether as a Bluecoat,, Cabaret performer or musician in a band or group. The list is legendary and many stories of their early beginnings (including mine) are told within the pages of this book.

Like the cliché says: *'Seen it, done it ... read the book!'* Well Jim has seen it, done it and now has written the book. It's a great 'behind the scenes' showbiz read and I'm in it! So need I say more??

Luv Ya' Jim,

Shane

CONTENTS

PROLOGUE

The evening's rush hour was approaching its peak and London's Euston Station reverberated with the bustling intensity of commuters homeward bound. The sounds were of carriage doors being slammed, attentive guards in officious uniforms waving green flags and blowing whistles with pompous glee and last-second travellers stuffing brief cases, overnight bags and finally, themselves into the rear end of trains already on the move. Their day was almost over – as was mine – and I settled into the comparative comfort of my seat in the first class section of the Pullman heading north and home.

It had been a long day spent in fractious negotiations with the Musicians Union to determine the scale of annual increase awards for the great many bands, groups and solo musicians under my control. As Entertainment Executive for the Pontin Holiday Group, I had sat with other representatives from the 'Big Four' – Pontins, Butlins, Haven and Warners – plus Band Leader, Phil Tate, to present our case. Phil, at that time was the Managing Director of Mecca International (the company that provided a great many of the quality bands that played on the Holiday Camp circuit), but was perhaps better known for his many hundreds of television appearances fronting his own orchestra – particularly for the *Miss World* contest which had been a regular annual event. Although a staunch Musicians Union member, Phil always sat on our side of the table and fought for our corner and I wondered often why the Union never considered revoking his membership! On this day, we had reached a very favourable agreement and I looked forward with some relish to informing the Board of the successful outcome.

The train lurched heavily, as if testing that its couplings were linked together before settling into a smooth gathering of pace as it moved into the darkness ahead, leaving the glow of the station lights in its wake. I fumbled in my case for something to read and remembering that I had purchased an *Evening Standard*, unfolded the tabloid and automatically turned to the section devoted to the latest in entertainment gossip.

In my capacity as Head of Entertainment, I was totally responsible for all that came into the category including the selection and booking of cabaret artistes, star performers, bands, groups, discos, sporting personalities, plus much more, but the one area of control that accorded me the greatest thrill and the deepest personal satisfaction was at the very grassroots of our business – the interviewing, auditioning and selecting of the Bluecoat Hosts and Hostesses to represent the company throughout its twenty-four Centres in the UK. A great many of these wonderful kids who apply for the position, graduate from the various Stage Schools in London and beyond, whilst others contact us, simply fired up with the talent and ambition to enter showbusiness, seeing us as the best possible way to progress. I cannot begin to tell you the pride I take in allowing them the opportunity to learn their craft by entering what we call the 'Bluecoat Academy' – a season or more in one of our Centres where we give them help, advice and training, plus practical stage experience, the most important factor of all. Watching them emerge from the raw cocoon of unfilled promise to the spreading of their early wings, their skills polished, their talent honed and their confidence high, is one of the highlights of my profession. The joy I receive from watching now established star names, both on the stage and on television, like Shane Richie, Brian Conley, Roger de Courcey, Amanda Reddington, Stu Francis, Bradley Walsh,

Mick Miller, Jimmy Cricket, Gemma Craven, Helen Chamberlain and others, in knowing they have all graduated through our Bluecoat ranks, is unparalleled.

As I looked through the 'What's on in the West End' column, I reacted with some disbelief, for what I was reading must surely rank as one of the great moments in my professional life. In the cold black and white newspaper print, the titles of five blockbusting musicals leapt out from the pages and burned into my mind – not because of the shows themselves, but for the fact that in each, the top name listed as the star attraction was the name of a former Bluecoat! A name that we had discovered, nurtured and sent on their way with our blessing, for us now to cheer, applaud and congratulate as they achieved the pinnacle of their careers in the West End of London: Brian Conley taking the title roll of *Al Jolson* in the musical *Jolson,* Shane Richie playing the male lead in *Grease,* Alex Bourne as *Buddy Holly* in the smash hit show *Buddy,* Andrew O'Connor staring as *Phineus T Barnum* in the musical *Barnum* and Gemma Craven with her name above the title in *South Pacific*. What an incredible achievement and each a headliner, each a star and each a product of one of the very few avenues left to aspiring performer today. I pondered, with pride, the enormity of our success and wondered how many more of these lovely, dedicated youngsters would follow in their footsteps?

The paper I was so engrossed in fell to the floor and I lay back in my seat and closed my eyes. The train thundered through the evening blackness and my thoughts woandered through my own early days when fate dragged me from my chosen career and decided to push me through the portals of showbusiness, with little to support me, except for an average singing voice, a love of the business and a mountain of ambition. I thought of the struggles, the triumphs and my slow rise to the top. The moments that made me laugh and those that brought tears. I reflected, with humility, the position of power I held within this crazy business that allowed me to mix with the star names, many of them my boyhood heroes, sharing their successes and their failures, negotiating with their agents for fat fees and giving lesser known names, perhaps, the big break of a long summer season and watching some emerge as stars in their own right. There were those who made the big time but equally there were those who didn't. All, however, share the same common denominators – faith in themselves, confidence in their ability, hope for their future and ambition by the barrow-load!

As the jumble of thoughts and memories, both high and low, flashed through my mind, I mused over my life. Most of it was spent within the spotlight of this creation we call showbusiness and was assured that amongst the precious memories that make up my life, there is a great story to be told. One day, yes one day, I am going to write it all down and share the fun, laughter and excitement of my career with anyone who cares to read it. I wonder if I really could? I wonder if I should? I wonder if I will? I wonder... I wonder...!

CHAPTER ONE

In the Beginning

Gluttony, in skilled hands, can be an art form, a science or simply a weakness. In my case, it was all three – being culpably to blame for my entry into the world of showbusiness! I was twelve years of age and still marvelling at the wonders of puberty and increasingly aware that such adolescent awareness required feeding, over and above the normal three meals a day one was allotted out of parental duty and so the battle of the larder began. The enemy, represented by my mother, assiduously hiding away anything that resembled a tit bit – biscuits, cheese, crisps and even tins of condensed milk (Oh, how I loved gorging on tins of condensed milk, armed with nothing more than a large spoon!). The war would last for years and even spread to outside the kitchen. After being sent to the bakers shop at the top of the road for a loaf of bread (called an Edinburgh plain, it stood twelve inches in height with the top rounded and crusted, whilst the rest was pure bread, still hot and doughy, fresh from the oven), I duly arrived back with only the crust left unconsumed. A feat of gastronomic endurance that passed into family folklore and indirectly pointed me in the direction of a showbusiness career. Let me explain further...

One evening, Mum and Dad were invited to an important function, which meant being away from home until the early hours of the morning. Much to their consternation, they discovered that sister Kath would also be away at the same time, thus leaving me at home on my own, with the larder and its contents entirely at my mercy. This was simply asking for trouble and desperate measures were called for. Poor Kath was asked – no told – that I would have to accompany her on her appointment – that of rehearsal and show pianist for an amateur Concert Party called The Vaudrams, run by an equally amateur impresario by the name of Charlie Williamson. Charlie was an avuncular, kindly man who formed the Concert Party to help entertain those in need of cheering up: pensioners, hospital patients and even prisoners in the local jail. Sadly, such was the woeful lack of talent and presentation, the complete opposite prevailed. The name 'Vaudrams' was a combination of the words 'vaudeville' and 'drama' and it was obvious to those poor, long-suffering audiences (especially the prisoners, who were captive), that neither was represented. If there had been a Trades Description Act in those days, we would have been out of business in no time flat! The poor pensioners anticipating an evening of melodic pleasures aged perceptively as the show dragged on, patients recovering in hospital suffered remissions, which resulted in the intensive care unit being full to overflowing within hours of curtain down and the poor malefactors incarcerated for crimes to the State sat there, enraged that *they* had been locked away and not us! Nevertheless, unaware of the company's infamy throughout and beyond the City of Edinburgh, I duly accepted the family demands and walked into the rehearsal room that was to sow a seed, to fan a spark and to eventually take me into the roller-coaster world of professional showbusiness.

Rehearsals were in full swing for The Vaudrams *Show of the Year*, the one week in the calendar that they actually charged admission. The profit for the period would support the company for the rest of the season, thus allowing them to work totally free of charge for all the best causes. There were rumours abounding that some of the more affluent societies paid money into the coffers in order that we should stay away, but that has yet to be proved. In any event, Charlie had this wonderful idea for an opening. The curtain would rise to reveal an empty stage in total darkness. Slowly, as if to represent the rising of the sun and the breaking of dawn, the lights would come up and the music would swell in unison. A haystack would come into view and a tramp, suddenly appearing, would wearily climb to his feet, yawn and trudge off. Brilliant! The problem was, however, that no one was available, or willing, to play the vagrant and the flash of inspiration that had lit Charlie's waking hours for the past few days, seemed doomed. The finger of fate that was to determine the course my life suddenly decided the time had come and Charlie's beady eye fell on me. There was no argument from either of us. Charlie, flushed at making his inspiration a reality, and I, somewhat bemused, totally astounded and I guess rather flattered, accepted the situation. I was in showbusiness!

The show, as usual, was an unmitigated disaster, but because that week the audiences were made up of families and friends of the cast, they clapped and cheered the efforts of those known to them – at least until half way through the first half, when realisation dawned that the show had started off badly and was rapidly going downhill. Euphoric nepotism gradually gave way to a form of communal 'Family at War'. Nevertheless, my appearance which opened the entire proceedings, allowed me the opportunity to bask in applause which saturated my soul and filled me with a longing to repeat the dosage again and again. I was hooked!

Much to my delight, Charlie decided that such was the success of his 'spellbinding' opening to the show, the sequence would remain unchanged for the next year and I was to retain my starring role. Every show night, and to be fair there was quite a few (bearing out the argument that people will put up with anything no matter how bad, so long as it's free), I was filled with excitement at the prospect of appearing in front of a live audience, albeit briefly and I played my part diligently. I experimented, too, in a great effort to expand the character. I wore a false beard, followed by an equally false moustache. I wore shoes with the soles ripped off and socks riddled with holes. What *was* happening though, although I didn't realise it at the time, was the beginning of a learning curve that was to build and build over the next few years into an abstract substance called experience. I watched every movement on stage and studied the way performers performed. I noted their styles and particularly the response from the audience. Much of it was bad, as I have said before, but nonetheless, I absorbed all that I saw and in time was starting to segregate the better bits from the simply abysmal.

One momentous evening, en route to another extravaganza, Charlie whispered in my ear that his partner in comedy (?) had failed to turn up and did I know any of the sketches in which he appeared? Did I indeed? I knew every line of every song, every sketch and every joke in the show and I was promptly drafted in without rehearsal. Mind you, there was never ever a script in Charlie's shows. He would describe to you the part he wanted you to play, making sure that the comedy role was to be his, then follow up with words of directorial genius: "You say this and I'll say the other. You walk downstage and I'll follow. I'll say this, you reply with that and I'll get the big laugh at the end." That was all there was to it – and I made the transition from being part of the scenery to bit part player with aplomb. And so it followed that when any member of the cast took ill, or left the company to seek satirical asylum elsewhere, I was given the part and soon I was in every speaking role there was – except Charlie's!

The joy of reaching my fifteenth birthday was unabated. I left school ready to face the world with a sense of relief and little foreboding. I had never raised any eyebrows during my scholastic career but always did just enough to succeed. At the end of my primary school days, I must have sensed the importance of the exams and lifted my competence level to a higher ratio to gain a bursary which allowed me to attend Trinity Academy, with no fees involved. Once settled at the new school, I sank back into mere oblivion and forged my way to the fourth year, which was to culminate in the Lower Leaving Certificate examinations. Such was my desperation to succeed, I once again climbed to giddy heights and passed (the equivalent of today's O levels). So on a warm May afternoon, I finally wiped the dust of my formal education from my shoes and set about finding a job and at last, earning some money.

I was rescued by an uncle who was Managing Director of A&A Crawford Ltd, the blenders of one of the best loved quality Scotch Whiskys on the market at that time – Crawford's 'Three Star' and 'Five Star'. After discussion with my Father, they decided to take me on board, to work in each department (including the blending process) and end up with a possible Directorship. A glowing prospect for one so young and a great relief to my Mother and Father, who had begun to despair for my future. It was a particular delight to Dad whose knowledge of the product was vast from personal experience and was, indeed, his favourite tipple!

The plan was put into operation and worked well. I had to attend Night School to further my education, but on the evenings we had a Vaudrams show, there was never any contest and showbusiness won hands down. As if I hadn't enough distractions to my work and studies, I was also playing local football and at the age of seventeen, signed for Edinburgh City, then a nursery club to the Heart of Midlothian FC, one of Scotland's premier sides, and one of the great loves of my life. Ambitions to succeed within football dictated that I neither smoked nor drank in an effort to stay fit. I was a little apprehensive when my employers informed me, that to further my experience and knowledge of the industry, I was to be transferred to the sales division, and start the following week as a sales representative. My area was to be the Southwest corner of Scotland, taking in the countryside around the Solway Firth covering towns from Dumfries, Dalbeattie, Newton Stewart and Stranraer. It was a beautiful part of the country and to say I took the trade by storm, was an understatement. Bar managers could not believe the new 'rep' who spent the morning extolling the virtues of Crawford's Whisky to finally confirm an order, but when offered a 'wee dram' of the said brand to celebrate the deal, were met only with a pulled expression of disgust and the words 'Good God, no thanks, never touch the stuff – bloody awful!' Whether being the subject of so many jokes within the trade helped or not, everyone wanted to see this freak of a Scotsman who sold whisky for a living but couldn't stand the taste. Whatever the reason, my order book was always well filled to my Uncle's delight and to my complete and utter astonishment.

Things were now settling down and the routine of my life was unfolding when, somewhat expectedly (but nevertheless, a shock to the system), a letter arrived one morning in a large brown envelope addressed to me and bearing the official stamp on the top left hand corner – *OHMS*. My time for National Service had arrived.

CHAPTER TWO

National Service – The Brylcreem boys

I had to report to an imposing building on the Queensferry Road, Edinburgh, near Daniel Stewarts College, for a briefing and IQ test and was surprised at the simplicity of the questions asked. More difficult, indeed, was the answer required to the somewhat loaded query – 'Which branch of H.M Forces would you like to be considered for?' I desperately wanted to serve my time in the RAF as I did not fancy the other two one bit – but having been pre-warned as to the way the military minds work, I decided on a bit of cunning and played them at their own game and for my first choice carefully wrote...ARMY. The idea of actually wearing a Khaki uniform filled me with loathing: foot-slogging, mud-wading automatons that I figured had little pulling power with the girls – Out! For my second choice I wrote...NAVY. A slight improvement and although I was aware that they owned quite a few ships, my inability to swim (I hold the record of being the only living soul to sink in the Dead Sea!), I felt, would prove disadvantageous. My third choice (actually my *first*, if your still following the plot), was the RAF and I made it clear that this was very definitely the *last* service I would want to serve in! I kept my fingers tightly crossed and three weeks later, received my official posting and to my delight, I realised that my subterfuge had succeeded. I was to report to RAF Padgate for induction to the Royal Air Force on 28th January 1953. I could see myself being kitted out in that sexy shade of blue and fighting off the girls as they swarmed around me. The thought warmed me and softened the anticipation of the drastic change to my life that waited just around the corner, but as the day approached, any feelings of excitement that remained began rapidly to evaporate and be replaced with a growing sense of dread and apprehension.

My day of destiny finally arrived and I stood on the doorstep of 81 March Road, trembling at the thought of what I was about to undergo. I waved goodbye to all and sundry and set out on the ten-minute journey to the bus stop. The realisation that I had finally severed the umbilical cord of my Mother's apron strings struck me like a thunderbolt and I walked slowly up the road with tears flooding (resembling from behind, I am sure, one of the water carts that spray the roads in hot weather to keep the surface cool). Despite my tearful vision, I managed to correctly identify the bus that would take me to the Waverley Railway Station and the train that would transport me over the Border to a land as yet unknown to me (but if my history books were accurate, filled with crazy Sassenachs, sheep stealers, cattle rustlers and strangers that spoke with foreign tongue). For the first time in my life, at the tender age of eighteen, I was in England!

My first sight of Padgate was one of huge aircraft hangars and parade grounds. Everywhere I looked were groups of young men marching, what appeared to be aimlessly and dressed in an assortment of civilian and military apparel. Some were wearing the countenance of extreme bravado, swinging their arms with gusto and defying anyone within eyeshot to speak out of turn. The majority, however, by their sheer body language, sent out the message that they were frightened little boys, torn from their families and asked – no ordered – to become men, to learn to fight for their country and to kill. Their lives would be changed forever.

I was directed to 'Registration' and escorted to a long hut where, entering at one end with empty arms, you exited at the other grasping full military kit which, visually at any rate, transformed you from civilian to a fully fledged member of

HM Fighting Forces. The method of providing you with the clothing and kit required, proved a far throw from the joy of buying a suit of your own choice from the local branch of John Collier. No measuring tape was ever seen or even mentioned. The Godzilla behind the counter simply looked at you for a mere moment, muttered under his breath the size he thought you might be and hurtled the garment at you with some force. On the early part of my journey down the line, it proved a simple task to catch the missile, but as you progressed it became more difficult, (especially in the masochistic way the Air Force have in dealing with raw recruits), as the object thrown became larger and heavier. The size ten military boots saved for last nearly took my head off and could have terminated a promising career before it had even begun.

Staggering under the weight of newly acquired belongings we were finally taken to our quarters – a rounded hut resembling an old 'Anderson' shelter, housing twenty rusting worn beds, with a small wardrobe on one side and a bedside table on the other. On each bed lay a pile of sheets, blankets and pillows and underneath them was a mattress that I swear was filled with straw. The whole room was dominated by a large pot bellied stove conveniently placed in the centre and being January, was unlit. This was to be my home for the next seven days. That evening, like condemned prisoners, we huddled together, commiserating, sympathising and generally getting to know each other, each with his own thoughts, fears, hopes and apprehensions but outwardly trying to convey the confidence that none of us really felt. I was sharing my bedroom with nineteen strangers, all with stories to tell in unfamiliar accents, the tall and the short, the thin and the fat, the loud and the quiet, but all sharing the same fate and similar futures. Throughout it all, the forced laughter and the high pitched voices, betraying their inner nerves. Throughout the cacophony of human presence I felt alone, I felt threatened –

I felt oh so lonely – wishing I was in my warm familiar bedroom back home in Edinburgh where I was safe and loved and welcomed. The tears, never far away began to reform but thankfully, the stresses of the day proved too much and to my relief I fell asleep.

The world about me exploded! A searing electric light blazed into my face and my sleep shattered into wakefulness. My scrambled brain tried to decipher the shouting I could hear. As consciousness slowly penetrated my being, I noted to my horror, the time. It was barely 5.30am. The stove, coaxed into life the evening before, had burned itself out and the windows were patterned with the mosaic design of thick frost, both inside and out. At the end of the dormitory stood the figure of a man in full uniform, boasting the double stripes on his arm, indicating corporal to those qualified to recognise, but to us, the terrified conscripts, he was nothing less than the devil himself. "Feet on the floor, you horrible little men," he screamed and followed this tirade by ordering us to remove our hands from the only part of our bodies that was still giving out warmth.

We struggled into the perpendicular position and were then instructed to dress only in our new trousers, socks, boots and vest. We formed a line outside the hut and clutching our toilet bag and towel, were marched in double file and at double time to the ablutions hut for a wash and shave (for those less endowed it constituted a de-fluffing). The fact that the water was ice cold simply compounded the horror of it all! By now the outside temperature had risen to minus five and we all looked forward to our first full day of National Service with growing panic, trepidation and downright fear.

Breakfast was minimally better. Once again we marched, this time to the mess hall. Swinging our right arm freely, we deposited the left arm behind our backs, whilst grasping the utensils necessary for the forthcoming operation – namely, a mug, knife, fork and spoon. We lined up clutching an empty plate and offered it to the portly red-faced chef who was guarding three large metal, deep-filled trays, each filled with traditional breakfast fare (fried eggs, fried bacon and beans). A selection of each was slapped on to the proffered plate and we retired to the nearest space available to consume the contents, washed down with tea dispensed from a monster urn, which, like the horn of plenty, never needed filling. The beans were stodgy, the bacon fatty and the eggs swam in grease, but it was hot and we wolfed it down as though it was the Last Supper.

Throughout the next few days, we underwent tests both physical and mental and were grilled by NCO's and Officers in an effort to find the area to which we would be best suited to serve for the next two years. If that was to prove traumatic for some, then surely the visit to the station barber was to prove equally so for many others. Carefully groomed hairstyles that had taken years to nurture, vanished in a moment with one sweep of the barber's blade. Bribes were made by those who cherished their locks and, had he been so tempted, 'Sweeney Todd' could have taken *very* early retirement and gone to live in Australia shearing sheep, but he was loyal to the Crown (the sovereignty, I hasten to add and not the head of the victim) and did his dirty deed without favour to all who sat before him. As if consumed by guilt at the havoc he was wreaking, he never spoke a word, merely grunting to signify his intent to commence and repeating the grunt to signal it's completion. To some, it was a moment when the tears, bravely overcome in the last few days, threatened to re-appear and to others (thankfully I counted myself in the latter set), it was a time to smile at the discomfort and reaction of those proud peacocks who had sported the exotic hair fashion of the day with a pride, which in this case, particularly, came before a fall. What this one thing did however, beyond any other, was to bring home the realisation that we were now members of HM Forces and had the uniform and the haircut, to prove it!

If we thought hard done by from what we had endured so far, worse was yet to come. One morning, we were shepherded onto a large transport vehicle and transferred to RAF Wilmslow in Cheshire to begin eight weeks of what was commonly known as 'square bashing'. In reality, it was a period designated to transforming us from raw recruits into highly polished, fully trained fighting machines and once again (but more forcibly this time), fear was the method used to instil the discipline demanded. We did not have long to wait. Hardly had we been deposited into our quarters when the door of the barrack room smashed back against the wall, sending a shower of plaster fluttering to the floor. A short, stocky NCO appeared, sporting the dreaded two stripes of Corporal and screamed at us. "I am in charge of this unit. I will get you through this course if it kills me. I have never seen a more helpless, moronic crowd of cretins in my life. You will stand to attention every time I enter this room. My name is Corporal Gartside...spelt B.A.S.T.A.R.D and don't you forget it!"

I have, of course, only written the gist of what he was trying to convey but do be informed that each sentence was liberally sprinkled – nay loaded – with the most descriptive of Anglo Saxon invectives, which made his total diatribe one to strike terror into the toughest of us.

Life, under this tyrant of a man was, for the next few weeks, almost unbearable. I doubt if he knew how to talk normally and can only imagine he owned shares in the company that produced throat expectorant, for he screamed and yelled continually and never seemed to suffer. Amazingly though, as the weeks went by, an almost imperceptible mellowness began to appear. Needless to say we sailed through the 'passing out' parade at the end of the training period, with honours. Corporal Gartside greeted our success with some pride and his invitation to a celebration in the mess, made us feel that a miracle of some magnitude had entered his soul, transforming him into this gentle, kindly being. It was only when we heard him greet the new recruits with the same welcome he had reserved for us, that we realised that nothing and no one changes.

Two memories stood out from that period and both affected me. The latter, to this day (and even now), makes me go cold at the thought. The first was the injection we were given to safeguard us against typhoid. Given in two doses, known as a '75' and the obvious weaker one as a '25', the reaction was sheer agony. My arm swelled in pain and I flinched when someone came within 50 yards of me and after suffering the first infusion, I was very apprehensive about undergoing the second. To my surprise and delight, there was no reaction whatsoever and the following day, happily accepted an invitation to watch the great Manchester United at Old Trafford that afternoon, along with forty thousand others. All was well until the second half got under way when suddenly, I sensed a throbbing in my left arm. Within seconds I was in agony as the injection took hold, albeit twenty-four hours too late. Never has Manchester United enjoyed such vocal support, for every time they attacked the goal we stood behind, the crowd surged forward in excitement and the screams that emitted from its ranks was one of acute and agonising pain and not, as the team imagined, of hero worship!

The second memory is the stuff made of nightmares. The weather was windy and wet, ideal we were told, to attempt the deadly assault course and duly rigged in full battle dress (including the back packs), we progressed through each horrific test of endurance. With the feeling that I was at least holding my own, I felt a confidence that was to prove totally misplaced as I approached what was nothing more than a hole in the ground.

"Down you go!" screamed you-know-who. "Headfirst!"

I hesitated to absorb this frightening instruction but before I could react, was forcibly pushed into the gaping hole. The ground angled downward for about six feet, then straightened out into a long black tunnel which stretched unlit for a full twenty feet – the longest twenty feet of my life. I was flat on my stomach, inching my way forward and could feel the roof of the tunnel touching my back. The sides, too, touched my shoulders and I feared, with rising panic that I could be stuck and unable to move forward or back – effectively buried alive. Wildly, I grabbed the ankle of the guy in front and held on grimly. How it never broke, I will never know. Claustrophobia was closing in fast and I can't begin to describe the feeling of relief that flooded over me when at long last, a tiny speck of light appeared, signalling the end of the tunnel and the end of this nightmare. Never before has daylight and fresh air been more welcome! Cold sweat was pouring from every part of my body as I emerged and, although I can appreciate the reasoning behind such a test, it was, and remains to this day, one of the most frightening moments of my life. Nothing would make me repeat that short journey unless my very life depended on it and even then, I would probably hesitate.

What excitement there was as the postings were pinned to the board (similar I guess, to students awaiting the final exam results). Having conquered the pain of homesickness, for the moment at any rate, I was now hoping to be given the chance to serve overseas. Ideally, Hong Kong topped my list, but it was not to be. When my name finally rose to the surface, I had been posted to serve at RAF Alhorn in Northern Germany, an operational night flying station that flew NF7's, NF11's and Canberra bombers. News of this dissolved the initial disappointment in not being sent to the Far East and I felt the excitement well inside me at the prospect of being at the sharp end – an RAF unit that actually flew real live aeroplanes.

A few days at a transit camp near Lytham St Annes, allowed me to review the brash and breezy excitement of nearby Blackpool before we were convoyed to Harwich and the overnight troop ferry to the Hook of Holland. I slept little and at the first glimpse of dawn, I went on deck to a sight that thrilled me more than anything I had known. The ship was easing its way into its dock and behind the area of goods wagons, mobile cranes and low slung buildings, I could see windmills, dozens and dozens of windmills. I knew then that, without doubt, the little lad from Edinburgh, whose only journey outside the Capital City was the annual holiday across the Forth Bridge to the Kingdom of Fife, was in Holland. I was abroad and at that moment, I loved it! Military police guided us to the awaiting trains, each recognisable by a colour coding and soon the blue train slowly snaked northwards, on the last step of the journey to my new home.

Alhorn was a pretty German village lying to the south of Hamburg, with its inhabitants heavily outnumbered by the RAF station personnel. Whatever their thoughts on this invasion by a foreign force, it was something they kept private but, later on, I was able to gauge that the majority, if not all, welcomed us with open arms. Memories of the war were still fresh but there was little resentment – remember it was a mere eight years since hostilities ended. It was clear that they, and millions of other German citizens, had not wanted confrontation and had lived in fear like many of us did in Britain, praying that one day, sanity would return. Happily it did and our presence was the price they had to pay. If we, however, were no great inconvenience, then surely they could not have been too enamoured at the sound of screaming jet planes that roared over their rooftops when darkness fell and never ceased until the first light of dawn appeared on the horizon.

Life at Alhorn settled into a fairly peaceful existence and apart from the morning and evening parades and the occasional billet and kit inspection, one could have almost been back in Civvy Street. It was natural therefore, that my thoughts looked back to the days in Concert Party and I realised, quickly, that to recreate The Vaudrams on the station would probably restart the war, but, nevertheless, the ambition to present some form of light entertainment in this closed community might prove a welcome distraction. I approached one of the Officers who looked as if he might be interested and was given clearance to hold auditions, which we duly did. Surprisingly, there was much hidden talent amongst the ranks and after careful selection, finally presented our first variety show. My own lack of front cloth talent prevented me from promoting myself as star attraction (or any other attraction come to that), but, in a way, it provided me with further knowledge and experience in presenting a show. I gloried under the title of Producer and as the weeks and months passed by, I began to establish a reputation (admittedly amongst those who could maintain and fly jets but knew less than nothing about showbusiness) as an impresario. My biggest problem with show presentation was the lack of girls. However, we managed to overcome the scarcity, by encouraging one or two of the male company to cross-dress. I must admit to some surprise in finding the level of enjoyment they extracted from the transformation, and the care and attention they took on the preparation, caused many a rumour to circulate that was difficult to refute.

The outcome and the range of shows we delivered, plus the successes we enjoyed, further encouraged me to look beyond my two years in service and I tried harder than ever to figure out a way in which I could enter the wonderful world of showbusiness and survive without any tangible talent. Not an easy one to answer, I surmised.

On the sporting front, my time in Germany was a joy. I managed to hold down a place at right back in the Squadron Soccer Team and we travelled around a good deal playing local sides. To my utter amazement, I was contacted by one of the sporting Sergeants who was organising a local RAF Scotland v England international match and was selected to play for my home country. What an honour and what pride to wear the jersey – until I found out that there were only eleven Scots available to play on the station and this took some gloss off the moment. I would love to say that my performance justified my selection and that we went on to thrash the Auld Enemy but I can not tell a lie. I was instructed to tightly mark their outside left and I made every effort to do so. Unfortunately, for me (and the team), I never saw him for the entire ninety minutes. He absolutely roasted me on the inside and outside, in the air and on the ground. His very being was a blur and I was chasing a shadow. It was only after the game was over and we had been walloped 4-0, that I learned he was signed up by Wolverhampton Wanderers and was on the verge of England honours. So ended my internnational career and the humiliation stayed with me for some time – until the next match at any rate.

As for my period of training, two memories remain of my stay in Germany. I had always been, and still am, a Big Band fanatic and when we heard that Woody Herman and the Third Herd were to appear in Hamburg, we lost no time in organising tickets. I can remember little about the show itself except that it was superb, but what did implant in my mind was the journey through the outskirts of this once huge and impressive city. The entire landscape, where once had stood houses, churches, shops, restaurants and bars, was flattened. It was a scene of total desolation and depression. You could recognise where the streets had been from the outline of the footings and the occasional broken wall or part ruin. It was as if an atomic bomb had been dropped and wiped out the whole population. Instead, the sad, sad sight we witnessed, was the result of night after night of relentless bombing by the RAF, bringing death and devastation to those unfortunate enough to live in this doomed thoroughfare. I was aware that similar scenes encircled London, Liverpool, Coventry, Glasgow and many more towns and cities in the UK, but it was no consolation. It brought home to all of us that saw this terrible destruction, the horror, the stupidity and the futility of war. Only the sight of the centre of this proud city, where new buildings were beginning to spring from the ruins of the old, did we sense the feeling of hope and the knowledge that within the scourge of death and ruination, the flame of life still flickered.

If that particular moment burned into my memory, another more light-hearted event made its mark, in more ways that one. I was given the tip-off by one of the pilots, that a series of cross country exercises were to be undertaken by both squadrons of jet fighters and because they were superfluous to the training programme, the navigators were to be grounded. This meant, in effect, that with the pilot occupying the front cockpit, the rear cockpit would be empty. Would I – came the invitation – like the experience of flying as number two? Would I, indeed! I, who had never been higher than Edinburgh Castle ramparts, was about to get my 'wings'! There was little doubt that my inclusion in the flight crew was to be taken seriously and I was told to report to the crew room to be kitted out. This involved the wearing of flying overalls with a badge on the left breast picket, denoting that I was now a member of 256 Squadron, coupled with a flying helmet complete with intercom, so that I could communicate with the pilot or vice versa. As I walked to the aircraft, my imagination took command and I assumed the role of my childhood alter ego Squadron Leader 'Biggles', preparing to do battle with the dreaded Hun. I was brought down to earth before I had even left it by the Chief Mechanic who made it clear he was not in favour of 'sprogs' setting foot in his beloved craft. "Ten bob [50p] if you use the sick bag," he growled, "and one pound if you miss it!"

With that delightful thought in my mind, I clambered into the empty space behind the pilot and was shown the connecting jack plug which opened up the communication channel. I was absolutely staggered at the bank of instruments that faced me but before I could raise a finger, my headphones crackled and the voice of the pilot warned me not to touch a thing. "Keep your hands by your side – hold on to the side rail and you'll be fine," he instructed.

The final buckle snapped me into place and the engine fired. The noise, even with the helmet on, was deafening and we moved on to the runway. I had never heard of centrifugal force before and my introduction to it was quite dramatic. I could feel the flesh being pulled away from my face and my whole body flattened by a massive invisible force that threatened to push me backwards through the padded seat and beyond. Suddenly we were free and the earth fell away below us.

"Okay?" yelled the pilot and I could only nod stupidly.

For a while we darted above and below the wispy clouds, touching speeds of nearly seven hundred miles per hour and the whole experience settled into one of amazement, peace and wonderment. Soon, however, it was all to change – causing me to recall the warning given by the mechanic. Afterwards, I began to form a very deep and unshakeable suspicion that the money gained from those with stomachs made from anything less than cast iron, was donated to some worthwhile charity, or perhaps it was the personal prerogative of the pilot to share the spoils amongst his colleagues later that evening in the bar. Whatever the reason, the plane suddenly dipped and proceeded into the most superb display of aerial acrobatics that anyone on the ground must have thrilled to. We rolled to the left, did a back flip and rolled to the right. We flew upside down, the right way up, flew horizontal and flew perpendicular. We targeted a family enjoying a quiet picnic on a small island a mile below and we dive-bombed them, only pulling out at the very last second. They loved it! They laughed and waved and I tried to laugh and wave back, but I was too busy making a hefty donation to the pilots charity, much to my embarrassment as an airman and my personal financial disgust as a Scot! Finally, the pilot took pity and to my utter relief, I saw the runway get larger and larger until a gentle bump told me that my very first flight was over. I climbed out the cockpit with legs trembling and settled my account with the grinning mechanic.

The pilot approached. "How was it – young Kennedy?" he asked with an evil smile on his face. I would not give him the satisfaction, I vowed, even though I knew that he knew he was well in pocket for the trip.

"Fantastic!" I lied. "When can I go up again?"

One of the great moments in my life as a leading aircraftman, was being awarded the 'Flag of Demobilisation' as my time in uniform came towards its close. Since my arrival, many months ago, I had, like all others, drawn up a demob calendar and each day was religiously crossed off. The days became weeks and the weeks became months, but regardless of the number of crosses collected or indeed the number of virgin dates yet to be scored, you were never really coming to the end of your time of conscription until you received the demob flag. To fly the ensign at the head of your bed was the signal for all to see – you were the next to go! The evening before the great day was one of celebration and ceremony. A festive occasion to say farewell to friends and acquaintances and a ceremonial duty to hand over the flag to the next one in line. I well remember the envy as I watched and indeed, took part as, one by one, the time arrived for those who had served out their two-year stint in the Armed Forces. I suffered pangs of jealously as I saw that flag change hands again and again. I was aware of it planted proudly above beds that always belonged to someone else and inwardly, I ached for the day when it would be mine. And one day it was. I took the symbol of impending release and freedom back to my bedside and unashamedly slept with it that night, in the fear that it would be stolen. I revelled in the looks of envy afforded to me by others and especially the new arrivals whose demob calendars were fresh and clean and unmarked and wondered, with hindsight, at the speed and alacrity in which the period had passed. I looked back on the early days of induction at Padgate, the instilling of discipline by fear at Wilmslow and the eventual emergence of the required standard of excellence required and demanded, by HM Forces.

As I left the gates of the RAF where my final demobilisation papers were rubber stamped and signed, I reflected at the change in my own personality. Gone was the immature adolescent who wept his way from a small street in rural Edinburgh and in its place was an adult who had grown up through the ranks of the military system to become, in such a short space of time, someone capable of standing on his own two feet – of making his own decisions and above all deciding on his own destiny. There can be little doubt that whatever the foreboding, the fear and the apprehension experienced at the beginning of this two year adventure, I know of no one who endured the experience, who will say anything other than National Service made them into men. When I look at the youth today, with some exceptions, I admit I feel saddened that this character-building period of time in their young lives has been denied to them.

CHAPTER THREE

Happy Knights & Baronets

Whatever maturity I gleaned in the time I wore the uniform, however, it scorned all reference to common sense, for although I was welcomed back into the folds of the Scotch Whisky trade, my brain assured me that such a move was an inspiration, providing a future that was secure, well rewarded and long lasting, whilst my heart meanwhile refused to acquiesce and steadfastly assured me that my longing was still in the world of showbusiness. With that knowledge, coupled with the prompting and little prodding from the fickle finger of fate, I decided to keep the spark alive and do something about it.

I recommenced work with A&A Crawford Ltd (much to Dad's delight, having greatly missed the perks of the trade), on February 5th 1955 and also recommenced my evening studies at the Royal High College. I undertook to gain the National Commercial Certificate and to do this, had to pass in six subjects – Mathematics, Economic History, Bookkeeping, Commerce, History and English. The course was to take five years to achieve and to pass, would mean an almost certain seat on the Board. I set to with ambition but the bug implanted by the sound of applause in my early days as a 'Vaudram vagrant', began to gnaw at my soul and I finally made the phone call that was to play right into the hands of fate and change my life's direction, once again.

His name was George Bartleman – a pianist of some local notoriety, who attacked the ivories as if trying to settle some long running vendetta. In addition, he dabbled in comedy and although not in the Premier League class, was good enough to enable him to combine his talents and earn a very useful additional income to his job with the Gas Board. It also allowed him to produce, direct and appear in a Concert Party called The Happy Knights. Similar to The Vaudrams, in that they played to the same type of audiences, any further comparison would be slanderous, for The Happy Knights were as good a touring show as The Vaudrams were bad. They were certainly up to semi-professional standard and beyond and recognised, not only in Edinburgh, but also throughout Central and Southern Scotland as the very best around. And so, aiming for the highest peak available, I rang George and poured my heart and my ambitions into his ear. To his credit, he didn't put the phone down, but listened sympathetically. Yet again, the setback came when he asked what sort of an act I had. I had to confess that none existed. I did, however, tell him about my starring role with The Vaudrams and he stifled (I am sure) the urge to convulse into hysterical laughter. Nevertheless, he invited me along to the next rehearsal of the show to meet the 'gang' and talk further. This I did and watching them work on that Sunday afternoon, was a joy to behold. Although it did nothing to fuel my glowing aspirations, I jumped at his offer to join the stage crew, responsible for the loading and unloading, the setting up and the operating of the lights and sound equipment plus complete control of the costumes – their cleanliness, condition and distribution. I felt, without doubt, that being connected in any way with a company of this stature, was a hundred times more preferable to being the leading light in a troupe with the reputation of The Vaudrams. In a sense, it was the classic case of taking two steps back in the fervent hope of progressing three or more steps forward and so it was to eventually prove.

The talent on show from the company was superb. Led by George himself as comedian and keyboard accompanist, it featured Marion Reid, a vocalist who combined show songs with the popular chart toppers of the day and The Raymond Brothers, a mime act, who specialised brilliantly in recreating very funny routines to standard pre-recorded songs by top artists. Their technique was so well performed that I vividly recall, after they had cavorted as two Red Indians mouthing the voices of Jeanette McDonald and Nelson Eddy in the classic *Indian Love Call,* one particular old age pensioner grabbing my arm in the interval of the show. "Here son – that big Indian, that's just been on...what a great voice. Will you ask him if he'll sing Scotland the Brave in the second half?"

No greater compliment – I'm sure!

The male vocal was a slim good-looking young man, yet a teenager, called Jackie Dennis. Shortly he would be 'discovered' by a major recording company – Decca – and whisked off to London in a five figure deal to be re-presented as The Kilted Rock'n'Roller. He had quite a few hits to his name – the biggest being *Lah Dee Dah,* which went to number four in the charts and *The Purple People Eater* which peaked at number twenty nine. The latter, staying in the top fifty for nearly seven months. It only goes to prove surely, what wonderful talent we displayed within the company.

The remaining two acts were both bands but totally contrasting in style. The first was Bobby Jack and his Scottish Country-Dance Band and if you closed both eyes, you could be listening to the great Jimmy Shand himself. Bobby was only a youngster, but the way he handled his button key accordion was pure magic. Why he, too, was never discovered, I will never know – he deserved to be. I watched, many an evening, as the band took the room by storm and marvelled at the audience of poor old souls who had struggled to their seats at the beginning of the show, suddenly being infected with this toe tapping music and shedding the years with clapping hands and feet become possessed as the rhythmic beat sent their blood pressures soaring – a joy to behold.

Last, but not least, was our skiffle group, led by Billy McKenzie. Billy was a character and if truth be known, on intimate terms with most of the Edinburgh constabulary, but on stage he led the group with a voice reminiscent of the late Jim Reeves – rich, deep and resonant, but when required, a gentleness that belied his self styled image. They, of course, catered for the style of that period but, again, delivered with quality and class.

The team was completed by singers Danny Cairney, Bernie Foley and Terry Whiteman, plus dancer Sandra Bell, two girls whose names escape me (forgive me ladies!), who took responsibility for the costumes and a young man by the name of Brian Hall, who, with myself, looked after the heavy humping and all things technical. Brian was in the stationary business by day but had agreed to work as stage crew for reasons similar to mine. In his case, that of frustrated singer who was unable to gain a permanent 'spot' in the show because of the talents of the aforementioned Jackie Dennis. Finally, the hard work in dealing with the secretarial and administrative duties fell to a very capable young man by the name of Charlie Innes.

So that was our line-up during the mid and late fifties and such was the pride we had in belonging to such a talented and polished group of performers, we actually talked George into purchasing black blazers for everyone (including, I'm glad to say, the back stage crew), proudly displaying a breast pocket badge woven in gold wire depicting a knight in armour on a rearing horse with the words underneath which read – 'The Happy Knights'. And so they were!

Our mode of transport to and from engagements was always by coach and George insisted that we all met at a given meeting point – usually our place of rehearsal (Dalry House off Gorgie Road) – so that we would all arrive and leave together – a sensible precaution. On these journeys to places like Tranent, Haddington, North Berwick, Moffat and Dumfries, it was the tradition, especially on the journey home, that those who required the healing power of sleep would occupy the front seats and the more raucous members of the company would retire to the rear of the coach, to vent their musical frustrations in song. In these early years of my life, I qualified for the latter and was ably supported by Brian, my stage crew compatriot and, probably because we had been vocally suppressed during the actual show itself, took our revenge on the long trail home, accompanied most times by Billy McKenzie on vocal and guitar. There was never any one moment during these impromptu sing-songs when I can point a finger and say with certainty that, at that particular second of time, The Baronets was born but it started to dawn on us that, even to our inexperienced ear, a blend was beginning to emerge that was exciting to say the least. Whilst I did not possess a singing voice able to sustain a solo career, I discovered a completely natural ear for singing harmony and with Brian showing a similar skill, we wound ourselves around Billy's rich baritone voice and without any planning, began to produce three part chords that sounded very satisfying and very professional. George, always with an ear for talent, began to take notice and encouraged us to keep going, but Bill, ever loyal to his skiffle colleagues, constantly refused to commit himself and showed little interest in appearing with a three handed singing group. In the late fifties, fair to say, vocal groups were in their zenith. Groups like Stargazers, The Polka Dots, The Ames Brothers, The McGuire Sisters and particularly the brilliant Four Freshmen and the Hi Lo's. Perhaps George sensed that a vocal group within the show would add to the scale of variety it already contained and he continued to support what we had started. To our great delight he invited Brian and I to rehearse a ten-minute act with the promise of a slot in the show. The great moment arrived, not with great success, but not with abject failure either. We performed well but we were lightweight and we both knew it. Having seen us take this major step forward, however, fate was not going to allow us to fade into obscurity. It was but a few weeks later that the mystic finger of fate stirred an argument within the skiffle band, so fierce that they decided to call it a day and Billy finally agreed to join us – The Baronets had been born!

The voice of Billy McKenzie transformed The Baronets from a lightweight duo into a 'tour de force' threesome, not overnight but certainly within a few weeks. The joy of quite suddenly becoming one of the major players in this talented team was unbelievable and we rehearsed every possible moment. Suddenly, however, I began to experience the tug of war within my conscience as I realised the difficulty in combining my studies with performing. It was a battle between head and heart and I have no shame in admitting that the head lost convincingly. By this time we had increased in numbers by adding our own piano accompanist to the fold, by the name of Bob Burns and this was a major help to us, especially with rehearsals. Our reputation began to proceed us and before long we were beginning to take bookings outwith The Happy Knights. I recall one such engagement at the Alhambra Cinema in Leith, who began staging a series of live Sunday Concerts designed especially for the younger element. We were booked as one of the supporting acts to The Black Adders, one of the top skiffle bands around at the time and needless to say, the place was packed, mainly with their fans. The Baronets went on prior to The Adders, and as the curtains closed in order for us to set our mikes, the audience mistakenly assumed The Adders were next appearing and screamed and yelled their excitement and approval. An off-stage announcement was lost in the bedlam and the curtains opened to reveal three lads in pristine white shirts, striped ties and immaculately creased trousers singing *Love is a Many Splendid Thing.* We brought the crowd to its feet – but not in adulation. Everything they could lay their hands on was propelled in our direction – peanuts, orange peel and I counted the armrests of at least three front row seats as they mercifully sped harmlessly past our heads. It was probably the shortest show we ever did!

On a more peaceful note, we started entering the numerous talent shows that proliferated at that time and soon began to pick up the various cash prizes on offer. This greatly added to our experience and we were thrilled to be included on the same bill as the great Billy Fury, at the Caird Hall, Dundee. Adding to the excitement was the fact we were sharing the dressing room (it was actually a caravan) with Billy's backing group. The house was a sell-out, for Fury was a huge star in the late fifties. Throughout his tragically short career, he totalled an amazing two hundred and eighty eight weeks in the UK record charts, but never had a number one hit. Unbelievable! We were to experience, too, what these Rock'n'Roll icons suffered off-stage, for as the crowds poured out of the hall, they espied the caravan in which we were changing and, assuming that Billy was inside, started to rock the vehicle to-and-fro with increasing vigour in an effort to dislodge the great man. It was the first time in my life I feared a mob of fans and we were only rescued when the police waded in. It was the first time, too, that I felt seasick after a concert.

Carroll Levis was, I suppose, the forerunner to Hughie Green (he, too, was Canadian) and auditioned throughout the UK for talent to include in his weekly television and radio shows. Both were extremely popular and when it was advertised locally that Levis was to appear at the Edinburgh Empire for a full week, the tickets sold like hot cakes. His idea was to use the weekday show to showcase as many local acts that he could squeeze in and from those he would select two winners each evening to appear in the grand final on the Saturday evening. The winner would be featured on the *Carroll Levis TV Show* and the runner up on the radio equivalent. To support the amateurs, he enlisted two unknown 'pro' acts and a comic female impersonator by the name of Mrs Shufflewick. It certainly was a rather odd supporting bill, but nevertheless, we decided to take the plunge and duly appeared on the Tuesday evening and much to our excitement, went through to the Saturday final in style. We arrived at the theatre for the big night in plenty of time, but were somewhat taken aback to have to navigate around the body of half-man and half-woman, who lay sprawled across the stairway, audibly cursing and mumbling unintelligible profanities, whilst struggling to consume what was left of a bottle of 'aqua vitae'. It was Mrs Shufflewick, oblivious to her surroundings and most certainly unable to do her normal act that evening. Whatever her loss, it proved our gain for the instruction was passed for all finalists to add a second number to their repertoire and, in addition to the extra opportunity to show off our talent, it was such a great thrill to extend the time allotted to us, to appear on that wonderful stage and in that superb auditorium. We won the final that evening, with the runner up being a particularly attractive young lady vocalist, and we waited in great anticipation for our very first TV appearance. It never came. Instead we were offered a radio broadcast and although disappointed, we naively accepted the invitation and our first media appearance took place in the *BBC Light Programme* on Wednesday 2nd June. It was much later that we discovered that the young lady who was runner-up to us, was featured on the TV as a new 'Carroll Levis' discovery. I wonder what it was he discovered?

Our television appearance was not long in coming however, and we were thrilled to be chosen to represent Edinburgh in a *Top Town* TV show, which featured selected towns or cities in the UK battling against each other. Each side was given thirty minutes to present their talent. A panel of Judges awarded scores and the winning towns progressed through to the next round. We were drawn against Leeds and the neutral ground was the BBC studios in Manchester. Our team travelled south by coach and the luggage compartments groaned under the weight of bagpipes, bass drums, kilts and the like – the traditional fare offered by the majority of Scottish teams who competed. I felt that, all patriotism put to one side, the theme had been overdone – and so it proved. We were soundly thrashed and as we crept back to Edinburgh the following morning, our sporrans sadly drooping and tails between legs, I was heartened to read in the *Daily Mail's* TV review of the show 'Edinburgh overdid the heather and kilt syndrome much favoured north of the border and paid the penalty. Nevertheless they presented the best act of the evening – The Baronets, who could have a future to look forward to'. I've bought the *Daily Mail* from that day onwards.

We decided to spend a week's vacation at Butlins Holiday Camp in Ayr for two reasons. The first and main force was the fact that we were four young and healthy males and it seemed, at the time, to be the place to go. The second was the incentive to enter their talent show, open to bona fide weekly guests, with a first prize of £1,000 to the outright winner. We packed our stage suits (we had progressed from the white shirts and striped ties) and set off for the Southwest corner of Scotland, filled with excitement and anticipation. We duly entered the heats and found ourselves in the weekly final – the standard of which was quite frankly, appalling. We were up against a male singer (who's vibrato was so pronounced, planes from nearby Prestwick Airport were being diverted), an escapologist who was tied into a sack by four over-enthusiastic members of the audience, and forty eight hours later had to be labelled and sent home in a Royal Mail van, and a vocal impressionist who sang *It Was Just One Of Those Things* and shouted out the name of the singer he was about to copy every few seconds. In thirty seconds he portrayed Frank Sinatra, Dean Martin, Nat 'King' Cole, Tony Bennett, Frankie Laine and Johnny Ray. He would have been a sensation but for two things. One – he couldn't sing in tune. (He produced such a superb display of chronic modulation that the pianist who had seen and heard most things in his short life, bravely stuck it out until the reprise before slamming the piano lid down with a bang and storming off the stage to find solace in the nearest bar). Two – each and every artiste sounded the same – not unnatural in view of his vocal limitations. When he ended his set by announcing '...and this is me!' (before finishing in the same voice as all the rest), the audience went wild – many of them demanding their money back or free vouchers to spend on hard liquor, as compensation for what they had suffered. With that sort of competition against us, we secured first place and on the Friday, walked proudly on to the floor at prize giving to receive a hairbrush and a small bottle of Babycham (to share!). The main award, however, was an invitation to appear in the end of season finals in which each weekly winner would compete against all others for the title 'Act of the Season'.

Once again, in late September, we returned and once again (this time the competition was much stiffer) we ended with the top prize. Now we were getting into the big time and headed for the national talent semi-finals (north) at Butlins Metropole Hotel in Blackpool. A similar semi-final was being held at the Ocean Hotel in Saltdean in Brighton, for those winners who had progressed from the southern-based camps. Six acts would be chosen from each of the two semi-finals to appear in the National finals at the Apollo Theatre, in London. Once again, our luck held and we were listed as one of the six acts to go through to the London Final. To say we were excited was an understatement and we were given quite a bit of press coverage. *The Sunday People* who sponsored the event, printed our picture in their publication and we received equal publicity back home – slightly tainted by one local newspaper whose headlines proclaimed '*Coronets* Crown Their Success'. Ah well – no one's perfect!

One other event took place during our stay at Blackpool and this, so fate would have it, further shaped my showbusiness aspirations. We were sitting in the lounge one afternoon, relaxing after an arduous rehearsal with the local band, when a gentleman approached us and asked permission to join our table. "Have you heard of a forthcoming radio talent show to be called 'Make a Tape' sponsored by Currys – the National Electrical Retailers?" he enquired.

We confessed that we hadn't and the proposition was put to us that he (the gentleman, whom I assumed represented the sponsors) would record us on the tape machine he just happened to have with him and enter the resultant tape into the contest.

At this time of our career, we were beginning to pick out the real from the phoney, whose opening lines always started with..."Hey you guys are great. You are just too good for this place! I have contacts – I will make you stars..." etc., etc.

We were, maybe, just a little suspicious of this stranger, what would *he* get from it? Were we being stitched up? We finally decided that it would cost us little and as long as we signed nothing, what had we to lose? The way it turned out we had *nothing* to lose and what we gained from an acceptance to do the recording was another hefty dig in the back from the fateful digit, another step forward and an invitation to make the ultimate move and turn professional.

The National Talent Final of 1960 was a glittering star-studded occasion, which was a joy to be a part of. Compered by Don Arroll (the current host of ITV's *Sunday Night at the London Palladium*) and judged by eminent showbusiness luminaries, Earl St John (film Director), Bernard Delfont (agent), Vera Lyn, Geraldo, Carole Carr and Jimmy Jewel and Ben Warriss. When we looked around, apart from the other contestants, we were the only ones we'd never heard of. The sixteen-piece pit orchestra was led by Al Fried, a short Jewish man with an acerbic sense of humour. We had spent over £100 on orchestrations for the big evening and when, during the band call, the musicians had trouble with a rather difficult musical passage, Al threw the conductors part high into the air and yelled at us. "Take this load of manure back to Woolworth's and get your money back!" Only he didn't say manure...

The musicians dutifully laughed, but I was mortified and thought Mr Fried was a nasty, horrible, little man. By the strangest of coincidences, I found myself, a few years later, working with Al Fried as his manager and I soon realised that, far from my first impression, he was a warm, generous and delightful man and we became close friends. I should have realised the extent of his humour during the actual show when we took the stage, almost frozen with nerves. I glanced down into the pit and there was the cherubic face of Al Fried, beaming up at us, his left hand enclosed around our musical score and his right hand extracting imaginary chips from the paper and putting them in his mouth. We had to laugh and the tension fell away.

Sadly, when lots were drawn to determine the running order for the show, we drew the short straw and went on first. Our second of the two songs each contestant was allotted, was a parody on the Lonnie Donegan hit *My Old Man's A Dustman* and we had re-written the words to get even bigger laughs than the original, along with silly props, intended to compound the action. The fact that we appeared on stage whilst some members of the audience were still being shown to their seats and still in the process of settling down, meant that we found it difficult to make the impact we had hoped for. Nevertheless, it was fair and we had no complaints. We did not get a place amongst the prize-winners but shared a memory with a few others that will remain with us for the rest of our lives.

The disappointment we experienced did not last long however, for within a week we had a letter from Currys informing us that the tape we had made in Blackpool (and had forgotten about), had been accepted and we would be featured on the first show of the series on Radio Luxembourg at the beginning of February 1961. We told everyone we knew to listen in and on that Monday evening, we huddled around the radio and heard (for the very first time), our vocal arrangement of *Autumn Leaves*. At the end of the programme, a theatrical agent had to give a brief summing up of what he had listened to and announce the winner. To our surprise and delight, he went on and on in highly favourable terms of our efforts and announced that we were the winners and would go through to the semi-final in six weeks time. The joy of being on a competition of this nature was the fact that the work (or so we thought) had finished and we simply had to sit back and listen. The same rules applied for the semi-finals and we, once again (and getting more excited by the second) listened to not one, but two agents agreeing The Baronets were the best act of the evening and so, for the second time in two months, we reached a major final. To our surprise however, bearing in mind the competition was based on making and recording a tape, we learned that the final was to be a stage show and broadcast live on radio. The venue we were told, was the beautiful Gaiety Theatre within the Butlin Holiday Camp at Bognor Regis. I could not shake the feeling however, given that Butlins kept coming into my life, that fate was guiding me in a direction without any assistance from me – and so it was to prove!

The recent experience at the Apollo Theatre in London conspired to ensure that when we took the stage at Bognor, it was a much more relaxed quartet who performed. We certainly had a great advantage over the other finalists who had produced tapes of talent and quality but perhaps, lacked the stagecraft required to project their work, so, in that alone we were able to score extra marks.

The compere of that special evening was top broadcaster of his day, McDonald Hobley and I could not believe it when, as the show neared its close, he dropped me a wink and whispered in my ear. "You've done it, old son. You've won!"

The result was duly announced and we took the stage to receive the plaudits and the prize vouchers. Once again, the difficulty of sharing a prize proved a handicap, for the first prize was a magnificent radiogram costing nearly £1,000. Short on purchasing a power saw and reducing it into four equal musical sections, there seemed no solution until Curry's offered us gift vouchers to the value and we happily accepted. The distribution of the spoils however, lost its importance compared to the events that followed. At the reception following the show, we were approached by a delightful gentleman sporting a large moustache, who introduced himself to us as Wally Goodman. Wally was the Entertainment Executive for Butlin Holidays and he wanted us to join the resident Entertainment Team at Bognor Regis for the summer season of 1961. He wanted us, bluntly, to turn professional. As a further carrot, he mentioned that the resident band on site for that season would be the Eric Winstone Orchestra, with resident singer Lisa Glenn and Bill Forbes and there would be every opportunity to sing with them. Eric Winstone, at that time, was a household name, due to radio, TV and records and I must admit my stomach turned over at the decision I knew I had to make. To make things worse, I had, believe it or not (despite the multitude of various counter-attractions), managed to complete my studies at home and was about to sit the final examinations. I begged time to think things over and although the other three lads tried to convince me to take the plunge, I really felt that I owed it to myself not to waste the five years of study I had put behind me. At the back of my mind, too, was the thought of what my Uncle would say, notwithstanding my Mum and Dad. I had reached the major crossroads of my life and I had to decide which direction to take. I had to get it right!

CHAPTER FOUR

Stars in Redcoat

I sat the exams in May of 1961, but although I had crammed as hard as I knew how, my heart was not in it. On the day of the final examination, I felt empty and it was as if I was watching someone else undergo the ordeal. When the bell rang to end the day, I put down my pen and paper and felt utterly relaxed. The content of what I had written seemed good but the combination of relief, nervous exhaustion and a burning anxiety to know my results, simply did not exist.

Incredibly, three months later, whilst working at Butlins, I received a brown buff envelope – the contents containing the news that I had passed in all subjects and was now in proud possession of the National Commercial Certificate. I could not believe it and wondered – if the document had arrived sooner, would I have made the same decision? Fate has a lot to answer for!

As always, I confided in my Dad and he came into my bedroom a day or so later, minutes after I had settled down for the night. He sat on the side of the bed like a family doctor about to pronounce a diagnosis and spoke the words of a Solomon. "I know the dilemma you are suffering," he said. "You must do what you feel is right...whatever that is, your Mother and I will totally support you. You must make me a promise however..." and he paused. "If you decide to accept the offer to make singing your career, give it two years and if it hasn't worked out by then and you haven't progressed any further, you will give up the thought of showbusiness and come home. I have spoken with your Uncle Bob and in that event, a job will still be open to you."

I could have hugged him and for the first time in a long while, I slept deeply. In the morning I rang the boys, then phoned Wally Goodman to inform him we were pleased to accept his offer and what date could we start?

Fate never gave me a chance. I was now in showbusiness full time – whether I liked it or not. I had thrown away the mantle of safety and opted for a business that was fraught with insecurity, risk and a grave danger of unemployment. Fate! Fate! Fate! What the hell have you done to me!

We arrived at Bognor late evening and apart from a brief introductory meeting with the Entertainments Manager, Roy Markwell, met no one until the following morning. The accommodation was a cultural shock – a single bed, a bedside table, a sink and a brick wardrobe was all it contained. In order to make the image more palatable, however, the designers had opted for a montage of pretty little yachts that cheerily sailed on anything that moved – the bedspread, the curtains and the piece of material that acted as a wardrobe door. I'm sure that there were other things that moved in the chalet also, but they were too small for us to check whether they, too, were covered in these bloody yachts and in any event, we were too tired!

It appeared that we *would* be singing with the Winstone Band but it was required that we wore the Butlin Redcoat uniform whilst not on the stand – helping out with the various aspects of entertainment – bingo, competitions and sports, which I particularly enjoyed. On that very first morning, we again reported to the Entertainment Office and were promptly packed off to the Reception (we had to ask the guests how to get there!). When we arrived, the Redcoat in charge immediately dumped me into the 'Ask Me' desk, leaving me to direct the new arrivals to the places of importance. I am sure there are to this day, guests still wandering around the Bognor Camp sporting long hair and straggly beards, who followed my instructions how to get to point A and are still frantically trying to find their way back. Nevertheless, it was a quick learning process and by the time evening fell, I knew where everything and everywhere was, as if I had lived there for months. What followed was one of the happiest periods of my life. We sang our hearts out on the ballroom stage with the Eric Winstone Orchestra, in the theatre when Eric presented his own *'Band Show'*, supported the major stars who topped the bill on the *Sunday Evening Variety Show* and in the Redcoat show, where we had to repeat the show five times (!) per evening, such was the demand for seats. With nearly eight thousand guests on site, divided into four huge dining rooms each catering for first and second sittings, the shows had to be well staggered. The first show was 5.30pm to 6.30pm, then 7.00pm to 8.00pm, 8.30pm to 9.30pm, 10.00pm to 11.00pm and a special midnight show finishing at 1.00am. Exhausting work but I would have done it seven days a week.

The Redcoats in the early sixties were legendary – we were demi-gods. If we had demanded that the guests walk to the end of Brighton Pier and throw themselves into the sea, most would have done it. The marketing juggernaut that created the image of the Butlin Redcoat had, in some ways, created a monster but how we loved it! We posed for thousands of photographs, signed a multitude of autographs and had enough invitations to visit guests in their home towns and cities to last us into the next century. Whenever we appeared on stage, even before we opened our mouths to sing, we were being cheered to the echo. It was so easy to forget that we were mixing and mingling with these lovely people morning, noon and night and became their 'buddies' and so the support they gave us was more by way of friendship on a personal basis, rather than an appreciation of us as performers. It was heady stuff and we almost began to believe our own publicity.

There was no doubt however, that in those days, the up and coming cream of undiscovered talent was flocking into the Redcoat ranks and we worked with many who have become today's great stars. I remember two Irish brothers named Johnny and Dave O'Mahoney who took the camps by storm. Johnny stayed in Redcoat for many years and became a legend of comedy with the loyal guests, but Dave decided to take the plunge, left Butlins, changed his name to Dave Allen and never looked back! Des O'Connor, too, wore the jacket of fame and although I never worked with him at Butlins, I shared a meal with him many years later and we had a wonderful evening reminiscing. Mike Newman was a lovely man and he, too, excelled in comedy (he starred for many years in the TV game show *3-2-1* with Ted Rodgers and Chris Emmett). He had, though, a wicked sense of humour and when he entered the dining room on any given evening, you could be certain that the meal would disintegrate into a glorious bread roll fight with everyone involved. You can imagine the apprehension amongst all the Reds if Mike chose a Sunday evening to join us, for the dessert that day was lemon meringue pie, pre-set – one to each table. The local dry cleaners had a field day each Monday morning, until we persuaded the powers that be to give Mike the Sunday off!

Many other familiar names of showbusiness fame owe their success to the experience gained wearing the famous jacket – names like Charlie Drake, Michael Barrymoe, Ted Rodgers, and a young singer called Harry Webb who changed his name to Cliff Richard.

We were surprised, one day, to be informed that instructions had been received from high places, that the best Redcoat Act from Bognor was to swap places with the best from the Butlin Ocean Hotel at Saltdean, near Brighton, each Saturday for a six week period. To our delight, we were chosen to represent Bognor and we enquired who was to replace us from Brighton.

"Some cocky young comedian from Liverpool," we were told. "Called Jimmy Tarbuck."

Wonderful stuff and a great comic!

Today, an artiste can supplement his nightly fee by selling tapes or CD's directly after they finish their performance and in many cases can top up their contractual figure, particularly if other items of merchandising are included – T-shirts, baseball caps, pens, key rings and in the case of some well known ventriloquists, dolls. It is now not only accepted but indeed, expected. Go to any pop concert these days and you will be harangued by stall-holders selling everything that carries the name of the artiste or group. Back in the sixties, however, it was seldom, if ever done. We decided to have a go and before commencing our season, booked a studio and a local band to record a 7" record which would feature on the 'A' side, a great version of *Ball In The Jack,* made famous by Danny Kaye. We gave it a twist rhythm and renamed it *'Twistin' the Jack'*. It was going to be a winner and we coupled it with a slow harmonic number called *Autumn Leaves*. We waited with some excitement for the record to be released but one week before we left for Butlins, we were informed that the song *Ball In The Jack* had been copyrighted and the company who owned the rights had taken out an injunction to prevent us using it. We were devastated and with visions of a fortune in sales, not to mention the possibility of it sneaking into the charts, fading rapidly, we decided to still issue the record, moving *Autumn Leaves* onto the 'A' side and using a jazzed up version of *Scotland The Brave* on the other. When I listen to the record today, I cringe in embarrassment and only play it to punish the dog, but on the day, we packed the boxes of records into the car and headed off to Butlins to make our fortune. To our dismay, Butlins refused us permission to sell the discs on site but even without their help, we watched the record soar to the number one spot in the charts within weeks... in Bognor Regis!

What we did, with Butlins refusing to assist, was to approach the manager of the local branch of WH Smith's and – bless him – he agreed to hold stocks of the record on a 'sale

Our first record goes on sale. Note the price .... 6/7½. It rose to be Number 1 in the hit parade .... in Bognor Regis!!!!!!

or return' basis. We then persuaded Eric Winstone to write us a most beautiful arrangement of the number *Autumn Leaves* and heavily featured it in the *Band Show*. With that sort of musical backing behind us, we simply couldn't go wrong and when taking the applause at the finish, I just happened to mention that what they had heard was our latest recording and copies were available from WH Smith's, High Street, Bognor. The sales were brilliant and it was one of the great moments in my life when I passed the shop front towards the end of the season and saw standing on the pavement, by the doorway, a billboard which read –'This weeks Top Twenty Records, based on sales achieved by this branch'. Holding the number three position was Cliff Richard, *When The Girl In Your Arms*. In the number two slot was Elvis Presley, *Wooden Heart* and sitting proudly at number one was The Baronets, *Autumn Leaves*. Why is it I never have a camera handy when I most need it?

We were approaching the end of the season and it hit us quite suddenly that there was no work from October onwards. From the lofty position of early June, the feeling was that the show would go on forever and without end. The warm glow emanating from this knowledge wrapped itself around you and implanted in your mind a false sense of security. Fate, however, after driving me into this business, had a trump card to play in the shape of a rather smart, elegant man who approached us one evening and asked if we would meet him the next morning for coffee. Intrigued, we agreed and he introduced himself as the Managing Director of the William Galt Theatrical Agency, based in Sauchiehall Street, Glasgow. He wanted to know our plans at the end of our current contract and when we told him, he asked if we would be interested in joining the *Here's To The Tartan Show* at the Tivoli Theatre, Aberdeen, the Monday after we closed in Bognor. Would we indeed! I'm sure his hand still bears the teeth marks as we nearly bit it off to get to the contract. The show was to run for four weeks – change of programme each week – and would star Scottish comedian Aly Wilson. The relief of the moment was pure and, in addition to the work it was to provide, I was thrilled to have been recognised by the Galt Agency, who cast some of the biggest theatres in Scotland at that time. At the back of my mind however, was the thought that for the past five and a half months we had, in a sense, been cocooned by the warmth and friendliness of the Butlin audiences and we were now about to be exposed to the other end of the spectrum – to be thrown to the lions, as it were, and experience the coldly expectant atmosphere of a paying audience. A very different proposition and I wondered if and how long we would survive. It wasn't long before we were to find out!

CHAPTER FIVE

On the Road

The season finished with the expectant bang and it was a rather sad group of singers who loaded the car, bade farewell to our many new found friends and headed northwards and home, albeit for a very short time. Instructions had been received from the agency that rehearsals would commence at 10.00am sharp at the Tivoli Theatre in the Granite City and we had to report to the Producer – a Mr Claude Worth. My first duty then, was to check the train times for the following Monday morning and I was disgruntled to learn that the first train out of Edinburgh arrived in Aberdeen at 10.18am. I had the choice therefore, to risk the wrath of the Producer or take the train on Sunday afternoon and have to fork out an extra night's accommodation, which I could ill afford. Given the choice today, there would have been little problem and the Sunday train would have had one extra passenger, but in those days, although I had respect for my new profession, I had a greater regard for my state of finance and chose to travel on the Monday. The train rolled into Aberdeen Station, more or less on time and I was pleased and relieved to discover that the theatre was only a hundred yards away and I covered the distance in double time. I entered the auditorium practising my carefully prepared speech of apology, only to be met by the enraged Claude Worth. He pulled himself up to his towering height of five foot four inches and proceeded, in front of the entire cast, to give me the biggest dressing down of my life. If the Academy of Dramatic Art had been anywhere in earshot that morning,

Claude would have been immediately nominated for an award, such was his performance. He left me cringing in total embarrassment and completely speechless, but filled with admiration for his dramatic and oratory skills that would have received – and deserved – a standing ovation in less traumatic circumstances. The other members of the Baronets, who actually drove up the night before (I *did* have the choice to join them) sat smirking at my great discomfort and if their haloes had been just a fraction lower, I would happily have strangled each one with the angelic symbol. I kept out of Claudes' reaches throughout the morning for by now, like Corporal Gartside in my 'square bashing' days, I was now in terror of the man with the acerbic tongue and superb command of the English language. We finally broke just after lunch with the show set for that evening and indeed, for that week. Tuesday morning would be free and from Wednesday morning onwards we would start rehearsing for the new show to commence the following Monday.

We were staying at the charmingly named Kittybrewster Hotel – a temperance hostelry that upset Billy and Bob greatly – and after completing the signing-in routine, the receptionist really made my day. "Oh", she said, conversationally. "You're with the show are you? We've got someone else staying with us from the Company!" I just *knew* before she told me the name of the person and prayed I would be wrong. "Do you know a Mr Claude Worth?"

My heart sank and the anticipation of a wonderful first season in the real outside world of showbusiness collapsed like a pricked balloon. As it happened, nothing could have been further from the truth. Claude turned our to be the most delightful of men and a great raconteur of showbusiness memories. Night after night, when the show had finished and we returned to the hotel for the inevitable 'mince and tatties' (we learned later that the building was nick-named 'Mince Castle' by the showbusiness fraternity), we would sit in the lounge and just listen to Claude speak –

regaling us with stories of the shows he had been in and the 'old pros' he had worked with. On many occasions, the sessions would last until 4.00 or 5.00am, but he was a joy to listen to. The bad start I had suffered with him was quickly forgotten and we became very dear and close friends. Years later when, sadly, we had lost touch, I was invited to The Argyll Theatre in Birkenhead to audition two acts that were appearing there and was so thrilled to discover that the Front of House Manager, resplendent in full evening wear, was none other than Claude Worth himself. He greeted me like a long lost son and could not do enough to make my stay more enjoyable. Sadly, not long after, he passed away. He was one of the old school of theatrical gentlemen – a breed that no longer exists in this modern age and he was and still is, I am sure, greatly missed.

We arrived back at the theatre an hour before the curtain rose on our twice-nightly debut and I gazed with some excitement at the queue that wended its way around the theatre building and beyond. Showbusiness is *so* easy, I told myself. From the packed houses of Butlins, here we were, about to take the plunge and yet again, the customers had flocked to see us. At that moment, life was grand and the feeling of euphoria lasted all of sixty minutes. I heard the orchestra tuning up and we filed onto the stage to await curtain up. The moment arrived and, despite the glare of the stage lights, I was able to determine that the front three rows of the stalls were filled to overflowing, whilst the rest of the large theatre echoed to the sound of emptiness, I could not believe my eyes or my ears. I had the feeling of being drenched by a bucket of icy water. Where was everyone? Where had they all gone? A stagehand provided the answer. "Ah – that'll be the new Bingo Hall next door", he said in that lilting Aberdeen accent. "They always do well on a Monday!"

The business went from bad to dire but we struggled on, grateful to be working and, despite the lack of support from the locals, enjoyed the experience. One member of the

Mum & Dad celebrate their Golden Wedding Anniversary

With the 'Brylcreem Boys' – Leading Aircraftsman Kennedy. J. (2582755). Germany – 1954.

My first cap for RAF Scotland. A proud moment but little did I know that there was only 11 players to chose from!

The Happy Knights on the road – 1958. The Concert Party was one of the best in Scotland and many of the performers featured in the show turned professional. Producer/Director George Bartleman is fourth from the right (wearing the bow tie) and I am standing to the left of centre.

Big sister Kath plays piano and I try to sing. Other members of the Happy Knights look on and listen in admiration.

The 'Kilted Rock'n'Roller' – Jackie Dennis with Perry Como.

Me – a smiling Redcoat!

We finally make the 'telly' – photographed by a fan in South Wales as we battle for the title 'Top Town'. BBCtv 1959

'The Baronets' – 1959.
(L to R) Bob Burns on piano, Jim Kennedy, Billy McKenzie, and Brian Hall.

A soccer 'Superstar'! The only player to have scored a hat-trick in an FA Cup Final at Wembley. The legendary Stan Mortensen.

Bringing in the New Year in the South Pacific. Cruise Director on the P&O 'Arcadia' – 1973

company stood out for a reason, well separated from the great talent he possessed. Each evening he would arrive at the theatre in such a state of inebriation that he would fall into his dressing room and all but pass out. Minutes before his part in the show was due, two stage-hands would arrive at his dressing room door and literally half carry and half drag the unfortunate man to the side of the stage. They propped him up in the wings carefully, for if they had not done so, he would surely have fallen over into a heap on the floor. The stage crew would proceed to place his clarinet and range of saxophones on the stage to await his 'off stage' introduction. When it came, and his intro music sounded, the most amazing transformation took place. He would slowly draw himself up and walk, as steady as a rock, onto centre stage where he would then play the instruments with skill, dexterity and with great feeling. Without fail, the audience would rise to his talent and after taking his well deserved curtain call, would leave the stage. As soon as he left the spotlights glare, he would resume his alcoholic state and collapse into the arms of the waiting stage crew who, quickly and efficiently, returned him to his dressing room to await the next call. Yet again, this flawed, but so talented entertainer was to reappear much later in my career but with a happy ending: I was searching for a quality big band to appear in the ballroom at the Pontin Centre at Ainsdale, near Southport, when to my amazement, he turned up fronting a group of eight musicians who were pure class. He had completely given up all alcohol and now, concentrating totally on his great love of music, formed this band. When I listened to their sound, I knew my search was over. I offered him the contract and he and his band played superbly for the many thousands of Pontin guests who danced to his music year after year after year. Well done and thank you to the brilliant Harry Bence!

The four weeks of the show went so quickly and once again, I was haunted by the fear of being out of work. The

Fairy Godmother, in the shape of Jean Baird from the Galt Agency in Glasgow, saved the day, however, leaving it to the Wednesday of the fourth week before being able to offer us a further four weeks at the Palace Theatre, Dundee – this time with the superb Scottish comedian, Johnny Beattie. Of course, we accepted with great joy and made the short journey south for the Monday opening. The pressure of changing the programme each week was bad enough but to have to perform a completely different act put quite a strain on our material. It was not just a case of selecting four or five new numbers and singing them – each song had to be arranged and the completed work given to an orchestra, who would write out the band parts. The cost of this could be

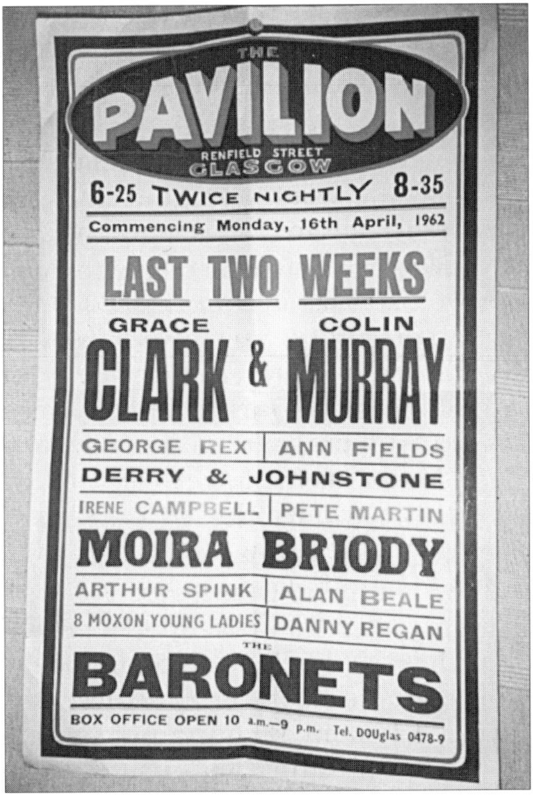

The end of another wonderful season with Clark & Murray ('Mr & Mrs Glasgow') at the Pavilion Theatre, Glasgow. The Theatre still operates to this day and is one of the very few Variety Houses left in the UK.

quite prohibitive – the Musicians Union has a set rate per bar of music – but thankfully each pit orchestra usually contained someone who would do it at a very special rate, or at least enough to cover his beer money. The result may not always have been a Peter Knight arrangement but it got us by. Mind you, sometimes we began to suspect that many of these (part-time) musicians really *couldn't* play the music that was put before them. We arrived at the Dundee Theatre on the Monday morning to go through our band call for the evening show. Try as he might, the trombone player kept playing notes on his instrument, that were never written. Exasperated, the Musical Director stopped the proceedings and the poor man looked up at us towering above him and smiled a sheepish grin, which showed clearly, he did not have a tooth in his head. "I'm sho shorry", he said, showering the whole brass section with a fine spray. "It'll be aw right the night cosh I'll have ma new teeth in!" and it was – he was note perfect!

Once again, the weeks flew by and, once again, came that haunting feeling that re-appears when the phone remains silent. That dreaded piece of plastic covered electronics, that refused to impart its joyful message that someone with good news wanted to speak with me. How often did I lift the receiver simply to check for myself that the damn thing was still connected – but it sat there, mutely mocking me! We rang our agent Jean Baird, of course, and whilst she sounded sympathetic, the message was still the same. "We're looking at every possibility but nothing has come in yet."

So the moment I had feared came to pass – I was out of work! I don't know who suggested the idea, but regardless, it was decided that if the mountain would not come to Mohammed, then Mohammed must go to the mountain. In our case, we targeted Manchester as being the centre of the many clubs that were springing up in the early sixties. We arrived with renewed hope and some optimism but I began to suspect that the fates which, up until now, had been so kind to me, had gone absent without leave. Manchester, anxious to retain its reputation put on its most dismal and dampening of welcomes – the rain lashed down and, to my horror and great discomfort (you would never believe this if you had read it in a book), my shoes were letting in water by the flood. To sum up therefore – we had no work, nowhere to stay, it was pouring with rain and I was soaked to the skin! What lunatic said showbusiness was easy?

We were finally given the name and address of a lady who took in 'theatricals' and found the terraced house in a back street, hidden by what had once been a cotton mill. I guess it was somewhat brave of her to take in four lads who each spoke with accents even more foreign than hers, but she did and split us into two double rooms – I sharing with Brian. The bed was one of the very old fashioned kind with an iron frame and headboard and I was positive that the design had been stolen from a French prison, in the days when torture was legal! The mattress, too, was a work of art, which burst into a cacophony of squeaks, groans and squeals if you did nothing more in movement than raise an eyebrow. The wooden floor was probably built by the same craftsman, for it, too, joined in the 'anvil chorus' – even when you weren't walking on it. The lady of the house then had the gall to warn us of severe penalties should we be discovered entertaining persons of the opposite sex in our rooms. On that floor? In that bed? The mental picture of the scenario such a clandestine adventure would present, sent us into mere hysterics and cheered us up immensely. "Finally", our hostess added, "there will be no breakfast." (She didn't rise until noon and the household was expected to follow suit for fear of further retribution). "Lunch will be at 2.00pm and evening meal will be when you return from your show – sometime around midnight." We didn't have the nerve to tell her we didn't have a show, so we nodded and tried to look as if we cared! On the advice of those who professed to know these things, our first stop was to register at the

Labour Exchange. As I queued to receive my pitiful hand out, my thoughts turned to my Dad and my Uncle and I thanked the power above that they couldn't see me now. We were informed that we had to sign in at 10.30am every Thursday and we tried to explain to them that we were not allowed out of bed until noon but, understandably, they wouldn't listen. And so began the weekly farce of us tiptoeing across the creaking floor boards each Thursday morning, climbing through the window and descending to the ground courtesy of a large oak tree which grew conveniently close. We would sign on and repeat the hazardous journey in reverse before climbing back into bed and lie there waiting for noon to strike.

We finally made contact with an agent by the name of Madame Ace, who sounded more like the proprietor of a house of ill repute than an agent providing work for desperate artistes. She got us four paid engagements in all – each one in a Church hall with an audience of Christian Methodists, who shouted out requests for us to sing great songs like *Onward Christian Soldiers* and *Fight the Good Fight*. By the time we had been paid, put a contribution into the collection box which was compulsory in order to leave, settled our commission and paid our expenses, we had little left to buy the fish and chip supper on the way home and things were getting desperate.

It was at this time, that fate, fresh from wherever he had been over the past many weeks, decided to re-appear in the shape of an agent called Gerry Millman. Gerry ran a very successful business with his partner, ex-wrestling champion Bill Benny and to our great delight, took a liking to our act. Almost immediately, better work with better pay began to materialise and we began to realise that there *were* some better clubs in the area. We were now appearing regularly in places like the Cabaret Clubs in Manchester and Liverpool (this was expected, as they were actually owned by Gerry). The Levenshulme, The Derby, The Northern Sporting Club and The Casino Club in Bolton. We went to one club in Manchester and were met by the owner, a chubby round faced man with a great sense of style and humour and I remember thinking he would probably make more money as a comedian than as a club owner. I did not realise at that time, that he was already combining the two and still is to this day. The club was The Embassy Club and the great guy in question was Bernard Manning.

We met so many artistes during that spell, some on the way up and many on the way down. I recall, one evening playing the College Club and being introduced by the compere, who sported the biggest handlebar moustache I had ever seen. It must have measured at least three feet across, so big in fact that he had to enter the stage from the wings sideways, to avoid it being snapped off. He brought us on to great cheers from an audience well on its way to happy-land and we, mistakenly, thought it was going to be one of our special evenings. As we moved into our opening number, the entire audience rose to its feet as one and moved towards us. Fear and panic set in and my past began unfolding before me, until I suddenly realised that the menacing mob were now indulging in what thinly passed as dancing to the sounds of our singing and were totally oblivious to our superb harmonies, great arrangements and choreographed routines. I felt insulted, yet had to give in to what they craved and we changed our programme song by song, discarding the slow ballads and replacing them with up beat throwaways. We drew that one 0-0! Top of the Bill that same evening was a handsome, sexy, young man called Gerry Dorsey and we were relieved to note that he, too, suffered the same fate. After the show we had supper with him and we departed his company, promising to keep in touch and to watch for each other's careers. We had no difficulty in keeping up with his for, shortly after, he changed his name to Englebert Humperdinck and never looked back. He is probably still looking for ours!

And so, we struggled through the winter – sometimes in work and other times, renewing our acquaintance with our friends at the Labour Exchange. I cannot admit to liking the clubs in which we worked. Occasionally, we would come across an establishment that was run on theatre lines and these were a joy to perform in – clubs like Wakefield Theatre Club, Batley Variety, Caesars Palace in Luton and Lakeside Country Club. But, all too often, we would have to play second fiddle to the Bingo which ruled the kingdom then (and now) and be subject to many of the legendary concert secretaries who wielded such power from behind their sound desks and yet knew nothing about the serious business of entertainment. They would think little of cutting you off mid song to shout for quietness"or to admonish someone for a minor discretion. In any event, it was all filed into our bank of experience and when Butlins rang to offer us another season, we were delighted to accept.

Once again, we reacted to the wonderfully warm reception from the happy guests and singing with the Eric Winstone Orchestra was such a delight after suffering 'Fred' on the organ and 'Charlie' on the drums throughout the dark months. Eric was an inveterate smoker and always had a cigarette protruding from his lips which, coupled with a nervous head twitch, played havoc with his beautiful stage suits. It was usual for his right shoulder to be a beautiful midnight blue whilst his left shoulder, a delicate ash grey. As the season wore on Eric spent less and less time on stage with the band. He would open the proceedings by fronting the opening number, usually a 'quick step', then would hand over the reins to the wonderful Roy Marsh (one of Britain's top vibraphone players), before returning to the stage piano to play the last waltz – always *Stagecoach* which he wrote himself and was the bands signature tune. I guess you can get away with it when you're the boss!

Towards the end of the season, Eric approached and asked us to sign up with the London agency he managed called

New Century Artistes, run by a very efficient lady by the name of Josephine Baker. The office was in Great Portland Place, just off Oxford Street and the thought of having a London agent with such a prestigious address, proved irresistible to us and we happily put our names to the contract. We now looked forward to the type of work we felt we deserved but, for a while, the phone receded into its normal state of winter hibernation and sat there, sullenly and silently, staring at us, each daring the other to make a move. Suddenly, it relented and the call invited us to meet the agent and show director Alan Blackburn at the Max Rivers Rehearsal rooms in London to audition for some possible work abroad. Auditioning at the same time, was a brilliant young impressionist called Peter Hudson and we felt sure that Alan would book him instead of us. Peter made the mistake of including mostly British artistes within his repertoire and this proved totally unsuitable as, we discovered later, the shows were to be structured for the American Forces serving in Europe. Our programme was deemed by Alan to be ideal and at first he had us pencilled in for a season of shows in Beirut, but later changed the venues to Southern Germany.

With that in the bag, we confidently turned up for our second audition that week, at the famous Windmill Theatre in London. We were asked to perform our act for Sheila Van Dam, the talented daughter of the legendary owner and aware of the type of shows presented in this establishment, we nurtured a wonderful mental vision of sharing backstage with all the beautiful, scantily clad and naked young ladies. I felt sure, at long last, that my Dad would finally forgive me for denying him the perk of a weekly bottle of Crawford's best and would settle for the compensation of a backstage pass whenever he was in town. But the bubble of all our collective hopes in this particular arena burst when Sheila Van Dam rang to say we weren't suitable. Maybe she felt that four strapping young guys would be too much for the customers who preferred a more feminine figure wearing much less, to be on view. Or maybe she thought we were simply not good enough but, be that as it may, it was one job we *didn't* get. Never mind Dad, we can dream can't we?

CHAPTER SIX

Germany Calling...Again!

Once again, I found myself in Germany, but this time the reasons were entirely by choice – my choice. We arrived in Weisbaden, a beautiful town in Southern Germany, not far from the Black Forest and reported to an American Air Force Sergeant by the name of Charlie Clopp. Charlie was housed in a dingy building that was laughingly called The Union Jack Club and we were quickly told that if we wanted to use the establishment we would have to pay a year's subscription. Being as we were only there for four weeks, the cost did appear rather stiff – made even stiffer when we were informed by Charlie that our yearly subscription would have to be renewed on the 1st January – only two weeks away. It was at that moment that I began to suspect our Charlie of having not a bad little business going, but worse (or better, depending which side of the fence you were on) was to follow. It was Charlie's job, we were told, to sort out the incoming artistes into 'mini' shows consisting of three or four acts and these shows would both travel and perform together throughout their stay, visiting all the American Air Bases in the area. Charlie also took it upon himself to negotiate with each of the bases, a fee for the show. The British acts were paid from the UK on a weekly basis and therefore, he owed us nothing – so everything that was paid to Sergeant Clopp went into his back pocket. I am sure that others were involved and they, too, had to be the recipients of little brown envelopes, but regardless, Sergeant Clopp stood to make a fortune! I do not know how long the scam lasted but somewhere today in the United States of America, there is an American ex-Sergeant, who is living in the lap of luxury and who never needs to work again. On the other hand, if there is any justice, he is in some State Penitentiary, breaking rocks during the day and arranging prison concerts in the evening – but somehow I doubt it!

We were coupled with a black American comedy duo called Stump and Stumpy, veteran English comedian Maxie Bacon and a female vocalist, whose performing talents didn't amount to much but her physical attributes assured her of rapt attention from the GI's. Our first and opening show was at Rheine-Meine and it was obvious that Stump and Stumpy, who topped the bill, were going to struggle, whilst Max Bacon found the differences in sense of humour, an obstacle difficult to overcome. The lady singer raised the temperature, if not the roof and it was left to us to carry the flag. I never ceased to marvel at how inconsistent our business can be. On one hand, we presented great songs that were rich in harmony and arrangement – numbers that had taken months to rehearse, only to receive polite applause. On the other hand, we literally threw in one song that had taken us two hours to complete, with no harmonies and night after night, stopped the show. The song was *Donald – Where's Yer Troosers?* and we loaded in some comedy lines and festooned the lyrics with visual props – kilts, glengarrys, bagpipes etc. It was total and utter rubbish but the Yanks loved it. Within days, we replaced Stump and Stumpy as top of the bill, Max Bacon had to return home because of ill health and our lady singer was overcome with a rash of bright spots (probably German Measles!), which added colour to her act but could do little for her vocals.

The Bases were quite superb, particularly in the Officers' mess where it was not unusual to be backed by a Big Band and the only drawback was the travelling. On New Years Eve, we had a long, long journey to Stuttgart and did not return to our accommodation until 7.00am on New Years morning. The journey had been horrendous with falling snow, ice on the roads and patchy fog and the mini bus we travelled in slithered and skidded, at one time losing the road completely in the poor conditions. We collapsed into bed exhausted but, within forty-five minutes, the 'New Years Day Parade' started the route that was to take it past our bedroom window. Band after band wended their way into our befuddled brains as we tried, unsuccessfully, to shut out the noise. Some were good but most were bad and for three hours we were tortured with the sound of out of tune bugles and manic bass drummers. It was the nearest we got to starting World War Three!

Our journey throughout the Fatherland finally came to an end and we returned to Blightly, buoyant after an unexpected success and looking forward to meeting Josephine Baker once again, and learning of the huge amount of work she had accomplished for us in our absence. We felt sure that word had carried over the channel and although we didn't quite expect *Sunday Night at the Palladium*, we did anticipate a surge of interest in view of what we had just done, and harboured hopes of at least a tickle from the moguls of television. We were in for a shock! We sat there, faces bright with expectancy – our diaries opened and our pencils poised. Jo shattered our hopes and ultimately our careers, when she told us simply that we had been offered another summer season at Butlins with a minimal increase in salary and that would commence on the 28th of May – four months away. "No," she confirmed. "There is no other work before then. Sorry lads!"

I have always been a slow burner but this was exceptional and my blood pressure took off like Apollo 13! It would appear, that in our absence, the agency had signed two very with-it male singers who had blended together as a duo and had had a very minor hit record (nothing compared of course to our Bognor Regis sensation) and whenever enquiring clients had professed an interest in booking a vocal group, the two boys were given priority. We spilled out into Great Portland Street still fuming and retired to a coffee shop to make decisions. I had already make up my mind by now and informed the guys that, regardless of what they thought, I would not put up with the constant ebb and flow of showbusiness any more. I had had enough. They attempted to talk me out of my decision but eventually withdrew when they realised how serious I was. It was then I blessed Mum and Dad and my Uncle Bob for driving me to fulfil all the extra studies I so hated.

With the fire still burning inside of me, I walked out of the café and turned right onto Oxford Street and kept walking. Suddenly, I stopped and, looking up, found myself standing outside the Marble Arch offices of Butlins Ltd. I was overcome with that eerie feeling of being driven on by forces unseen as I approached reception and in a voice that seemed to come form someone else, I asked to speak with Wally Goodman. Again fate played its part, because Wally was *never* in his office – he was the most difficult man ever to get hold of, even if you had an appointment. Yet there I was sitting face to face with this entertainment icon, telling him of the groups demise and my desire to rejoin his Company in an Executive capacity! I rattled off my precious qualifications and Wally mused over my somewhat fierce and self-opinionated application for a top management position for what seemed an age. He was probably taken aback in some ways at the transformation that had overcome me, but I was still burning at the sudden down turn to our singing career and how unfairly we had been treated. Worst of all however, was the thought that maybe – just maybe – I would have to return to Edinburgh, my tail between my legs and admit to Mum, Dad and Uncle Bob that I had failed. I had been a fool and I had suffered! I could already hear the sniggers and the snipers sharpening their knives. Oh, that bitter foul taste of humble pie and I thought – 'No, not just yet, I'll give it one more go.' And so, sitting face to face with

Wally Goodman, I awaited his answer, knowing it would be my last chance to stay in this unpredictable, uncompromising and very unfair business – yet one I was beginning to love with a passion, one which was beginning to consume my every waking moment and one which I was now so desperate to be a part of. His reply took a lifetime but was so sweet in content. He was offering me a single step on the ladder to success and although it was the very bottom rung, my right foot was already in position as I accepted his offer and, once again, my career had taken a dramatic turn. For better or for worse, it would soon become apparent, but in the meantime I had to digest two further conditions, one good and the other not so. The good news was that the job, providing I proved successful over the forthcoming season, would be permanent and the bad was that the position of Assistant Entertainment Manager would not commence until the 28th May 1964, still four months away. With the prospect, however, of a pay cheque being guaranteed on a regular basis, this was not going to be a problem. To bridge the period of waiting I eventually took a job with the retail electrical giants, Civic, at their branch in Wimbledon and each morning, my first job was to sweep the floor, dust all the shelves and counter stock and wash the entrance and adjoining pavement. I cannot tell you how often I looked over my shoulder during that time, dreading the thought of seeing anyone who knew me from the days when we appeared on stages throughout Britain on our way, we felt sure, to success and international stardom. How they would smile to themselves and think what a fool I had been with my head in the clouds and my feet of clay and just look at him now. Thankfully, I saw no one from the past and if I had, I am sure now, that unkind thoughts would not have entered their heads, but then, young and still rather foolish, pride has so much control over mind and imagination. Everyone, you are certain, is so concerned about you and the way you lead your life and it is only when you reach later life with its wisdom and maturity, that you realise that nothing could be further from the truth. And so I cleaned and dusted, scrubbed and polished. I mended electric irons for little old ladies and spoke with commanding authority on the virtues of radios and gramophones – something I knew absolutely nothing about.

As much as I enjoyed the experience, despite my fear of recognition, I longed for the weeks to pass by and for May to arrive and soon it did. Once again, I headed for the bright lights, the fun and the gaiety but this time it was different. Gone was the red blazer and the white slacks and in its place was the subdued tie, the obligatory clipboard (which told me nothing but had to be carried everywhere to show authority) and most important of all, the suit. I had arrived, I was on the rung – I was a boss!

CHAPTER SEVEN

Boss at Butlins (Almost)

I learned in the first few weeks, how difficult the transition was from being one of the gang to being the one in control and I almost blew it. Not for me, the disciplinarian, the hard, unbending martinet from high command – no, I would be the gentle, kind, ever-understanding, everyones-uncle type of controller and so I was. I revelled in the banter with the Reds, the jokes we told and the endless cups of tea we shared off duty. I enjoyed the popularity I had from the boys and girls, but slowly, I began to realise that the one thing missing from the various emotions afforded to me was the one thing I needed more than anything else to be a success in my new lofty position – respect! If I walked into a bar, or a ballroom or theatre, I would see the kids stiffen when they realised that a 'suit' was present but just as quickly relax into stand-down mode, when they realised it was only me. It was then that I decided that things had to change and change quickly if I was to be accepted by the hierarchy and processed from full-time employment elect into full-time employment permanent. This may have been more difficult than was possible, given the start I had made but thankfully, in the early part of July, I was transferred to Skegness and was able to drop the word 'Assistant' from my title and replace with 'Deputy' – a step up indeed!

Skegness is a town steeped in holidaymakers from the turn of the last century and sad to relate, the fare enjoyed by them in that bygone time, has changed very little. There is an almost archaic air of stagnation permeating amongst its shops and cafes and yet to some, it is that, more than any other characteristic that gives it its quaint appeal. Surrounding the town centre is the myriad of small hotels and boarding houses and beyond them are the flatlands of Lincolnshire, heavily impregnated, particularly in coastal areas, with caravan parks and camping areas. How they must have felt, when the foresight of a young entrepreneur by the name of Billy Butlin descended on their tranquillity, and decided in 1936 to build the first piece of the jigsaw that was to become an empire on their land, offering accommodation to over seven thousand guests per week. The amount of revenue it brought into the town surely saved the resort from possible extinction and we can only assume that those who make a living from the tourist industry, are forever grateful.

I drove my new, but very second hand car (a Morris Minor, bought to compound my managerial status), through the main gate and quickly settled into the new routine. Office work has never frightened me and I revelled in the organisational skills required in producing details, charts and running orders for the shows. The *Sunday Startime Show,* was always a great thrill for me, for not only did I enjoy watching the performances of the top of the bill artistes, but in my new job capacity, it was my duty to meet them on their arrival, take them through their band calls and, best of all, join them for an after-show meal (and drinks) before they faced the long drive home. (Anyone who has visited Skegness will know that, no matter where you happen to live, *everywhere* is a long drive home!) How I looked forward to *my,* 'Sunday night with the Stars'. Each week, I would be in the social company of household names such as Donald Peers, Charlie Chester, Vic Oliver, Jimmy Jewell and Ben Warriss, Anne Shelton, Ruby Murray, Tommy Trinder and dozens more. I was always so amazed to find that these superstars from radio, stage, record and latterly TV, whom I expected to have two heads and speak with an alien tongue from another planet, were simply ordinary people, with bills and mortgages to pay, with worries, no different to you and I and who did the basic things common to everyone else, despite rumours to the contrary! A good example was the first time I met Leslie Welch, TVs' 'Memory Man'. I felt sure his act was 'fixed' and when he asked for someone to shout out a question from the audience, I was certain I had him rumbled. Not so! His act was to ask the audience to fire any question at him involving sport and he would rattle off FA Cup winners, give the teams, the referee and even the ball-boys. He would recall events going back over one hundred years, not only on football but on cricket, boxing, athletics, speedway, golf and horse racing. His only fear was, like that of every other Artiste, not having a good 'get-off' – his big finish, so to speak – and he asked for someone, when given the cue, to ask for the winner of the Grand National of 1932. Leslie not only gave the winner but also listed the first three past the post, the jockeys and the betting prices. Then he did the same for 1933, 1934 and so on up to the present day, walking off the stage to thunderous applause from a totally amazed audience. The man was brilliant, with a photographic memory, but the bubble burst for me at any rate, when he shook me warmly by the hand as he left the centre, only to return an hour and a half later, muttering audibly to himself as he passed through the gate. "Silly me – I left my bloody pyjamas in the chalet!"

Another great performer who appeared regularly, was the wonderful Dickie Henderson – adored by the Butlin guests. The problem before, but more particularly, after the show, was the crowds of autograph hunters and although most artistes were always happy to sign, we always steered them away from the main body of signature seekers to avoid the possibility of a mass mobbing. On one occasion, we had successfully guided Dickie to his car near the main gate when out of the gathering gloom, two girls appeared waving autograph books in the air. As they rushed towards us,

Dickie smiled, resigned to being tracked down and slowly walked towards them, taking out his pen ready to oblige.

The girls passed him as if he wasn't there and to my utter embarrassment, grabbed me by the arm. "Mr Kennedy," they said breathlessly. "We've had a brilliant holiday, will you sign our books for us?"

At that moment, I just wished the earth would have opened up and swallowed me, but Dickie just laughed. "Who's looking after who?" he asked.

It was at this time that I interviewed and auditioned a young lad from the south coast of England, by the name of Jack Harris. Jack had a really broad southern burr, with an equally broad smile and warm personality and when he presented himself to me, he explained his ambition to be a top magician. He had brought his best effects with him and, for the next thirty minutes or so, I was subject to his full repertoire of tricks and illusions delivered with a series of one line gags and observations. It was nothing new or original and, to be frank, I had seen it all before, but nonetheless, I warmed to his personality and took him on as a Redcoat. He proved popular with the guests, but struggled with his act – especially in the theatre where most of the shows were held. The Chinese rings, floating silks and producing cards from a shuffled pack may have proved popular in his front room at home, but meant nothing in a theatre which held one thousand five hundred people. So we had to remove him from the running orders, much to our regret and his disgust. The solution appeared quite suddenly, and quite tragically, when Uncle Boko, our well loved children's entertainer who had been a stalwart – indeed almost a legend within our department – passed away, leaving a massive gap to be filled. A great many of our younger guests persuaded their mums and dads to take a holiday at Butlins, Skegness for no other reason than to be in the company and be entertained by the great man himself. It looked to be an almost impossible task – until I thought of

Jack Harris. At first he withdrew at the very thought of being with upwards of one thousand children each week and gave me every argument for him not to be considered, but he eventually, on careful consideration and notwithstanding the generous rise in salary we were offering, decided to give it a try. He took to it like a duck takes to water and the kids loved him, despite the Chinese rings, floating silks and producing cards from a shuffled pack. The reason I mention this pleasant but unremarkable incident, is that Jack stayed as resident Children's Uncle for three seasons before deciding not to return. I was extremely disappointed but held no grudge – it was his decision and he was entitled to make it. I was surprised, however, to learn that he had taken a job with the opposition – Pontins – and was attached to the Entertainment Executive, David Lever as his 'gofer' or general dogsbody. I filed that information at the back of my mind for possible use in the future and I was surprised at the speed in which this new contact in high places was called upon to re-direct the course of my life yet again.

For three years I had established myself in the position of Deputy Entertainment Manager, working at Skegness during the summer months and transferring to the winter club at Margate from November to March. Each year, I dutifully rang Wally Goodman to discuss the following summer season and possible promotion to full Entertainments Manager and each year, Wally would reply with the same dreary and well-worn script. "Not yet son – you need another year!"

He was so wrong and I knew it! I was ready for the top job. I was confident and I was ambitious. Nevertheless, each year I accepted, with disappointment, the wisdom of this Head Office sage and turned up yet again for another season as number two.

In November of 1966, I rang Wally expecting the same answer and, to my utter amazement and delight he, at long last, fulfilled my dream and invited me to spend the next summer at Minehead as a fully blown Entertainments Manager. I was ecstatic and spent the cold winter months preparing my programme and the show productions but was horrified when a letter arrived in late February 1967 from Head Office informing me to report to Skegness for the summer, once again as Deputy Entertainments Manager. I rang Wally immediately, expecting him to assure me the letter was a mistake but he curtly apologised and muttered something about a 'change of plan'. Once again my blood boiled and after replacing the phone from Wally, I picked it up immediately and rang Jack Harris. Jack spoke with David Lever and it was arranged that I should meet David at Belle Vue, Manchester the following week where he would interview me as a possible Entertainments Manager. If Butlins didn't want me (their loss!), I felt sure that Pontins would and my optimism was totally and completely justified.

CHAPTER EIGHT

Blue is the Colour

David Lever was a delight. He carried a great deal of weight both in his professional life and on his physical being. He smoked incessantly, enjoyed a drink and spoke in a staccato voice that gave the wrong impression to those who didn't know him. He had a heart of gold and although, in many ways, he was a rogue, he was a very loveable one and had very few, if any, enemies. I should have hated the interview, I should have been nervous, I should have made a meal of my fingernails but I did none of these things. David and I chatted like old buddies and when we parted company, he had offered me a choice of two centres – Blackpool or Bracklesham Bay in Sussex. I chose Blackpool (wasn't that the entertainment capital of the UK?) and started work as Entertainment Manager on 1st April 1967. I had made it at long last!

The Centre Manager too, was newly appointed as part of a clean sweep, for the camp at Squires Gate had suffered greatly in previous years due to incompetent management. The out-going Entertainments Manager, by the name of Barney, had more fiddles than the London Philharmonic Orchestra and was well on his way to making a personal fortune. One of his pet 'scams' was to hang around reception on Saturday afternoon (intake day) and collar one of the many disappointed families being turned away. In those days the camps were filled for the summer by the end of February but the odd few turned up each week, hoping for cancellations. Barney would swoop, taking them out of reception and therefore out of earshot and would offer them a chalet for the family for 25% less than the going rate. The families would accept with great alacrity and blessing their good fortune, would follow Barney to their chalet allocated them for the week – *his* chalet! He merely moved in with a friend and the deal was done. A quick word and a folded note to the Catering Manager and the family were given their table in the dining room. The deal was done but Barney, the General Manager and many others, parted company with their employers, leaving the door open for myself and the new General Manager – Bill Armistead.

Bill was a thorough Lancastrian – stocky, bluff and loud with a face of granite but underneath that fearsome exterior was the family man with a heart of gold. He and I hit it off immediately and enjoyed a working relationship that grew stronger and stronger as the months and years progressed. Bill almost never used the internal phone – he simply opened the window of his office and bellowed out the name of any person he wished to contact. Once, he shouted out my name and fourteen Jims arrived at his office – two from as far away as Preston, fifteen miles to the east. In addition to his prolific vocal prowess, he was also a grafter who would think nothing of rolling up his sleeves and diving into the kitchens to cook and serve the meals if they were under pressure. It goes without saying that with all these laudable characteristics, it was inevitable that he would enjoy a pint – or maybe more. He had his own stool situated at the corner of the bar and woe betide anyone who occupied it – staff or guest! He would sit there night after night, like the Lord of the Manor, surveying his subjects and supping steadily. Friday evening was the worst, despite the fact (or probably because of it) that he had to appear with me on stage at 11.45pm to say the farewells to the majority of the guests who were leaving for home the following day. I would bring all the Bluecoats to stand in a line in front of the stage and introduce Bill, who by now would be suffering from an overdose of liquid refreshment. At this stage the ballroom would be packed to overflowing with guests who would press forward to listen to the speech from someone, no less, than the Camp Manager himself! Bill would solemnly take out a folded piece of paper roll from his pocket and start his speech by pointing out that the wonderful holiday they had just experienced was totally due to the wonderful staff he employed and reading from the roll, listed each department one by one. It was not long before the guests cottoned on to what was happening and they slowly drifted away, leaving only the staff patiently waiting for their own department to be mentioned before giving themselves a huge cheer, prolonged applause and disappearing into the night air. Forty five minutes later, the only people left in the huge ballroom space were the waitresses (he always left them to last because he knew that there were a great deal of them!), the Bluecoats trying hard to smile and yawn at the same time, Bill, myself and the band who had their heads down, scribbling away on the back of cigarette packets in an attempt to work out their rapidly accumulating overtime earnings. Bill would then dispense with the girls from the restaurant, wait for the massive roar they always allowed him and carefully refolding his list would retire once again to his stool at the bar to receive the congratulations from all those still capable of coherent speech. The one and only time the ritual changed was the day that Bill, who was never ill, suffered from a particularly nasty but very brave virus and it fell to the Assistant Camp Manager to make the speech. He moved to the microphone and addressed the expectant hordes of guests and staff alike. "It's been a wonderful week, we've enjoyed having you here and the staff and I join me in wishing you a safe journey home!"

And with that he was gone leaving everyone, including the guests, who had been told what to expect, in a state of limbo and shock. The band never forgave me for it and were convinced it was done deliberately in an attempt to cut their wages.

One of the saddest days I can remember during the five years I spent at Blackpool was the day of the air crash. A team of twelve German air technicians had arrived that morning by chartered private jet and had spent the day working at the British Aerospace experimental base at Warton, near Lytham St Annes. They were due to return to Germany the same day, from Blackpool Airport – which backed onto the centre – with a take off scheduled for 6.00pm. By the time they lined up at the end of the runway ready for departure, the time was reading 6.10pm. The plane, tragically, never left the ground. It was discovered later that the locking pin, which held the yoke (or joy stick) in a rigid position, was still in place and the aircraft smashed through three lines of chalets, killing everyone but two passengers outright. By the Grace of God, every single guest was in the dining room enjoying their evening meal when the crash happened and every chalet was empty. But for that, the death toll would have been much greater. First to the scene, was the English national number one Table Tennis champion, Dennis Neil and his playing partner English coach, Colin Deaton, who had been playing an exhibition match only an hour earlier. They had been in their car and ready to leave the site when they witnessed the terrible accident and raced to the scene. Despite the carnage and the ensuing flames, they managed to pull out the two passengers still alive and it was their unquestionable bravery that saved their lives. A year later, the two survivors returned to meet Dennis and Colin and present them with an award for courage.

What had happened cast a pall of gloom over everyone and I had to rearrange the evening programme in an attempt to lift everyone's spirits. Pivotal to the events was a Bluecoat show and I spent nearly an hour with the kids getting them into the right frame of mind to perform – not an easy task.

With every tragedy, however, there is always a moment of humour and in this case, it was provided by the warmth of an East End Cockney called George who approached the General Manager. "I just cannot believe it! I lived by London's Dockland throughout the war and the Germans bombed me day and night and the house survived. I then moved to central London and the Germans still bombed me day and night and the house survived. Now we're at peace and I come to Pontins in Blackpool for a holiday and the bloody Germans have just flattened my chalet!"

For the first time at any Pontin Centre, I was allowed to audition and select my own Bluecoat team. Normally, the Blues were chosen by Head Office and it was they who farmed out those who were successful to each of the twenty-four centres, but for some reason I was allowed to advertise and choose who I wanted myself. I was aware that, because of Barneys indiscretions and his panache for making money, the standard of entertainment (and indeed every other department), was at rock bottom and I had been tasked to raise the standard up to a level commensurate with the Camp, which boasted 'Blackpool' within its title. Perhaps that was why I was given the Company's confidence, but in any event, I tackled the task of bringing together a team which had talent, personality and an ability to work under my control. The resultant search of characters proved so successful and indeed enjoyable that I continued the task year after year until my eventual retirement thirty-two years later. Whether it was pure luck or maybe some little skill on my part, but I 'discovered' quite a few talented kids who moved through the ranks of our training schedules, gaining wonderful experience in the complex world of entertainment and emerged at the other end to become major stars of stage, film and especially TV. That, however is another chapter, which I will write about later.

No mention of my early years at Pontins, Blackpool would be complete without a mention of my 'special' find – Ken Skelton. At first, I simply could not believe I had taken the lad on. He was quiet, introvert and lacked everything required for the job. I suspected I had made a big mistake in offering Ken the season, for in comparison to the others, he was an also ran. During my time at Butlins, it was the norm for each Centre to employ a camp comic – not the stand up variety but more in the shape of the village idiot type. The kind who always dresses in 'scruff', who always creates havoc wherever he or she appears and whose comedic value is almost entirely visual. Pontins had never used this tool before and I was desperate to be the first to introduce it. Easier said than done, however, for these characters are born and not bred. Everyone on our team had a specific role to play and could not be spared to 'roam' around as required by our funny man and so I looked long and hard at Ken. Once again, I could not believe my decision but I eventually pulled him aside and after explaining to him the sort of role I wanted him to play, asked whether or not he could handle it. He said he would give it a go and I let him loose on our unsuspecting public. I expected little or nothing and confidently anticipated that within two weeks, I would be reeling him back into obscurity and an almost certain early end to his season, if not his career. What happened was sensational! A complete metamorphosis took place and Ken changed from the unassuming, retiring person that he has been, into the funniest, most gregarious personality it has been my good fortune to know. If Ken had been around in Hollywood at the start of the 20th Century when silent comedy was king, he would have topped the list of greats – better than Chaplin, Keaton and Lloyd. He took Blackpool by storm and I am sure put thousands more guests into the camp. In the Saturday 'Welcome' show he arrived on stage by swinging on a large rope, dressed in a leotard and yodelling the Tarzan call. He got away with murder! I introduced a late night scary film for all the horror addicts. When the plot climbed to its crescendo and every guest in the cinema cowered in terror at what they were watching, Ken would creep into the auditorium and clamp a huge false hand, covered in hair and dripping in false blood, on the shoulder of an unsuspecting young lady. It became so bad we had to ask the first aid centre to stay open during the film to administer oxygen and cardiac massage to the victims. We asked, too, for the laundry to remain open for obvious reasons!

Another great area for Ken to work was the professional wrestling ring. We attracted many great names of the grappling game and each week, we watched the likes of Big Daddy, Jackie Pallo, Giant Haystacks, Mick McManus and many more. It was always agreed that the final bout would be the 'goodie' versus the 'villain' and when the match was at its climax, with the baddie being screamed at by the 'fans', in would walk Ken who would start by baiting the evil one. Cheered on by the guests, he would intensify his tirade until he would be chased around and finally trapped, in the centre of the ring. Ken was slightly built but, in actual fact, was an extremely good gymnast and to the delight of the crowd, would throw the 'unsuspecting' victim all over the arena before pinning him to the floor for the count of three. The wrestlers of course, were in on the fun and indeed had coached and rehearsed with Ken and the resultant combat made him a hero. They talked about it for days after.

Ken however, didn't monopolise all the fun alone. We instigated a number of running gags, which the guests loved. The best was, without doubt, the 'Cannon of Death' and this was strongly advertised in the weekly programme – 'Sunday 10.30pm – The Cannon of Death', it proclaimed, 'See a man fired from the sensational Cannon of Death from one side of the ballroom to the other and be caught in the safety net'. Naturally the ballroom was packed and first on stage was the compere who introduced the (mad) professor who had invented this great spectacular weapon. He spoke with a rich European accent interspersed with a mad maniacal laugh and after describing what was to happen, introduced the 'brave, brave' person who would undergo the feat. Enter Ken unrecognisable in frogman's suit, helmet, goggles and flippers and he was then checked over by a physician in white coat and by an undertaker in black. Finally, came the arrival of the Canon itself hauled by four strapping lads, stripped to the waist. The Cannon was, in fact, three dustbins with the bottoms removed and welded together to form the barrel. The bottom of the barrel was covered by a black cloth and the whole tube was fitted onto a flat base with four large wheels. Obviously the barrel was angled upwards and Ken climbed a ladder before disappearing down the tube feet first, waving farewell to all and sundry as he disappeared from view. Amidst the ravings of the mad professor and the ballroom band playing suitable raucous music, the firer now entered the scene. Four Bluecoats held the net on the far side of the ballroom and the fuse was lit. Slowly the sparking fuse reduced in size until it disappeared into the fuse box...and fizzled out! There was great panic amongst the players and eventually the professor announced a technical fault 'which would be repaired' and the whole thing would be re-enacted on the Tuesday. All day Tuesday, all that could be heard was, 'Will they? – Won't they?' and the whole scenario was repeated with the same result. Thursday was the next date set for the event and this time, it *did* go off. The flash of magnesium blinded the audience for a few seconds, corresponding with the lights in the ballroom being extinguished and they therefore did not see the figure dressed exactly like Ken and resplendent in frogsuit, helmet, goggles, etc., run out from a hidden door and roll into the net. Meanwhile the cannon with Ken inside was pushed up against the dressing room door and Ken would slide through the curtain at the base of the barrel and out. When the lights went up and his double climbed from the safety net, the audience would react with laughter, applause and shouts of 'fix' and worse. Great fun though and one we did for two seasons.

Two more gags we did with success were 'The Long Distance Runner' and the cash 'Bingo' fraud. The Long Distance Runner was introduced on the Saturday evening and the announcement explained that a long distance runner was going to attempt the Pontin Marathon, starting at Blackpool on the forthcoming Friday when he would endeavour to run to and through every Pontin Camp in the UK – twenty five in all. He would be in strict training throughout the week and – please – hinder him not! Every event from then on, including the evening shows in the theatre and even the swimming gala, would see this figure in running shorts, shoes and vest jogging through each presentation and creating havoc with the participants. On the Friday afternoon, he would turn up at the starting point with probably 90% of the guests on hand to cheer him on his way. He would adopt the starting crouch, the starter would produce his starting pistol, count down with the command, 'On your marks – get set – go!' and fire. The runner would fall over, apparently shot and from nowhere a van would appear, two 'orderlies' would scoop the body onto a stretcher, throw him into the vehicle and roar away, leaving everyone dumfounded, non plussed and wondering what the heck was happening.

Finally, the cash Bingo gag, which was operated during the weekly Bluecoat show. Each guest arriving at the show was handed a Bingo ticket as they arrived and told to hold onto it and an explanation would follow. Half way through the show, the compere would tell everyone that Pontins at Blackpool had won an award for the best entertainment and had received a cheque for one thousand pounds. Unable to decide how to use the money, it had been suggested that we call Bingo numbers during the show and the first person to shout 'house' on a line would collect the prize money. The old-fashioned cage and balls were brought on stage and the calling began. What the audience didn't realise, was that although every ticket looked different (the colour, the position of the numbers), each card contained a line of the five same numbers and the caller was reading the numbers from a script and not from each ball as it was drawn. When the fourth number was read out and each member of the audience realised that they were waiting for just one more number, the atmosphere became electric. We deliberately dragged out the tension before finally calling out the fifth and final winning number. The explosion of sound as over one thousand voices roared out 'house', sent the pigeons spiralling into the sky from nearby Manchester. There was a pause of five seconds or so as the brains worked out what had happened, followed by great roars of laughter as they realised they had been duped.

Sport always featured heavily in the centres and we specialised in bringing the top sportsmen and women to give demonstrations. From the world of snooker, I recall taking on one of the top players from Lancashire – a comparatively unknown player by the name of John Spencer. John lived in Radcliffe near Manchester and because he did not have far to travel, coupled with the fact that his appearance was during the daytime, his fee was very reasonable and more important to Pontins, affordable. Sensing I had got a good deal, I extended the contract to three years with an option for a further two. Hardly had the ink dried on his signature, when John entered and won the Embassy World Snooker Championship at Sheffield, not just once, but many times more. I cannot describe my joy (nearly as much as John's), when the last ball was potted and I realised that the Pontin guests would now be able to meet and actually play, the reigning world champion. John remained totally faithful to Pontins in the North (he also appeared at Morecambe, Southport and Prestatyn Sands), as did the superb Ray Reardon who worked on the Southern Centres. Both were lovely men and great ambassadors, not only for their sport but for themselves, too. It was also such a great privilege to meet the legendary Blackpool and England footballing great, Stan Mortensen. I contacted Stan with a view to making a personal appearance at the camp and he not only agreed, but also brought his personal film of the 1953 Cup final at

Wembley, to show the guests. It was known as the 'Mathews' final for obvious reasons but in fact, Stan scored a hat trick and, to this day, that feat had never been repeated. Stan refused payment to appear – he just loved the game, loved being with the fans and he sat at a table with only a microphone and answered questions until it got dark. He was a delightful man with a wonderful sense of humour. Bless you Stan.

With the combined efforts of Bill Armistead and myself bearing much fruit, we were justified in claiming the Top Centre award within the company. Fred Pontin acknowledged that we had lifted the camp from the mess it was certainly in at the beginning of 1967 to the high status it now enjoyed five years later. For that reason alone, I was Fred's 'blue-eyed boy' and I enjoyed a warm relationship with the 'Guv'nor' (as he was know by all his staff). He was undoubtedly a character and a larger that life personality and stories abounded of the man – some true and some debatable. In many ways he could be a bully if he felt you would not stand up to him and he loved the limelight and the chance to show off.

By now, I was allowed to book the supporting artistes on the Sunday night show although the Star names were always booked by David Lever at Head Office. Although trusted by Fred to find the acts to appear in such a prestigious presentation, there was no way he would allow me to sign their contracts. I would negotiate with each performer, working to a tight budget, type the details onto a contract and each Friday morning, would catch the very early train from Blackpool to London, arriving a 10.20am approximately, before taking the underground to Oxford Circus where Fred had his office, in order to receive his signature on each document. It was a ritual that had to be undertaken each week and, each week, he would have me sitting outside his office until late afternoon before he would see me. When the call came, I would enter his palatial quarters and if someone or some other people were still in the room, I knew what to expect. He would scrutinise each contract studiously and as he worked his way through them, would shout out remarks like "Never heard of him" and more often "I'm not paying that sort of money to a nobody!" Many times too, he would lift a particularly offending document and tear it into tiny shreds before throwing the pieces high into the air and watch them float down like confetti. On the other hand, however, if Fred was alone and there was no one to perform to – he was a joy! He'd ask me to close the door, then go to his hospitality cupboard and produce two glasses which he filled with the best wine (for him) and orange juice (for me). He would sign the contract like a lamb, then, feet up on the desk, would go into memory mode, recalling the early day of his life, which I found fascinating. I only fell out with him once and that was due entirely to his frustration at finding nothing to shout at in front of his friends. He had arrived at Blackpool for an unexpected visit (his visits were *always* unexpected but because he normally flew in by helicopter, we nearly always had advance warning) and I met him mid-afternoon. He informed me that he was bringing in a few friends and wanted me to reserve eight seats on the side balcony of the Theatre/Club for 10.00pm. He enquired who the cabaret was that evening and I fed him the information he required. He wandered off and I knew that, with his friends around him, it could be a stormy session. I was determined that nothing should go wrong and I rang that evenings cabaret – The Ukrainian Cossacks – and ensured that they would arrive in plenty of time. Next, I spoke with the resident band leader – Lennie McEllin – and asked him to change his schedule for that evening. It was normal for the band to break at 10.00pm in order to collect the band parts from the visiting cabaret and talk through any alterations or additions to the act. Just before 10.30pm they would then file back on stage, ready for the show scheduled to start at 10.30pm. If Fred had walked into the Theatre/Club at 10.10pm and found no band on the stage, he would have gone into orbit, so Lennie agreed to forfeit their band break. He also informed me that the uniform for that night, in honour of Fred's appearance, would be black evening suits and, as band leader, he would front in a white evening jacket. I was happy with that and when Fred turned up with his entourage, the place was jumping. The band were playing out of their skins and the ballroom floor was packed. The Cossacks took the floor dead on time and finished with a standing ovation. The crowd cheered and on cue, Fred beckoned me over and said he wanted to make a speech. The Chief Hostess escorted him onto the stage and the band blasted out *For He's A Jolly Good Fellow*. The audience was screaming their approval at Fred's few words and with adulation ringing in his ears, was led back to his table. His hand rose and beckoned me over. I went willingly, confident I was to receive his praise and congratulations and his audience of acquaintances leaned inwards so as not to miss a word. He didn't disappoint them. "Bloody shambles!" he yelled. " I have never seen a more scruffy band. Look at him". His finger pointed to the band leader, "Look at him! Can't he afford a black evening suit like the rest of them? Sack him!"

Fred's diatribe left me speechless and I turned on my heels and walked out of the building. For days I did nothing and said nothing and on the Thursday my phone rang. It was Fred. He could not have been nicer and the following day, when I went to London for the weekly signing fiasco, I was ushered straight in and we ended up at Verris restaurant in Regent Street for a very acceptable lunch.

There are a great many stories concerning this great character and I will relate those, especially the funnier of them, in a later chapter. Basically, I had a great love and admiration for the man. Yes, he had faults and yes he made enemies, but the guests adored him and it was a sad day for the Company when he decided to stand down. Working for him was being a part of his family and if you were ever in any trouble, he would be the first to offer help. A one-off and one I was proud to work for.

My admiration and love for the man, however, did not prevent me from making a move which resulted in me leaving the Company in the spring of 1972 and it was a further sporting link that caused the initial spark of dissension. We were delighted when British Boxing Heavyweight Champion, Jack Bodell, contacted us to enquire whether or not he could use the centre as his training camp, in preparation for a forthcoming fight to be held in the Tower Ballroom, Blackpool. We agreed and Jack and his entourage duly moved in. He trained each day and inevitably we got to know him well and planned to be there on the night to give him our support. Complimentary tickets were left with Bill Armistead for distribution to whom he thought fit but, when I confidently asked him for mine, he blustered and made excuses. On the day of the fight, I collared Bill in his office, still expecting at least one 'comp', but was met with a string of excuses, emphasising that my job was too important to be 'swanning' off to a boxing match and that I was needed on site. In short, he had given my ticket away to some lesser deserving recipient (my thoughts) and there were none left for me. If Bill had left it there and maybe apologised to me, calling it an oversight or an error or something, I would probably have got over it, but from his stool in the bar, he used it as a joke and soon everyone knew and continued to rub it in. I retreated to my office smarting from the hurt and fuming at the (I must admit), 'out of character' moment from Bill. Like all others in a similar position, my mind took over and raced away with imponderable schemes of retribution, from murder and incarceration to the more mundane act of simply walking out. But what would I do? What *could* I do? I glanced idly at the situations vacant column in *The Stage* newspaper and immediately my eye caught sight of an advert for Cruise Directors for P&O Lines. Applicants had to make contact with a company called Hubert Warren

Orchestras and still burning from the snub, intentional or not, I scribbled out a brief CV. In the cold light of the following day, I chastised myself for being so stupid. 'I should never have sent it', I told myself a hundred times, but each time I was consoled by the almost certain knowledge that I would most likely never hear from them, anyway. So it seemed and three months went by.

By now, I was back into the swing with all disagreements firmly buried and again, thoroughly enjoying the job, when out of the blue a letter arrived on 'P&O Lines' headed notepaper inviting me to an interview the following week in London. I could not believe this was happening to me and almost threw the letter in the bin, but good reasoning prevailed and having decided that I had little or nothing to lose, I presented myself to the selection board on the day, once again expecting the adventure to come to a natural conclusion. Because of the situation I was in and the fact that I was totally relaxed, I sailed through the interview, almost hoping that I would not be offered the position and I travelled back North assuming that I would receive notification within two days of my dismal failure to impress. No such letter arrived and I merely put it down to the old human failing of rushing around and overwhelming those whom you would want to recruit and ignoring totally those you wouldn't.

To my surprise (and growing panic) I received yet another notification fourteen days later, requesting me to visit London yet again, this time to appear on a short list of three. Once again, I wavered and once again I decided to see it through. The whole concept was beginning to assume nightmarish proportions and the earnest desire to rewind the clock was paramount in my thoughts. Surely, I reasoned, someone would see through me and realise that I was not capable of doing the job, but yet again I navigated the interview, answering all the questions thrown at me with some surety, yet pleading with them, mentally, not to like me. They did, however and I received their letter of intent two days later. The invitation was to join the *SS Arcadia* four weeks later as a 'supernumerary' Entertainment Officer, leaving Southampton for a two week Mediterranean cruise and thereafter as decided. The offer came as a total shock but I must admit to being flattered at being taken on to do a job most other people would kill for and I thought about the consequences and what it would involve – long and hard! It felt as if fate was playing into my hands and decisions were being made without any consultation whatsoever with me. An unseen hand reached into my brain, flicked a switch and immediately it all became clear – I knew what I was going to do and I suddenly felt at peace – fuelled by a slow burn of excitement for what lay ahead. I sought out Bill Armistead and told him of my decision to leave and, to his credit, he took the news phlegmatically, almost as if he had expected it. Fred however, was less stoical, indicating that to leave the 'Family' was punishable by the most extreme method of execution. But by the time the four week notice to finish had almost expired, he had regained his composure and paid me the extreme compliment of driving from London to Blackpool to wish me luck. "Do what you have to," he conceded. "Get it out of your system, but if, after two years, you decide you've had enough – your job will still be here and open for you." Maybe he realised that what he had just said could be taken as a sign of emotional softening for he quickly added, "Leave it any longer and you've had it – you're on your own!" It was so typical of the man and so appreciated by me.

CHAPTER NINE

Gone Cruisin'

I stood on the quayside at Southampton and gazed in wonder at the 30,000-ton monster of a ship that was going to be my floating home for the next period of my life. In comparison to other ships afloat at that time, the *Arcadia* was comparatively small but, to me, it was a giant superstructure of immense proportions and I felt like Captain Cook embarking into the unknown on a voyage of discovery. In the early seventies, the ship was divided into two separate sections – first class and tourist – and never the twain shall meet. I was seconded to the Tourist Entertainment Officer by the name of David Hall-Green, whilst the other 'super' went off to join the legendary Bill Alison, in first. Bill had been running the shipboard entertainment for the P&O fleet for more years than he would care to remember and during that time had fashioned a style of performance that put him in a class of his own. Many old hands swore that Bill took full control of whichever ship he was allotted and this included the Captain, Staff Captain and all others of authority. Nevertheless, his presentation of entertainment was of the highest quality and pure class in its conception and he accepted and wore with pride, an air of invincibility and total command that made even the sternest of passenger jump to attention when he spoke!

David Hall-Green was tall and studious and good at his job. He bade me watch, listen and learn and I did just that as he presided over the first evening of introductions, get-togethers and 'meet the Captain 'cocktail party. It was smoothly done with minimum effort from David and he invited me to run the evening Bingo session on the second night at sea to, as he put it, 'break me in'. This held no fears for I had done this a million times for the Pontin guests but what I hadn't realised was that during the day, prior to my grand debut, the *Arcadia* entered the notorious Bay of Biscay! The Bay is, at best, unpredictable and on days when you would expect it to be calm and benign, it can blow up a storm and vice versa. On this day, it must have known that on the large ship slicing through its swell, was a new officer minus his sea legs and it decided to show off its very worst mood. The waves, now battered by a howling wind, rose to great heights, as if to overpower all that dared to cross their pathway before crashing downwards into giant valleys and the *Arcadia* battled with the elements bravely, rising with the waters aft to stern then rolling from starboard to port as it fought to keep upright. The motion created is known as 'yawing' and even hardened seamen find it difficult to stay calm in these conditions. For me, whose only journey by water prior to this moment, was the ferry boat that carried passengers from South to North Queensferry over the River Forth, the end of my life was imminent. The world was tinged with a sickly green and the breakfast I had consumed with such relish hours before began to fight back and demanded an early release without parole. I retired to my cabin hoping for some solace but lying on my bed brought little comfort. I prayed for the motion to stop but was not heard – I begged for sleep to shut out the movement – even death would have been welcomed – but it was not to be and to cap it all was the increasing shame of wearing the officers uniform and being seen in this weakened state by passengers (admittedly not many) who seemed immune to the motion. I determined not to give in and bravely (but foolishly) strode into dinner and sat down wearing that forced smile that lights up the mouth but ignores the rest of the face. Minestrone soup was placed in front of me and bidding farewell to my table companions I retired quickly to my cabin for further contemplation. How would I manage to call bingo? What would the passengers think if I suddenly disappeared from the proceedings leaving prospective winners vainly waiting on one more number for a full house? I did not bear to think of it and when, at long last, the time came to make my public appearance, I did so with great trepidation. I looked out at the audience and wondered if they would be the privileged few who would witness the demise of my career within the next few minutes. Their respect for me, my position – indeed the entire Company – was about to be blown sky high and I hated myself for being the perpetrator and with this thought in my mind, I began to call the numbers. The miracle I had longed and prayed for came to pass – some would say rather late in the day – but I was in no mood to argue. A miracle is a miracle in any language and the feeling of euphoria overwhelmed the previous sensation of nausea, to my great relief. The more I called out the numbers, the more I concentrated on the game itself and the less I thought about the malady that had affected me. By the time I reached the half way game in the session, I was fighting fit and raring to go and that awful feeling of violent sea sickness had gone, never to return.

Later on, during my seafaring career, I recall the journey form Durban to Cape Town and negotiating around The Cape of Good Hope. The waves were so tall, they were breaking over the bridge of the ship – ninety feet above (a calm) sea level – and far from suffering alone in my cabin, I was on the promenade deck taking photographs to show the folks back home and enjoying every second. I actually began to look forward to rough seas, for a 'yawing' ship meant less passengers in the public rooms and restaurants and that, in turn meant an easier life and sometimes even an evening off! Am I getting indolent in my increasing years?

By the end of the two-week cruise, I realised how much I had enjoyed the experience and wondered what was to become of me. P&O answered my concern by sending a cable advising me to stay on *Arcadia* as Tourist Class Entertainment Officer for the forthcoming trip to Australia, followed by a further eight weeks of cruising through the islands of the South Pacific. It was a dream come true and Bill Alison (who remained as First Class E/O) and I began preparing our entertainment scheduled for the trip 'down under'. The accepted method of preparation is to compile a chart divided into the number of days the voyage will last and inserting the major events taking place, especially in the evening. Great emphasis is placed on 'theme nights' and on a ratio of one every second night, we entered on the chart events like 'Captains Cocktail Ball', 'Spanish Night', 'African Queen Night', 'King Neptune's Ball', 'English Pub Night', 'Wild West Night' and so on until we had filled all the gaps. In order to let the passengers relax and unwind from their exertions in helping decorate the ballrooms, we used the alternative nights for nothing more strenuous that Bingo or a quiz or a musical recital. The planning of the major events had to be completed before the ship set sail. Once we were under way, Bill and I met the Staff Captain in his quarters at 8.45am every morning at sea to finalise the rest of the programme of events, in the following days ships newspaper. My entertainment staff consisted of only one hostess – nothing more – and between us, we organised and ran every item of entertainment laid on for the passengers.

I remember devising and running an event on one of the 'quiet' days called 'Treasure Hunt', for the simple reason that the following morning, I was presented to the Captain and was given the mother and father of all rollockings. The game was to divide all the participants into teams of six and for each team to appoint a team Captain. On this particular evening we had a huge turn out – something like ten teams – and the idea was to run a total of eight rounds of furious competition involving every member of the team charging through the ship like persons demented. At the start of each round I would list five items to be 'found' and would allow them ten minutes to do the finding. The objects I requested were all very obscure – a half eaten apple, a book with a sexy cover, a man with a hairy chest, an alarm clock set to go off as it was handed to me, an Alka Seltzer fizzing in a glass of water containing a set of false teeth and so on. With the game at its height, I slipped in a beauty (or so I thought!), I requested a man and a woman wearing pyjamas and nightie respectively but also wearing a life jacket and flippers. Off the teams rushed to fulfil their task and as luck would have it, a little old lady had retired to bed for an early night – only to be wakened by the sound of people rushing past her cabin door, yelling and shouting. She looked out fearfully and her worst nightmare was awakened when she realised that those who were making the noise, were dressed in life jackets and she immediately put two and two in the wrong place and assumed that the ship was sinking. It took a long time of tough persuasion and a full bottle of the ships finest brandy for her to realise it was only a silly game the stupid Scotsman was playing and she was not about to emulate the tragic passengers on the 'Titanic'. I never attempted that game again!

We neared the approaches to Sydney Harbour in the early hours of the morning almost three weeks after leaving Southampton and I was advised by all – friend and foe alike – that I had to see the view of the City of Sydney outline, the Harbour Bridge and the 'soon to be completed' Opera House by the dawns early light. Grudgingly I set my alarm clock for 6.00am in order not to miss the big moment. The previous evening had been a hectic 'Grand Farewell' Ball and feeling fragile and extremely weary, I struggled into day clothes and made my way to the bridge for my first view of antipodean civilization. 'The vista will be breathtaking as the sun rises, bathing the buildings in its warm glow', I was told but the mist that hung over the city, like a pall, obscured everything. It was like Manchester in mid winter and I turned on my heel, retraced my steps and climbed gratefully back into bed. So much for Oz!

The sun did, however, show up and blazed the way for four two-week cruises travelling from Sydney, to Auckland, the Bay of Islands (New Zealand), the Friendly Islands, Fiji, Pango-Pango and Noumea (French Guiana). It was hard work but idyllic, travelling to places one could only dream of. I remember, vividly, arriving at Nuko'alofa in the Friendly Islands and as I stepped onto the open deck, witnessing a panoramic view direct from a Hollywood movie. As far as I could see stretched palm trees, fringing the sand bleached pure white from the hot sun. Interspaced in the shade of the giant leaves were grass huts shaped like small domes with little black children happily playing on the beaches and splashing in the aqua green ocean. When we stepped ashore, we were surrounded by the inhabitants of this wonderful island, the welcome both warm and inviting and the smiles on each and every face we saw compounded the very name given to this tiny dot in the Pacific Ocean – The Friendly Islands! I cannot imagine a better name for this most beautiful location.

The wonderful part of being on the entertainment staff was the very fact that, whilst the ship was at sea, we worked solidly with both daytime and evening events to organise and run but as soon as the ship docked into port, we were not required. Passengers took off on their many coach excursions to all the points of interest and providing there was seats available, we were allowed to join them free of charge. Indeed the company encouraged us to take these trips in order that we could describe at first hand to passengers on later cruises, the joys of what to expect.

One of the most exciting shore excursions I was privileged to make was *Arcadia's* inaugural voyage to Alaska – the first P&O ship to visit the USA's 49th State. We sailed from Vancouver (Canada) early evening and the following morning entered Alaskan waters. The first port of call was Ketchikan, Alaska's third biggest town and the entire population, fronted by the Mayor, was on the quayside to welcome us. 'Hiya All', their banners proclaimed as we inched towards the dockside. I say inched, for frighteningly, the quay was made of timber, as were the shops and the houses which ascended in rows, one above the other up the sheer hillside. One nudge from this giant liner would have collapsed the whole town like a set of playing cards and send it sliding into the deep and icy waters. We visited Ketchikan four times over the next eight weeks and the gentle control exercised by our Captain of this 30,000-ton monster was a joy to behold. I would be more than surprised if he had dislodged even one barnacle that clung to the blocks of wood supporting not just the pier but, in effect, the whole town.

One of the passengers who joined us on the next leg of the journey to Juneau was the boss of the local airline. Because there was no room for a runway, all his small craft were converted into seaplanes, with floats instead of wheels. His intention was to sell excursions during our next four visits and he accordingly invited me to experience the trip – and what an experience! We flew over tranquil inland waterways, swooped low over densely wooded hillsides to catch a glimpse of wild bears hunting for fish and in a moment, sped from peaceful scenery to that of rugged glaciers crushing all before them – rocks trees and vegetation – in its slow but inexorable journey to the lands end. It was a flight that was memorable and the photographs I took that day became a very popular slide show for passengers on later travels, as well as proving a great attraction for those passengers on subsequent cruises to this fascinating part of the world. The next day we spent anchored in Glacier Bay and watched in awe as the glaciers surrounded the area of water in which we sat. Every few minutes, a crack like rifle fire would fill the air and huge rocks of solid ice would break away from its parent and crash into the sea. It was a spectacular demonstration of nature at its very best and we felt very insignificant, but more than privileged, to witness the sheer majestic wonder of this natural evolution. Our final port of call was Sitka, once owned by Russia but now a firm part of the USA, before calling in to Vancouver Island with its wonderful Buchart Gardens, before docking back into San Francisco, on the completion of our Alaskan adventure.

I was looking forward to a three-day break in port and exploring the many places to visit in this exciting city when, just after 9.00pm, my cabin phone rang, much to my disgust! The voice on the other end informed me that I had visitors on the dockside and would I come down and meet them. I was convinced that I knew of no one in this fair city but curiosity conquered over the desire to slumber on and I made my way to the disembarkation point, to be met by a middle aged couple whom I swear I had never set eyes on before. They hailed me like a long lost son and demanded to know if I was ready. I was sure I was about to wake up from this crazy and very mixed up dream and my face must have registered total blank out.

"He's forgotten," shrilled the female half of the duo. "He's forgotten all about Las Vegas!"

What about Las Vegas? I tried to get my brain in gear but the engine had stalled. Suddenly a chink of light as my befuddled memory rewound the tape to seven weeks previous and the second day of our first voyage to Alaska. A social meeting with the passengers and a conversation with a husband and wife on their first cruise. Run of the mill chit-chat, making conversation and my light hearted remark to them that I would love so much to visit Las Vegas – six hours drive from San Francisco.

"We'll take you there," declared the man.

"Oh yeah? Thank you so much," I thought and moved the conversation on, finished and designated it to the mental waste paper basket somewhere in my mind.

"Are you ready?" they repeated.

I realised they were quite serious. I could not, then and still cannot believe today, the kindness and generosity of the home based Americans. Forget the brash, arrogant American tourists that let themselves and their country down. Everywhere I have travelled in the USA, I have met ordinary people who have opened their homes and their hearts – and in this case – their car to embrace me with kindness.

I quickly grabbed a small overnight bag and was soon crossing the Nevada desert on the way to the entertainment and gambling capital of the world. I had never experienced the pitfalls of transversing a real desert before – although I once got seriously lost in the sand dunes at Lytham St Annes, near Blackpool – but I wondered at the coolness of the air temperature. I was expecting great heat fuelled by a burning sun but I was sitting comfortably relaxed with no desire to stagger in search of an oasis for water or indeed, no inclination to induce a mirage, no matter how pleasant. How stupid can you be? Even in the seventies one should have been aware of in-car air conditioning and it was brought home to me just how hot it was when we stopped to refuel at an aptly named service station called Baker. Opening the car door was similar to opening an oven door to check if your Sunday roast was ready for consuming – the blast of red hot air almost singed my eyebrows and destroyed my coiffure (or at least what was remaining after nature had thinned out all the best bits!). A temperature guage registered 120°F and I scuttled back into the car to prevent my skin from peeling at the edges.

Las Vegas is an adults Disneyland. Hotels and, in particular, the casinos never close and clocks are conspicuous by their absence. They don't want you to know what time of day it is! People of all ages sit transfixed at one arm bandits, religiously feeding coins into its open mouth, their eyes glazed and their minds numbed to everything other than the desperately hoped for rush of disgorging coins onto the metal trays. The handles of these cash consuming monsters reach out wherever you go begging to be fed and it was no surprise to encounter their presence even whilst visiting the smallest room in the Hotel. For the more adventurous gamblers, areas heavily guarded to keep out sightseers are discretely placed in shaded corners and it is there that great fortunes are won and – more likely – lost. Gambling, for me, holds no attraction but I was still fascinated at the hypnotic spell the lure of the green backed dollar can exert over the most staid of men. Las Vegas, however, meant only one thing and that, not surprisingly, was the superb array of wonderful shows on offer. I would have happily drowned in a sea of showbusiness and died with a smile of contentment on my face. We decided to enter the magical world of Caesar's Palace to purchase tickets for the great Tony Bennett and, as we entered the portals of this Roman Coliseum, we were greeted by a large, black commisionaire who took my hand in his great fist and shook it – loosening most of my front teeth in the process. The man-mountain smiled. "Welcome to Caesar's Palace," he said in a deep brown voice.

At that moment, I thanked God that I had never been forced to meet this man in a boxing ring. It was Joe Louis – the Brown Bomber – ex-Heavyweight Champion of the World. It would only happen in Las Vegas!

Seeing Tony Bennett live, with the Count Basie Orchestra and featuring Louis Belson on the drums was a wonderful experience and so, too, was the hint to 'tip' the bell captain in order to get the best table. I dug deep into my pockets but the man in question had obviously never heard of Scottish generosity before, for he gazed for a moment at my contribution to his welfare and dumped us near the back and behind a pillar. I further enraged the staff by raising my pocket camera towards the stage whilst Mr Bennett and the band were in full flow, eulogising on his cardiacal misplacement somewhere in San Francisco, and dared to take a photograph. Within seconds a 'heavy' appeared at my shoulder looking for all the world like a reincarnation of

Bugsy Seigal and threatened to smash the camera over my head if I attempted such a manoeuvre again. I cowered back into my expensive seat and felt sure that I would awake the next morning in a bed having shared my sleep with a decapitated horse's head!

The two days I spent in this breathtaking sin capital were a joy and an experience I would hate to have missed and I was so fortunate in being able to return there many years later, hoping to find a star attraction big enough to top the bill at the Royal Command Performance at the London Palladium. Read on, dear reader and all will be revealed!

We arrived back in Los Angeles at the end of the second day and, on seeing the familiar shape of *Arcadia* still tied up and rock solid at the quayside, was filled with a flood of unjustified relief. There was no reason to have expected otherwise for we had checked and double checked the day and time of sailing but, like many other members of the senior crew, I was haunted by the constant nightmare of missing the ship. I recall one incident on leaving Vancouver when two passengers arrived at the embarkation point only to find that we had sailed twenty minutes earlier. The fact that they were well oiled, well endowed but particularly, well heeled allowed them to talk the local pilot into accepting an offer to give chase. He succeeded in catching us up after radioing our Captain with his intentions and as he drew up alongside, the master instructed with some venom *not* to lower the solid gangway steps he would normally have operated, but to use the rope ladder instead. The sight of the generously proportioned pair precariously ascending the side of the ship was a joy to behold and I marvel to this day why the liner, weighted down not only by the obese twosome but by some two thousand passengers lining the rails to shout encouragement and other forms of rude comment, did not accede to gravity and roll over on its side. The embarrassed pair made the sanctuary of the promenade deck and for the rest of the voyage were subjected to the cruellest of 'micky-taking' from everyone with whom they came into contact. If that should be the penalty suffered by the passengers, I shuddered to envisage the fate awaiting a ships Officer, should he dare to emulate a similar experience – especially the Entertainment Officer whose tasks were to mix, mingle, present and produce each and every waking hour with those who have paid vast sums of money for the privilege. The shame would be too much to accept and I still live with the nightmare of it almost happening to me!

Of course there was a woman to blame and in this case a very attractive beauty consultant sharing a short two-week cruise with us. I will not attempt to detail when and how the pathway of our ship-board romance unfolded, but nevertheless, I accepted her invitation to spend the evening with her family at their home in Sausalito, a seaside hamlet fifteen miles north of San Francisco. Aware that the ship sailed the following afternoon at 4.00pm, I accepted their offer to extend my stay until the following morning when I would be driven in plenty of time back to San Francisco to catch the ship. We left with time to spare but, to my dismay, we found ourselves grid-locked due to a road accident ahead and I watched with growing panic as the traffic and the minute hand of the clock inched forward. After what seemed hours, we were finally clear of the obstruction and in total fear of what was about to unfold, I grabbed the steering wheel, almost threw my companion into the passenger seat and set off for the Bay in a style that made Michael Schumaker's drive to win the Formula One World Championship look like Noddy in his pedal car. We hurtled over the Bay Bridge and, looking down, I could see the *Arcadia* ready to sail with all gang planks drawn except for one – and that was being untied. I raced through two red lights, expecting all the time to hear the siren of a police car and come face to face with Karl Malden and Michael Douglas. Finally we came to the dock gate. The uniformed guard held his hand up officiously in an effort to advise that cars were not allowed onto the quayside but I was in no mood to argue. I roared up the two hundred yards separating me from sanctuary, stood on the brakes and leapt onto the rapidly disappearing gangplank as it was hauled on board. I staggered to the top and stepped on to the deck with perspiration and relief flooding over me and to my abject horror found myself staring into the eyes of the Staff Captain who had witnessed the last few minutes of the Great Escape.

He summed it up perfectly and in the briefest of words. "You lucky bastard," he said and walked away.

That moment lived with me until this day and I still break out in a cold sweat in merely recalling it.

Despite that isolated incident of desperate panic, the eighteen months spent on sailing the seven seas were without doubt the happiest and most rewarding of my life. I was seeing the world in the most luxurious style and at someone else's expense and the uniform I wore, similar to the effect realised by the Pontin blue jacket, made me into a figure of reverence and glamour. The image was furthered heightened when I was transferred to the *Canberra* and promoted to the First Class section where I was able to meet and mix with film stars, politicians, sports personalities and stage performers. The entertainment on offer, too, had to become more upper crust with Bingo being replaced by Bridge, the afternoon 'jam' sessions converting to piano recitals and the traditional 'pub night' became an evening with Gilbert and Sullivan. Nevertheless people are still people and basically the same style of presentation, as I had used in the past, still proved popular. The accents may have been a little bit more 'cut-glass' but scratch away the surface and underneath, is still the same human beings who love a risqué joke and a good old sing song.

The period was one of sheer joy and again and again I had to pinch myself to make sure it was not all an exotic dream. I wondered, too, at the love affair I underwent with the ship itself – the *Canberra* was no steel encasement driven by massive engines and held together by thousands of strategically placed rivets. Instead, it was a wonderful lady of the sea, with a heart and a soul, devoid of temperament and who spread her giant girth to embrace and protect me from the dangers of the ocean. If ever I was to doubt my emotions, the sentiments flooded back when I sat at home watching on television, the Canberra return from the 1982 Faulklands war. I saw the ship ease gracefully into the Solent, battered, bloodied but in no way beaten. The white paint that graced its hull was peeling, the brass work was dulled and the deck pitted with the ravages of war. Through all that, however, the wonderful lady held herself proud. The Union Jack fluttered stiffly in the breeze and hundreds of small craft surrounded her in admiration of what she had achieved. Her body language spoke of patriotism and the unquenchable spirit of Great Britain, she had fought a battle and she had won. She was home and the crowds, thronging the cliff tops, cheered and waved their flags. She responded with a majestic salute from her siren and I dissolved into a flood of emotional tears. She was a member of my family home from the war and I felt so proud!

Without realising it, leave had accumulated and I was surprised to learn that I was due three months to be taken before my next trip out – the Christmas cruise through the Mediterranean. I looked forward to the break immensely and on arriving back in Blackpool rang Bill Armistead, not just for the pleasure in seeing him once again, but I suppose, like most of us returning from a holiday in the sun, for the opportunity to show off the tan and tell a few tales of exotic places. We faced each other over his office desk, sharing a pot of tea and a digestive biscuit (I know he was glad to see me for the biscuits only came out for Royalty and for Fred Pontin). It was as if I had never been away and we had been in conversation for maybe an hour when the phone on his desk rang and although he had given instruction not to be disturbed, he realised that the call *had* to be important – and it was! It was Fred Pontin and the two conversed over policies for a few minutes.

"You'll never guess who's sitting with me right now," Bill asked of Fred and, without waiting for his reply, handed me the phone.

Once again fate was up to his tricks prompting Fred to ring at that exact moment and he sounded delighted to hear my voice. I assumed from the way he spoke that he was expecting me to make contact as my two years 'unpaid leave' was now almost up and who, in their right mind, could refuse the invitation to return to the fold? Nothing, however, was further from the truth and I was prepared to tell him so but at that moment he threw me a bait so big, I was helpless to refuse. "Come and meet me," he ordered. "I'm over at the Hotel Pontinental in Torremolinos the week after next so get yourself over there, have a two week holiday as my guest and we'll have a chat."

The thought of a fortnight on the Costa Del Sol, doing nothing but lie in the sun proved too much of a temptation and I accepted. Take the holiday, I reasoned, and you can always refuse any offer he makes when we meet. Like many before me, I underestimated his powers of persuasion and fell for the five-card trick.

"I want you to re-join the company," he said "You will recruit all Entertainment Managers, Bluecoats and Lifeguards, audition and book all bands, cabarets and sports personalities for the Northern area and be responsible to me for the control of the budget. I will give you a company car and a good salary – now...when will you start?"

Perhaps it was the sun or perhaps the drink or maybe just the bombastic way he conducted his business but I found myself extending my hand to accept his offer and, before I knew it, I was outside his office door wondering what the hell I had done and could I rewind the tape and start the meeting all over again? It was then I glimpsed the face of fate laughing hysterically at my pathetic attempt to deflect his intentions and I finally and passively gave in, realising that once again the pattern of my life was about to change and I could not do a damn thing to prevent it. In retrospect however, it was to be the beginning of an extended period of my life which gave me such great satisfaction – an era in which I was lucky enough to discover and groom many of today's major showbusiness stars through the Bluecoat 'academy', as well as introducing up and coming professional talent to the Pontin cabaret circuit and watch them blossom into super stars with fees so great, we finally couldn't afford them. More of this to come...!

CHAPTER TEN

Go Pontin – and Pontinental!

I completed the Christmas cruise on *Canberra*, as contracted, and on February 1st 1974 rejoined Pontins as Area Entertainments Manager, based at Blackpool and shuttled between the four northern Centres, taking it all in and making my presence felt. My company car in which I plied my trade of great importance, was a Ford Escort of the most basic kind and many times during that year, I had to face the indignity of telling off a Bluecoat for some misdemeanour, before watching them drive to their next duty in a Granada or BMW, whilst I sloped off in my tin box on wheels. It was certainly an experience to prevent anyone rising above their station and it worked without a shadow of a doubt. The transformation, however, from the hectic do-it-all-yourself shipboard life to the more 'behind the scenes' lifestyle I had to become accustomed to, was proving difficult to accept and I approached Fred with this problem. It was, I guess, something completely new to him, to have a member of staff complaining that he had too little to do rather than the more common place 'too much'. He was understanding and came up with the perfect solution. "Would you consider, taking over the entertainment on the Pontinental sites as well as the North West?" he offered.

I nearly bit his hand off in accepting for, at that time, Pontinental ran fifteen centres, all situated in the sunniest places in Europe and America – four in Majorca, two on the Cost Del Sol, two in Greece, one in Italy, one in Sardinia, one in Tenerife, two in Yugoslavia, one in Morocco and one in

Miami, USA. The company was headed by Peter Hopper (Fred's son-in-law) and so began a very hectic period, involving almost non stop travelling which would have been fine but for two things which rather took the fun out of the experience. The first was the decision by Air Traffic Controllers in France to go on strike for the whole duration of that summer and the second was the discovery that I was terrified of flying – a phobia ideal for the job I was being asked to do! The best solution was to pump myself full of tranquillisers and, in theory, board the plane impervious to the dangers of flying through the air in a monstrous giant steel structure of many tons in weight, with nothing to support it above or below. The trouble with that ingenious plan, however, was the reluctance of the controllers to allow the planes to take off on time and by the time permission was granted and we rolled out on to the runway, the tablets had completed their course, allowing me the most peaceful and high flying rest on the floor of the airport lounge, to be replaced by the panic and fear brought on as soon as the aircrafts door slammed shut. At that time Pontinental exclusively chartered a company by the name of Court Airlines and their particular gimmick was that the livery of each plane was a pastel colour – all green, all yellow, all red etc., and I was always conscious that the entire contingent of passengers were all Pontinental guests. Inevitably, word would get around that a Company Executive was on board and many times, as I sat cowering in my seat, my eyes bulging in terror and my throat constricted as I pondered the worst, passengers would approach me.

"It's okay for you – you must be well used to this!"

The strangled gurgle I gave by way of reply must have been construed as a response from sheer boredom or the height of rudeness and for those subjected to my outburst of phobic utterances – I humbly apologise!

Now, I have no idea who Sod was, nor have I any inclination why he should make a law or even what the law was all about, but it came to pass, according to the legislation laid down by the Great Man that, what I feared most was about to happen! The strike had bitten once again, resulting in yet another forced wait of some seven hours in the sparse, austere comfort of Malaga Airport with nothing to sustain us other than the delights of some long forgotten sandwiches of indeterminable age, washed down with ersatz tea, which, had it been passed by the local bull, would have seen the animal shot. At long last the call came, like a reprieve from the death penalty, to board the waiting aircraft. We walked across the tarmac towards the plane and I shuddered to hear one of my fellow passengers, fraught with superstition, mutter to all within earshot. "My God – it's a green plane – that's unlucky – it'll never take off!"

The plane was indeed a delightful shade of pastel green and quite suddenly my fears, somewhat suppressed by the long delay, resurfaced bringing with it imagined scenarios of disasters about to fall in all their Technicolor glory – including a plane shaded in a verdant hue! The jet boasted two engines at the rear and as we roared down the runway, I digested every beat of the turbos, convinced that one or the other, (or both), was about to falter but neither did and we soared into the darkening sky and headed for home. I looked around me at the scene of normality and chastised myself for such infantile stupidity. The hostess happily dispensed drinks to eager passengers from the portable bar and there was an air of relief almost to the point of hysteria that, at long last, we were on our way. The Captain, too, anxious to share in the euphoria of the moment emerged from his secret compartment and moved between the rows of travellers like a God amongst his disciples, smiling, touching and reaching out. The explosion, as one of the two engines disintegrated, reverberated through the cabin and the plane tilted alarmingly to one side. The scene altered in a split second and the Captain, so previously serene and charming, wilted perceptibly as he disappeared into the inner sanctum of the flight deck. Fear and panic engulfed the cabin in a flash and confirmation that we were in serious trouble came over the PA system. An engine had failed and we were about to make an emergency landing at Bordeaux Airport. The hostess, we were told, would take us through the emergency drill. If this was designed to make us feel just that bit better, it didn't work for, no sooner had the senior hostess taken the microphone, to inform us what to do and what not to do before we plummeted into the ground, than her nerve gave out and she stood before us all, hands covering her face, weeping her heart out. That moment of spontaneity really cheered us all up and made the prospect of leaving this world behind much more acceptable. They say your past life flashes before your eyes – but mine didn't for I was too engrossed in what was about to come, rather than recalling what had passed before. Despite the lack of 'leading by example', the other hostess rushed up and down the plane advising us to remove from our beings anything that could leave us on impact – shoes, wigs, false teeth, glasses, artificial limbs and glass eyes and many a passenger decreased in size dramatically as they divested their extra baggage. I declined the invitation to remove my glasses (the only item that applied), on the theory that if I was going to die, I wanted to see it. I may never get the chance again! The bags and bottles of duty frees were removed from the overhead lockers along with the Spanish sombreros and the straw donkeys, and locked in the toilets and we sat with our arms covering our faces and waited for our fates to be decided. The plane slipped below the enveloping clouds and drifted towards the waiting runway, lined on either side by waiting fire trucks, police cars and ambulances and, by now, I was convinced my last moments had come. The aircraft powered only by a single engine settled onto the runway like a butterfly landing on the petals of a flower and the roar of relief, mixed with the tumultuous applause from the passengers in appreciation of the pilots feat of flying skills, must have been heard by Fred in his office at Oxford Street, London.

Fred naturally *was* to hear of my brush with death and, like the true humanitarian we all knew him to be, uttered the words of solace and sympathy that made me so proud to be a part of his family. "Poor sod," he empathised. "I'm glad I'm not paying his laundry bill!"

Regardless of the cleaning costs involved, however, it was a further blow to my already fragile nervous system in the art of air travelling and it was the most simple of experiences that delivered me from such a phobia and has since made flying much more of a pleasure than I ever hoped or expected it to be.

The occasion came at the end of my once-a-month visit, commencing with the flight to Malaga and the short journey to Torremolinos where Pontinental boasted two imperious hotels standing side by side just off the main beach. Using the company car, I then drove south through Marbella to the mini resort of Estapona, an overnight stay at our Holiday Village before continuing the journey by road beyond Gibraltar to the ferry port at Algeciras. The short ferry ride took me to the Spanish owned city of Ceuta on the North African coast where I was met and transported to M'Diq, another of our Holiday Villages, this one close to Tangier. It was early May and when I arrived at Tangier Airport for the flight home, I learned that the incoming flight from UK was the first of the season which meant that although full to capacity on the way out, the homeward flight would be empty as there were no passengers to pick up – with the exception of yours truly. Despite the usual misgivings and tablet consumptions, I was nevertheless thrilled to hear my name being called over the PA system and escorted to the plane by four delectable Air Hostesses. With such a bevy of beauties to look after me, it was ironic to be tightly strapped into my seat and then asked if there was anything they could do for me! The story of my life! Once we had left the ground and reached cruising height, an invitation to join the crew on the flight deck was extended to me and I made my way forward into the forbidden area in the hope that just maybe, some of its most hidden secrets, the ignorance of which had caused so much pain, fear and panic in the past, would be revealed. The Captain greeted me like an old friend and over the next two hours explained with great patience how each part of the flight deck worked – every switch, every dial, every lever – the complete package and after his insistence that I remain with him as we landed in Gatwick, I set foot on solid ground with the great phobia of flying totally punctured. I cannot say I am completely free of apprehension when I take to the air – who in all honesty really is? – but I can now look forward to travelling through the skies with an enjoyment of the experience – a feeling I never thought possible after the traumas undergone on the pastel green airbus!

CHAPTER ELEVEN

Tom O'Connor

The phone rang in my office one morning and I was pleased to hear the voice of an old friend, Billy 'Uke' Scott. Billy had been a well-known performer in the days of variety and was still a regular on radio programmes like *Workers Playtime* and *Variety Bandbox*. He explained that he was giving up much of his performing career to concentrate on the Management Agency he had just formed. "I'm taking on this lad from Liverpool", he enthused. " At the moment he's a teacher but Jim – he's going to be a star! Will you come and see him work?"

Of course I agreed and two nights later, I met Billy at a social club near the centre of Liverpool where his protégé was performing and I waited with, I admit, little confidence for I could not see me signing a part-time guitarist/singer/comic, no matter how good. I had set a high standard of professional entertainers throughout the northern Pontin Camps and each act was tried, tested and tried again. Many times I auditioned acts two, sometimes three times, before offering them work but Billy was a friend and I was anxious to see what all the fuss was about. The introduction was made and onto the stage stepped this young, very good looking lad holding a guitar gingerly in front of him, almost like a weapon, should the audience decide to attack. He had nothing to fear, however, and from the moment he opened his mouth he had the audience in the palm of his hand. His gags were as up to date as today's newspapers and the crowd roared their approval with great belly laughs. From one who has learned to live with the risqué humour of northwest comedians who plead that that is the only way to arouse the hardened audiences in this part of the country, I was startled beyond belief that the young man I was asked to view had not uttered one swear word or had resorted to one joke with even a distant double meaning and yet, the audience of dockers, engineers and shipbuilders who'd seen and heard it all before, adored him.

I looked at Billy. "Would he like to work at Pontins?" I asked.

The deal was done and Tom O'Connor never looked back. The rest, as they say, is history and to this day Tom has remained the same considerate, gentle, level headed person he was on the first evening I saw him work. Despite his well-deserved star status he now enjoys, he never forgets to send me a Christmas card each year with pictures of his lovely wife and children and the signed message 'From Tom, Pat and family with love'. Bless you Tom – a gentleman!

There is a wonderful sequel to this story and it happened quite a few years later. Tom had gone on to be probably the biggest name in British showbusiness and commanded large fees and quite rightly so. It was Christmas and, in deciding the cabarets to work over the five-day festive period, I was heavily requested by Fred Pontin to include a young man that he himself had discovered and had used extensively on the southern Camps, with great success I might add. I had seen him work on many occasions and agreed that he was an excellent talent but felt inwardly that, to bring him up North, would crucify him. His material was laid back and 'southern' in its style and the fact that he worked in a very 'camp' manner would be meat and veg to the rather raucous and drink fuelled late night guests of the north. However the persuasive powers of Fred, once again prevailed, much against my better judgement, and his opening night was planned for the Southport Camp on Christmas Eve – onstage at 11.00pm. It was the day the guests arrived and they were ready to swing and it was so important for us that their first evening at our Centre was a total success. The whole festive period in fact depended on it. For reasons which I cannot fathom, I decided to spend the day at Prestatyn but after the evening meal, the thought of my friend from the South facing his first Northern firing squad grew larger and larger in my mind and finally, I could stand the thought no more. I leaped into my car and, just before 10.30pm, I pulled up into the Southport car park facing the main reception. I had not even switched off the engine before my driver's side window was being battered by some maniac yelling and screaming. Bravely I wound down the window to reveal the white, pale face of that evenings star cabaret. "That's it!" he said in his high pitched voice. "I'm off! I'm not appearing in this dump. I'm going home – the band can't read my music, I'll die a thousand deaths – I'm off."

His hands fluttered as he reached the climax of his dramatic tirade and I waited for the storm to subside. Let him get it off his chest, I reasoned and he'll apologise profusely and go on stage meekly and without rancour. He jumped petulantly into his car and fired the engine but I was not to be fooled and waited confidently for him to re-appear full of remorse. My confidence began to wilt, however, when his vehicle reversed out of the parking bay and diminished rapidly from my sight as he sped towards the main gate. The last I saw of him was the red glow of his rear lights, doubling for a second as he touched the brakes to allow the barrier to be raised, before vanishing completely into the darkness of the night, heading for the sanctuary of his home three hundred mile away in Bournemouth.

I sat in silence with nothing to remind me of the drama I had just been subjected to, save for the lingering smell of the rather effeminate after-shave he always wore and pondered the implication. Twenty-five minutes to star cabaret time and no star cabaret! The room was filling up rapidly with guests looking forward so much, to the opening act of the festive season – a holiday they had looked forward to for so long and had saved up for so hard. Disaster was a mere twenty-five minutes away! I was joined by the distraught General Manager – David Gwyn, normally the most phlegmatic of characters but, realising the severity of the situation, was contemplating suicide and I threatened to join him. We commandeered the switchboard and without much hope, rang agents and artistes we knew who lived or worked within striking distance but it was, of course Christmas Eve and we expected, and got, no replies. With a final throw of the dice, we decided to ring the Southport Theatre, knowing there had been a pantomime performance that evening but not knowing who was in it. Maybe – just maybe, we could persuade the Fairy Godmother or the wicked Prince to make an appearance, sing a song and disappear. It may release us from jail – but we doubted even that.

The phone rang for an eternity and we were just about to hang up when this voice answered. "Backstage theatre."

I poured our my problems and although sympathetic, the Stage Manager doused the flame of hope by informing us that the show had finished nearly forty-five minutes before and everyone had gone – Fairy Godmother, wicked Prince and all. Even Cinderella's white ponies were back in their stables and locked away for the night.

"Hold on," he said and our hopes revived. "I can hear someone still in the number one dressing room."

"Bring them to the phone," we yelled and a few seconds later we heard the clumping of the phone being picked up and a voice I knew so well.

"Hello – Tom O'Connor here. How can I help you?"

It was the miracle of Christmas! Forget the Three Wise Men following the Star – these were two, far from wise men, who had found a Star.

"I'll be with you in five minutes," said Tom. "But I've no time to change – you'll have to accept me dressed as I am."

"I don't care if you're stark naked," I screamed. "Just so long as you make it!"

Tom did, by a few minutes and I will never forget the reaction when the compere walked out onto the cabaret floor and introduced him. "Ladies and gentlemen – its Star cabaret time. We promised you a star and tonight we've kept that promise. Will you welcome the fabulous...Tom O'Connor!"

The crowd went berserk and onto the floor stepped probably the hottest showbusiness property in Britain at that time. He simply tore the room apart for well over an hour and when he was finally allowed to return to the dressing room, I hugged him and embarrassed, brought up the matter of his fee. "I cannot pay you what you would normally earn," I said. "But all I can offer you is the fee we were to pay our departed friend."

"Jim," he said raising his hand. "You gave me work when I was starting out and needed it. I owe you for that – have this one on me!" and he was off.

We donated the money to charity but I have never forgotten that gesture from a great guy. So many of our major stars devote a great part of their lives giving freely without recognition or reward and it gives me great pleasure to repeat this story – one I have told many times in the past – in recognition of the side of showbusiness and the people in it who do not get the publicity they deserve. Tom – you're a star!

CHAPTER TWELVE

Finding Laughter – Plus Peters and Lee

On a funnier note, was the incident involving The Black Abbotts Comedy Showband. When we first started using the group, their drummer was a tall thin lad who would repeatedly leap from his drum kit and throw himself into manic impressions. His favourite was Tommy Cooper but he also excelled as the 'scoutmaster' and many, many others. It was clear that his talents were far reaching and so it proved when he decided to leave the band and go solo. He borrowed part of the bands name for his surname and so was created the brilliant Russ Abbott. Delighted with his success but sad to lose his great talent, The Abbotts recruited a young Blackpool boy by the name of Ronnie Baker to replace Russ on drums and, as a bonus, discovered that Ronnie, too, had a great feel for comedy. One of the highlights of their comedic routines was for the band to play a 'straight' instrumental number and every few seconds Ronnie would leap to his feet, crash the cymbals (effectively halting the band) and shout out a very funny 'one line' gag before regaining his position behind his drum kit and playing on as if nothing had happened. One of his favourite 'one liners', which got the biggest laugh, particularly in our centres, was (crash) "Fred Pontin's got piles," (crash) and carry on playing. Ronnie always swore he was referring to Fred's bank statement and not his haemarrhoidal collection and I believed him, going along with the joke. One evening, however, early in the season, Elsie Brown (Fred's sister), happened to be in the room and reacted violently to the remark. In point of fact, she went ballistic! She called me over (why am I always in full view when things go wrong?) and blasted me for allowing such a disrespectful joke to be used, ridiculing her brother. "I want that line removed," she raged. "Or you will sack the whole band – cancel their contract!"

I wasn't too bothered as I felt that Ronnie would have a whole library of jokes he could replace it with, but I hadn't reckoned on his stubborn streak.

"It's staying in," he said. "No one tells me what to take out. It gets the biggest laugh of the night, so it's staying in!" and he stormed off.

The following day I rang their agent – Tony Birmingham – and he promised to pour oil on the troubled water. "Don't worry," he said. "I'll speak to him – I can handle him. The line will be out next week!"

Of course, Tony had to agree to do something for if the band did lose their contract, then he (Tony) stood to lose a great deal of commission and so I felt confident that the matter was closed. I was horrified to receive a phone call from Tony a week later, admitting that he had used every threat known to man, beast and musician but Ronnie was still adamant and that the offending line was *in* and would be used that night! I had to be there, along with Tony Birmingham and the General Manager Don Green who had been instructed by Fred himself to ring him the next day and assure him that Elsie's instruction had been carried out. It was a long evening and I dreaded what was about to happen but eventually the *Black Abbotts* were introduced. The moment came as they swung into the number containing the contentious line and on cue, Ronnie leapt to his feet. Crash – as he hit the cymbal – then the words, "Billy Butlin's got piles – (crash) – Fred Pontin's been cured!"

The sight of Tony Birmingham, Don Green and I rolling on the floor, wiping tears of hysterical laughter from our eyes was one that must have puzzled many of the guests that evening and if you ever meet any of them and they bring the subject up – you can now enlighten them! Ronnie – you're a stubborn sod but nevertheless, a very, very funny one!

One of the most consistent questions I get asked after nearly thirty years of booking artistes from all the four corners of the Labour Exchange is 'Who was the best act you ever found?' – a question almost impossible to answer but one name keeps cropping up in my mind, whenever I think back over the period of my time in office and, surprisingly, it is not that of a major star. He remains probably as unknown today as he was when I first booked him for a Sunday evening show at Blackpool during the early seventies. His name was, and still is, Don D Williams (He added the initial 'D' so as not to be confused with the American Country singer of the same name.) The Sunday show, as always, consisted of three supporting acts and a top-of-the-bill, on this particular evening, Freddie Starr. I was horrified to learn during the afternoon that one of the supports had been taken ill. The fingers of panic began to caress my nervous system as I frantically rang all and sundry to find a replacement, but without success – everyone was working and I searched for the valium tablets that go with the job. Then – breakthrough! The voice of salvation came on the phone. "I can make Don Williams free if it will help?"

Now, like you probably, I had never heard of this artiste but every now and again, one had to close ones eyes and offer a prayer before taking a gamble and, in this case, that's exactly what I did. Don turned up with his band parts written on the back of the proverbial cigarette packet and I wondered what I had let myself, and the audience, in for. I completed the running order for the show and, after much deliberation, put him down for a fifteen minute act prior to the 'name' act, Freddie Starr, working on the theory that, with two acts before him to warm the audience up and Freddie immediately following him on stage, were he to 'die a death', any harm to the show would be covered. Don was duly announced and he wandered on and into the full glare of the spotlight, looking like a rabbit transfixed by a car's headlamp. My heart sank and when he started to strum an out of tune guitar and sing in a voice which wavered between the cracks of some unrecognisable melody, I began to count the paracetamol tablets in my possession and hoped I had enough to cover me on the way out. It got worse! He was now blaming the band for his musical disaster and begged the audience to understand the strain he was going through (*he* was going through?) and pleaded for them to help him recover. Slowly he recruited 'volunteers' from the bemused auditorium and, as he brought them onstage, as if by magic, musical instruments began to emerge from behind a curtain. A set of huge cymbals for a large lady with even larger bosoms, a euphonium for a little old man with no teeth, a trombone, a bass drum, a pair of maracas that kept falling off their handles, a trumpet and a set of Indian bagpipes, complete with chanter and turban. By this time, the audience were in an uproar and what followed was, without doubt the funniest most hysterical fifteen minutes of sheer slapstick comedy I had seen in years. When he had finished, the audience rose to a man and awarded Don Williams the ultimate tribute – a standing ovation – and I preened myself for having 'discovered' such a gem. Pride, however, came before the fall and within seconds, I was being pinned up against the wall by a very irate Freddie Starr. With his face red with rage and inches from mine, he screamed at me. "You bastard! Listen to them (the audience still cheering!). How the hell can I follow that?"

I totally understood what he meant and sympathised but I could do nothing to help – only Freddie could do that – and he did. Like the pro he is, he went onstage and tore the place apart like he always did but, on this occasion, maybe just a little bit more and I bet he enjoyed every last second of it.

With Don's success, however, I immediately signed him up for the following summer season and every show he did from then on was like the first. He is still working at Pontins to this day and still receiving standing ovations – I can't ever remember seeing him get less. His act increased in length as he added more routines and, on one magical evening at Southport, he took the stage at 11.00pm and never came off until 1.55am. The audience simply would not let him finish! To analyse his act was impossible – he struggled on guitar, he really could not sing at all well and he didn't tell jokes, but such was his sense of fun and superb personality, he was just brilliant. During his time with us (twenty-five years and still climbing), he met and married the lovely Doreen Savage and she immediately joined his act, adding excellent vocals between the mayhem, to strengthen the act even more.

Two more stories on the great Don before moving on...both amazingly at Southport where it always seems to happen! Don had now added a Frank Sinatra impression to the act (I *ask* you!) and, by his feet, lay a violin encased in a beautiful violin case. The song was *My Way* and during its haunting melody, as a break from the excruciating vocals, Don would reach down, extract the violin and would amaze everyone by playing the instrument beautifully, with great feeling and tonal quality. At the end of the passage, he would slowly take the violin from under his chin and bend down to replace it in its case. Suddenly the sound of the violin would boom out continuing to play the melody and Don would, in panic, try to place the violin back under his chin before anyone realised that the whole thing was a fake and the sound of the violin was a recording. It was near the end of the season and the band leader was a Yorkshireman by the name of Steve Gibbons. His zany sense of humour matched Don's and, by way of a practical joke one evening, he removed the violin from its case and replaced it with sand. When Don came to the part of the routine involving the violin, he struggled unsuccessfully to lift the case from the floor, such was its weight, whilst the band fell about uncontrollably on the stage. Don joined in the laughter and said nothing except, "Good one Steve. Well done – great gag!"

What the band didn't know, to their ultimate cost as it turned out, was that Don, prior to his showbusiness career, was a first class pattissier and confectioner and two weeks later arrived for his weekly appearance clutching the most beautiful and mouth watering chocolate cake, which he presented to the band. "Thank you lads, for a wonderful season. I hope you enjoy this small gift of appreciation from me."

Enjoy it they did, to every last crumb, not realising for one minute that the thick delicious chocolate that decorated the exterior was that of the very strongest laxative variety. As Don's act progressed, the audience were somewhat bemused as the members of the band kept dashing off stage with pained expressions on their faces and sheer panic in their eyes. Don, of course, admitted to the audience the nature of their discomfort and they joined in the fun by cheering each musician on his torturous journey off stage and cheering him back onto the stand to await the next call of nature. Never in its history has *My Way* been played so movingly!

Finally, the story of the memorandum from Fred Pontin decrying the use of swear words on stage by comedians – in particular the word 'bloody'. It had to stop, the memos said, and anyone using the offending word, or words, would have their contracts terminated. Don, of course, used the word extensively – not in a crude or nasty way, simply as an extension to his comedy timing and he was mortified when I told him of the instruction.

"I'll try very hard," he promised. "But if I slip up, please forgive me."

I would forgive Don anything but – would you believe it – the very next night, when Don was about to be introduced on stage – who should walk into the room but Fred himself. I rushed backstage to give Don the news and his face went white – even under the make-up. "I'll never do it," he said. "I'm finished – my career's over."

He started his act and it was almost a comedy sketch in itself watching and listening to Don doing the act without using the dreaded word. His face was pained and the sweat rolled off him in bucket-fulls as he weighed each sentence in his mind, cleansing it from all offending references before allowing it to escape from his mouth and be digested by an enthralled audience who were blissfully unaware of his mental torture. The end of the act finally came, releasing Don from the agonies he had endured and even he was dumbfounded, as he received his usual riotous, cheering reception. He took his curtain calls and he returned to his dressing room and slumped into a chair totally drained. At that moment, there was a knock on his door and the General Manager popped his head into the room. "Don," he said. "The Guv'nor wants to see you."

Once again the blood rushed from Don's face. "I didn't say it once," he croaked. " I didn't say it...did I?"

He gathered his courage and, like a man walking to the gallows, approached Fred at the bar. Fred looked at him coldly for a second then held out his hand. "Don," he said. "That was marvellous – bloody marvellous."

Don's face was a picture I'll never forget.

I would dearly love to claim the discovery of Peters and Lee and their subsequent introduction to the Pontin cabaret circuit as my own but, credit for this coup must go to Bridie Reid, my colleague responsible, at that time, for the entertainment on all the Pontin camps based in the southern areas of the country. Her phone rang one morning and the voice of Lennie Peters introduced himself and his singing partner Diane Lee, inviting Bridie to view their act at a local pub in the East End of London during the next seven days. As it happened, Bridie was due in London the following day to attend a meeting at our London office and decided to follow up Lennie's invitation to catch his act, despite some misgivings at venturing to an east end pub on her own. She half hoped that the establishment would turn out to be one of the more up market cabaret lounges but her hopes were dashed when she eventually found the building and pushed open the door. She was met by a wall of sound as dense as the pall of tobacco smoke that permeated the room, enveloping everything and everyone. Voices raised to the highest decibel, punctuated by shrieks of laughter, shouts of approval and encouragement for some macho pub game and above it all, the juke box blared out the voice of Ray Charles, singing his latest recording *Take these Chains*. Bridie recoiled as the cacophony reached its peak and her immediate reaction was to head back the way she had come and return to the comparative peace of her hotel room. Suddenly, she realised that the Ray Charles record, still playing, was not a record at all but the great soulful voice of a young man, wearing dark glasses, in the far corner of the room. She recognised immediately that she had found something special and her instincts were compounded when he was joined by a stunningly beautiful young lady, for his next number. The combination of the two total opposites in style and looks was irresistible and Bridie realised that the couple she was watching was, indeed, Lennie Peters and Diane Lee. She had found gold!

She asked then to meet her at the Pontin offices, off Oxford Circus, the following morning and they thrashed out a deal for Peters and Lee to appear at twelve Pontin Centres a week for the duration of the summer season (approximately twenty-two weeks), for the magnificent fee of £216 per week – which averaged out at £18 per show! In the event that you are confused over the number of shows contracted, bearing in mind that there are only seven days in a week, the conditions stated that the act would play two (or even three) Centres each day, for, at that time, many of the Centres were very close to each other, making such an arrangement possible. Lennie and Diane duly signed the contract with great delight, for they had never worked a summer season before and the thoughts of appearing in the plush cabaret venues, with stage lighting, backing bands and attentive audiences filled them with great excitement. With the deal done, they relaxed over coffee and Lennie casually mentioned that during the following month (April) they had been promised a TV slot on Hughie Green's *Opportunity Knocks.*

"We've no chance of winning but it will be a good promotional gimmick especially now, with the Pontin season to come," Lennie pointed out.

Bridie was happy with that and looked ahead to the weekly confrontation with Fred Pontin and the farcical scenario in attempting to obtain his signature on the pre-typed contract (she suffered the same battles I did, in getting him to agree our choice of cabarets etc.). The contract was duly presented and Fred went ballistic. "Who are they?" he shouted. "Never heard heard of them! I'm not paying that exorbitant fee for a couple of pub-singers!" Suddenly he saw the solution. " Tell you what – split 'em up, the bloke can do Broadreeds and the bird, Bracklesham. They can do six Centres each and look at the money we'll save. That's the answer!"

Birdie argued that an act of this calibre could not be split up but Fred was adamant, so she withdrew the contract and retired into her office to rethink. Now Fred had two great weaknesses – speciality acts and pretty girls and the following week the cunning Miss Reid presented the same contract to Fred, along with a photograph showing Lennie in evening suit and Diane in skimpy mini skirt. Fred's eyes lit up. "Who are they?" he demanded, obviously forgetting the previous weeks encounter. Bridie pounced.

"You'll love them," she said. "One of the best juggling acts I've seen in years!"

Fred signed and Peters and Lee were on the circuit.

What happened later, however, was the stuff that dreams were made of. Their appearance on *Opportunity Knocks* took the country by storm. The blind singer with the gravel voice and his lovely blonde partner who looked at him adoringly, whilst making wonderful vocal sounds, touched the hearts of millions and they won the viewers vote six weeks in succession.

By the beginning of May, the date they were due to start the Pontin season, they were household names and a few weeks later they were number one in the charts (both single and LP), with their version of *Welcome Home*. On the days of their appearances, the Centres were gripped by a 'Peters and Lee mania', with hundreds of our guests crowding the main gate and lining the roadways outside the Centre, hoping for a glimpse of their idols arriving for the show. In the cabaret venues where they were due to appear, the entire evenings programme had to be cancelled, with the exception of the show itself, because of the number of fans packing into the room. Chairs had to be positioned onto the ballroom floor, making dancing impossible, while the guests grabbed every vantage point available and simply waited with great patience for the great moment to arrive. All this and more, for the princely sum of £18 per show!

It had to happen, of course, and it didn't take long. Peters and Lee signed up to one of the biggest theatrical agents in the country and immediately, its Managing Director rang Bridie. He wanted them to star at the Opera House, Blackpool for that summer and requested their release from the Pontin contract, in order to fulfil the engagement. They were now being offered an incentive of £1,000 per night to go to Blackpool and Bridie was aware of what a temptation that would be for them. She needn't have worried. The following day, Lennie and Diane rang her, indignant that their new agent had been on the phone to Bridie without consulting them first. Bridie intimated that, although we had no commercial wish to, the Company would be prepared to negotiate a deal in order not to stand in the way of their spectacular success but Lennie and Diane would not hear of it. "No way," they said. "You believed in us when no one else was prepared to. You offered us our first summer season when no one else wanted us. Pontins have played fair with us and we will play fair with them. We will honour the contract."

And so saying, they climbed into their van and headed for the south coast and Broadreeds and two more shows that put another £36 into their bank account! Lovely people and a story I am proud to relate! Sadly Lennie is no longer with us but I'm sure his superb voice is still up their singing with the angels and his wicked sense of humour is reminding the Holy Ghosts – "Bloody 'ell – just like Camber Sands on a Friday night!"

CHAPTER THIRTEEN

Enter Jan – Stage Right!

The year was 1976 and Fred was now seventy years of age. Rumours abounded that changes in the Company structure were planned and with that information, rightly or wrongly, a feeling of unease descended on all of those whose living was wrapped up in the continued success of Holiday Club, Pontins. Whatever the foreseeable future held for us all professionally, my personal life altered dramatically on the Richter scale, when elegantly beautiful Jan Currey made her entrance. Jan was, without doubt, a super star in her home town of Blackpool. Years before, she had been voted Blackpool's 'Girl of the Year' and had since stayed in the headlines through her emergence as one of the UK's top singing stars. Once again, Hughie Green's *Opportunity Knocks* played a major role in presenting her to the TV public and they, in turn, responded by bringing her back as the 'Viewers Winner' four weeks in succession. The road was always upward from then on and she starred in the Nations Number One Theatres, both in pantomime and summer season, for many years afterwards. Hughie Green, and his team of Len Marten and Doris Barrie, made use of the Pontin facilities for many years to audition those hopeful of appearing on the TV show and, during the period, we became good friends. On this occasion, however, they had decided to hold their auditions at the Norbreck Castle Hotel but, nevertheless, invited me to sit with them on the 'judges bench' to view the aspiring performers go through their moments of agony. It was approaching lunch break and our thoughts began to veer from the talents on view and concentrate more fully on the menus that had been placed before us. It was at that moment when Jan chose to walk into my life. As a multi-winner on the programme, she, too, had formed a friendship with Hughie and the team and had merely called in to say hello. I remember the electric charge I received from that spiritual force that whispered in my ear that I was about to meet someone who was to play a major part in my immediate, and future, life. Introductions were made and I gleaned that she was now working on the club circuit and still making a good living. The agency who managed her talents was the prestigious ATS, controlled by Michael and Stanley Joseph, two brothers from Leeds who owned the world famous City of Varieties Music Hall. Jan, being Jan, had done a deal with Stanley Joseph to book her into all the premier clubs in the north of England (at that time, there were a great many to choose from) and she, in turn, would, after her performance, meet with the committees who booked the artistes and persuade them to use other performers managed by ATS. Like every good salesperson, she carried with her a portfolio of all those available, supported by 10″x8″ photographs, CV's and press cuttings and success in making a breakthrough would be rewarded by 2½% of the fee agreed. I was loathe to take my leave of her company that afternoon but had business to attend to and a conscience that kept sticking pins into my backside whenever I felt like being tempted by temptation. We shook hands and, despite the nagging force that insisted that this was one of the monumental moments in the pathway of my life's journey, I never really expected to see her again.

The phone rang two days later and it was Jan. "May I make an appointment to come and see you?" she enquired and I immediately cancelled every arrangement I had made, or was ever likely to make, over the next year and a half!

"Well," I mused. "I am rather busy, but how about...the next five minutes. I can just about fit you in!"

Of course, I should have guessed! My devastating looks and captivating personality were never, ever in the frame as she appeared in my doorway, lovely as ever, but wearing a business head of cool efficiency and carrying a briefcase from which she produced, like a magician revealing a large white rabbit, a portfolio containing 10″x8″ photographs of all the acts managed by ATS. It was not me she was after – simply that bloody 2 ½% commission she would receive from Stanley Joseph, should I book one or more of her acts. My world crumbled and my ego disintegrated, but little did I guess that my ethereal messenger, who advised me of the explosion to come, had done his homework and things were about to get better – much, much better!

We talked well into the afternoon and it slowly began to dawn on me that neither of us wanted it to end. We were enjoying the others company increasingly and on impulse, aware that I was committed to attending a showcase that evening put on by a local agent at the Leyland Tiger Pub in nearby Preston, I asked Jan if she would like to come with me. To my delight she agreed. Perhaps she was still thinking of it being a further outlet for her portfolio, but with confidence returning, I hoped and assumed that she rather liked the idea of being in my company. In retrospect, I wondered how I ever got off the ground! Here was I, taking her out on our first date and introducing her to a free night of sub-standard entertainment in the grotty back room of a street corner pub, but worse – I bought her a sumptuous meal of poached egg on toast at the Capri Café, washed down with a mug of hot steaming tea. I must have impressed her as the last of the big time spenders and I am sure that she left me that evening convinced that everything she had heard about the Scots was absolutely true. Something must have clicked, however, for we began seeing each other on a more regular basis and before long, I sensed that Cupid's arrow had buried itself in my heart. Jan too, must have experienced similar emotions for she decided to give up her beautiful home in Yorkshire and moved back to her parents home in Blackpool in order to be nearer to me. I recognised true love in the lady for I never did use any of the acts from her portfolio and still she wanted to be with me. What greater proof hath no man...?

Jan's talent as a singer was now equalled by her ability to recognise, nurture and manage other artistes and she decided to launch her own agency, called JC Management. The experience she gained from such small beginnings, coupled with the wonderful and invaluable tuition she received from the legendary agent Billy Marsh (with whom she partnered some ten years later until his death in 1995), resulted in Jan becoming one of Britain's top theatrical agents today, with an office near London's West End and a client list that looks like a 'Who's Who' of showbusiness celebrities.

One story, when our romance was beginning to blossom, typifies her dedication to the business she was now excelling in and her focussed eye for discovering talent. It had been a beautiful day in Blackpool – the sun shone steadily from a cloudless sky and the constant breeze, for once, had died to a mere whisper. In the early evening, we decided to drive away from the throng and bustle that is Blackpool in the summer and enjoy a quiet meal (no, not poached egg on toast!), at a country pub. As we headed out of the town, we passed one of the many clubs in and around the resort that present cabaret – or 'turns' as they are more commonly known in the area – and there, outside the entrance was a large poster advertising the grand final of their talent competition that very evening. I had no chance! Her hand grabbed the brake and the car skidded to a halt, much to the delight of the cars tucked in behind me. They were kind enough to shout their admiration of my skilful driving.

"Let's go in and have a look," Jan said. "You never know – we might find an act worth booking!"

"Fat chance," I thought, but always the gentleman (or was it coward?), said nothing and we duly took our seats.

Was it luck – or instinct or just sheer genius on Jan's part? – I will never be sure but it was obvious to us and, as it turned out, the judges, that it was a two-horse race, both female vocalists. The first of the two was a pretty, red haired singer with a great voice, a stunning personality and an Irish brogue that was strong enough to knock you over. Her name was Rose-Marie. The other was a sixteen year old with a pure golden voice that could transcend from a top soprano range to the pop standards of the day in the blink of an eye. Her name was Jacqui Scott and amazingly, in view of the location and its environment, both were to achieve fame through summer shows, radio, TV recording and in Jacqui's case – West End musicals. On this particular occasion, and I don't know to this day how the judges managed to split them, Jacqui was awarded the first prize and no sooner had the result been announced, than Jan was off her chair. Within twenty-four hours, after long discussions and promises made with her parents, her signature was put onto a managerial contract and another name was added to the growing list of potential stars under her guidance. I had no doubt she was heading for the top and future events have proved me right.

Despite her burning desire to succeed, and my great ambition to climb the Pontin ladder, Jan and I still found time to fan the flame of our courtship and on the 16th June 1979 (Jan's Birthday), we were married at Elswick Parish Church. Even on our wedding day, Jan remained the ultimate professional. At the reception, the band struck up their opening set and, true to tradition, Jan and I took to the floor, amidst rapturous applause, for the dance of the Bride and Groom. We held each other closely and Jan moved her mouth to my ear. I waited with loving anticipation, expecting words of tender devotion. "Jim," she whispered. "The band's too loud – Go and sort it out!"

CHAPTER FOURTEEN

The Guv'nor

What of the man and the many stories, some true, others fabrication, that built with his reputation? Tales, like his train journey from London to the Camp at Morecambe to see his long time friend Charlie Chester, who was starring that evening in the Sunday show. He arranged for his personal driver (six foot twelve and built like a brick out house, who revelled in the name Tiny), to meet him with car at Preston station and to transport him the rest of the journey by road.

Tiny was there waiting as directed and as Fred settled into the comfort of the back seat, touched his forelock with due deference, "Where to Mr Pontin?" he enquired.

Fred looked at him coldly for a second, wondering why no one had bothered to tell this idiot the reason for coming all this way but, suppressing his irritation at such incompetence, decided to exercise patience and spelt out his instructions. "We're going to Morecambe to see Charlie Chester," he said.

Tiny nodded his understanding and, as the car moved slowly from the station car park, Fred drifted off into a deep sleep. He awoke an hour and a half later and glanced out of the car window expecting to see the scenery that surrounded the camp, sights that were very familiar to him. The view he witnessed was unrecognisable and he knew instinctively that something had gone wrong. He slid back the glass window that separated him from his driver. "What's going on – where are we?" he yelled. "I told you we were going to Morecambe to see Charlie Chester!"

Tiny slammed on the brakes and slowly turned in his seat, his face and neck red with embarrassment. "Oh my God..." he said. "I thought you said we were going to Chester to see Eric Morecambe!"

True? I'd like to think so!

Fred was born in Shoreditch in the East End of London on 24th October 1906 and was christened Frederick William Pontin. He had a sister, Elsie and three brothers Harry, Len and Stanley (who sadly died at the age of ten). His first venture running his own business was to open a company called Smiths Soccer Totes Ltd, dealing in fixed odds Football Coupons, later diversifying into bookmaking. The war intervened and when peace was restored, Fred nurtured his idea to extend the military camps that so many men had had to endure, into catering and entertainment centres, the whole family could enjoy. He purchased a site at Brean Sands for £23,000 and in 1946 opened the very first Pontin Holiday Camp – soon to be joined by a second at Osmington Bay, near Weymouth. The time was absolutely right for such a venture and the public flocked to this new form of all-in holiday and before long, the number of sites bearing the Pontin Logo, had risen to twenty-six. There was no doubt that Fred Pontin was well ahead of his time. He was the first to recognise the need for chalets (now called apartments) to be built of bricks and mortar, to include en-suite bathrooms, fitted kitchens, carpets and TV sets.

In the early 1960's he ventured into the overseas market. The first Pontinental site was purchased in Sardinia and, once again, because of the Pontin promise of good food and entertainment plus the extra ingredient of guaranteed sunshine, others followed eventually totalling fifteen, in places such as Italy, Greece, Yugoslavia, Spain and even the USA. Sadly, in time, the centres abroad would diminish in number because of spiralling costs but it is interesting to note that, today, this type of British style holiday abroad is back in fashion and flourishing – further proof that Fred Pontin was many light years ahead both in thought and deed.

Two dates are firmly implanted in the minds of those who knew and cared for the great man. The first was April 1971 when an exuberant Fred Pontin watched, in disbelief, as his horse 'Specify', ridden by Johnny Cook, won the Grand National at Aintree. If Fred was thrilled beyond belief at the result, so too, were many of his staff who put a few bob on the nose at odds of 33-1. The other date of remembrance was 1976 when plain Fred Pontin became Sir Fred Pontin for his services to charity. The honour bestowed on him was shared by everyone who knew him and no one can deny how well deserved it was.

Nevertheless, it fuelled a further round of stories, and who else would be involved but the workaholic Chairman, who arrived at one Centre to witness an old gentleman dressed in clothes which befitted that of resident gardener, staring fixedly at a bed of flowers. Fred noted his position and when he returned to the same spot twenty minutes later, the old man was still there, not having moved. Fred hated laziness of any kind and characteristically blew his top. "I've been watching you for a full twenty minutes," he roared, "and you've never moved a muscle, I'm not paying you to do nothing. Pick up your P45 at the office and get out! You're fired!"

The old man slowly straightened up, looked Fred up and down and said, "Pay me? I'm paying you! I'm taking part in a competition to name the flowers in this bed and you can't sack me Mr Pontin, 'cos I'm one of your guests!"

That particular confrontation has now passed into folklore, as was another heated discussion with a guest at the aforementioned Pineta Beach Hotel in Sardinia. The press, always eager to spread any malicious gossip concerning the Pontin Empire, had headlined the rumours that the Pontinental resort was rife with food poisoning of the worst kind. Fred immediately arranged to fly out and face the 'problem' in person. He was met by the Manager, Franco Tressoldi, who informed him that there had been a minor outbreak of sickness, unrelated to the accusations levelled by the press, but thanks to the banner headlines trumpeted by the Sunday newspapers, there was a distinct feeling of unease amongst the guests.

"Right," Fred proclaimed. "I will meet you in the restaurant at seven o'clock this evening. We will be seen to be eating the same food as everyone else and it will prove to all that there is nothing to be feared from what is served."

When he appeared on site, however, one or two of the more avaricious minded holiday makers, sensing that here lay an opportunity to recover some compensation, proceeded to dog his footsteps, complaining loudly of everything under the Italian sun. Fred's blood pressure rose with the temperature and when he made his way to the restaurant, steam was beginning to envelop his well being. He sat down to consume his meal and, no sooner had he commenced eating, when a hand dropped on his shoulder. It was a guest. "May I have a word Mr Pontin?" he asked.

The pressure valve exploded and Fred leapt to his feet. "No you bloody well can't," he roared. "If you can't eat the food, or dislike the accommodation, or hate the entertainment, then you can leave first thing tomorrow. Your tickets for the flight home will be at reception at nine o'clock in the morning. Now leave me alone to enjoy my meal."

The guest hurriedly left to pack his bags and duly flew home to England the next day. The press of course had heard and were waiting. "What went wrong?" They enquired. "Was it as bad as we thought?"

"Bad?" said the guest. "It wasn't bad – it was brilliant! The food, the accommodation, the entertainment – brilliant! All I did was approach Fred Pontin to thank him for a wonderful holiday and he sent me home!"

Once again, I cannot vouch for the authenticity of these stories but I repeat them nevertheless for they make good reading true or false. One story that was without doubt completely true, concerned the beautiful beach at Cala Mesquida in Majorca and was the jewel in the crown for the Pontinental village that surrounded it. Unfortunately, however, on the very odd occasion, a particularly obnoxious type of seaweed would be washed in by the tide covering the bay with the dreadful substance. Normally it wouldn't last for long and it was generally acknowledged as being simply a nuisance. On one occasion, it arrived and considerably outstayed its welcome. Day followed day and the seaweed stayed, much to the despair and annoyance of the guests. Fred, unaware of the problem arrived on his regular visit, to be met by the Village Manager, Walter Rowley.

"They're gunning for you," he explained. "Their holiday's been ruined and they want to know what you're going to do about it."

Fred decided to meet a deputation that evening and they insisted that machinery and labour should be brought in to clean up the mess. Fred knew that was impossible for such a remote location and on a comparatively small island, but decided the only way out was to bluff. "I'll do that," said Fred. "By the morning the seaweed will have gone."

Walter Rowley buried his head in his hands, knowing it was all a bluff and very aware that by morning Fred would be well on his way back to London, leaving him to face the music. The guests were delighted and Fred was plied with drinks for the rest of the evening, whilst Walter considered all the options open to one about to be lynched. That night, the village was hit by a tropical storm. The surf crashed relentlessly onto the shoreline and when the morning dawned, not a speck of seaweed was to be found. Fred of course, decided on a later flight home that day in order to bask in the glory of his miracle and Walter Rowley wondered (in private), why he had booked a flight at all. "The man can walk on water," he breathed in admiration and five hundred guests agreed with him entirely.

A new decade had dawned and the seventies was an era of the past. No sooner had we settled into working for the Coral Leisure Group, than the Company found itself on the market once again and the new buyers turned out to be the brewing giants Bass. The battles were, of course, confined to the Boardroom and rightly so, but the sharp end of the business continued to flourish. Bookings continued to pour in and the camps were, as always, booked solidly. Trevor Hemmings had taken over as Managing Director and proved the ideal man for the task.

A Lancastrian through and through, he had formed an early link with Pontins through his building company Hemmings & Kent, who won the contracts to build the new holiday villages at Southport and Prestatyn, and his style of management was one of warmth, loyalty and an approachability that was second to none. Everyone knew him as Trevor but everyone knew he was the boss. Like Fred, but in a less formidable way, he was totally loyal to his staff and expected the same loyalty in return. If any of his employees fell on hard times or for any unavoidable reason, lost their jobs, Trevor would always be the first to offer help. He was, and still is, highly respected and well loved by the members of the staff who work with him. Notwithstanding the gentler side to his nature, Trevor was, and is, a formidable businessman with a sharp and even ruthless streak that has enabled him to run a multitude of contrasting companies. In addition, he sits on the Board of many more and is now listed as one of the top one hundred richest men in Britain today. His first move in my direction was to move my office from the Blackpool Camp into the Coral Island Complex on the Golden Mile and add the booking of that venue to my Pontin brief. This was a new venture for me, for now I had to present entertainment for customers who had to pay to get in. The type of clientele, too, was rather different to the more sedate guests on the camps and the acts and bands I booked had to reflect this.

The Guv' nor – Sir Fred Pontin.

No sooner had I got to grips with this particular problem when I was on the move again – this time to Park Hall Leisure Centre, part of the Camelot Theme Park, situated near Charnock Richard in Lancashire. Once again it was a step up, for part of the complex was a superb night club, featuring top live artists and it became part of my ever increasing remit to book the star names. I began to feel an important cog in the wheel of the company as I contracted some of the great names in showbusiness – Bob Monkhouse, Tommy Cooper, Little & Large, Les Dawson, The Drifters, The Rockin' Berries and the American country singer, Billy Jo Spiers. I was now enjoying the challenge thoroughly but Trevor had further surprises in store and this one was a cracker!

The event was the National Finals of the 'Elegant Grandmother' competition held at Southport and, as always, we were anxious to appoint judges capable of recognising good winners. Who better, I thought, than Jan and obviously, she was delighted to oblige. She performed her duties with great aplomb, the results were announced and we retired to the bar for drinks and the 'Hunt the Twiglet' scrum! Trevor approached us and I introduced him to Jan, watching his eyes light up at the sight of my elegant spouse. As is usually the case in these free-for-alls, we were separated although I did notice Jan and Trevor in deep and earnest conversation.

"That bloody portfolio again," I mused. "She's trying to sell him some acts!"

It was however, more traumatic than that would ever be and I was not to find out the outcome until just before our time to leave. Trevor beckoned me over and came straight to the point. "You're doing a fine job," he started and I immediately sensed danger, recalling the numerous scenarios played in the Boardroom of soccer clubs all over the country, when the Chairman assures the hapless team manager (and the hovering press), that his job is safe and his position with the club is secure for life, before delivering the 'coup de grace' the following day by presenting the victim with his P45. I waited with breath that was extremely bated. "A fine job..." he repeated. "I feel, however, that with the extra work you have recently taken on, you should have an assistant." He didn't wait for my agreement or otherwise, but ploughed on with what proved to be a 'fait accompli'. "I've found the perfect person for the job, she can start on Monday!"

There standing before me was Jan looking just slightly embarrassed but nevertheless, obviously excited and eager.

"Well – what do you think? Will it work?" he asked as an afterthought, perhaps feeling just a mite guilty.

My mind whirled. *Would* it work? Would being together twenty-four hours a day be healthy? Would I *really* be the boss? Would it affect our marriage? I faced Trevor and said, "Ah well...erm...urr...I urr..."

"Good lad – I knew you'd see sense!" he said clapping me on the back and with that, he was gone, leaving me and my Assistant facing each other with mouths wide open.

It did, in fact, work – it worked very well. Jan took over the entire recruitment of the Bluecoat staff, reorganising the advertising, interviewing, auditioning and, best of all, the training and the system she introduced was the benchmark for the way it is done today. She loved the involvement with the kids and they, in turn, adored her for the way she cared and looked after them. She was, in her own words, the 'mother hen', protecting and nurturing her own family – always intent on improving their wages, their accommodation and their uniforms. She carried the flag, she fought their battles and there is no doubt in my mind, she would have killed for them had it been necessary. The standard of Bluecoats increased dramatically during her reign and has remained the very highest to this present day. The Bluecoat 'Academy', as I like to call it, has now become almost akin to a stage school – like something from the film 'Fame' in which the boys and girls are encouraged to indulge in the Performing Arts. The Bluecoat shows, at one time alternating between 'Wild West' shows and 'Old Time Music Halls', have now become top class professional productions. The company, realising the incredible impact this type of show has on its guests has, at long last, seen the light and is now pouring many thousands and thousands of pounds into sets, costumes, lighting and sound. I say, without contradiction, that, particularly in the larger Centres, to view the Bluecoat show, whatever its title, is not far removed from watching a West End production. I am proud that I played a major part in the later renaissance and the spectacular improvement in the standard of the presentation was greatly encouraged, when I persuaded the Board of Directors to make the whole thing competitive by awarding a large, suitably engraved, silver cup and generous cash prizes to the winning team. One of the great joys of my life, I have to admit, was in judging the best of the best and to watch the faces of the boys and girls as they performed – so full of passion and hope and fulfilment – brought a lump to my throat. The evening when we announced the winner, usually done at the end of their show without the knowledge that we were on site and with no inkling that they had won, was like the opening shot of *This Is Your Life* as I walked onto the stage to make the announcement. Their mouths would drop open, realisation that they had won would dawn on them and their world would explode into hugs, kisses, champagne and screams of sheer joy. The poor guests, bravely reflecting the euphoria in front of them, were totally ignored for a goodly measure of time before sanity and professionalism returned, but I am sure they understood and shared the same pleasure as that shown by the kids in Blue.

Let it be understood, however, that the basic duties of a Bluecoat still remain – the mixing and mingling being paramount – but there is no doubt that the emphasis is now heavily weighted towards the 'show' in showbusiness. With that carrot to dangle, we are now attracting the best of the boys and girls with talent to spare. The Actors Union, Equity, have also acknowledged the impact the talented Bluecoats now have in the world of entertainment and finally agreed to allow selected performers to gain the highly prized and coveted Equity Card – a breakthrough that I worked for, and am very proud to have achieved.

With that in mind, it would seem the ideal place to reflect through the years and mention just a few of the Bluecoats who benefited from the system, the training, the experience and the opportunity to blossom from the raw recruits who applied for the position and ended up as one of the star names we regularly view on our television, radio and theatre stages.

CHAPTER FIFTEEN

Stars in Bluecoat

Carol Lee Scott was one of those who found fame after a fairly long apprenticeship and when it came, it was not so much under her own name but that of her alter ego 'Grotbags' the Witch. Carol had been working on a small, privately owned centre in the south west of England but was decidedly unhappy, for no one recognised her talent as a comedienne/vocalist. Frustrated, she rang Pontins Camp at Brean Sands and was startled to find herself speaking to Fred Pontin himself, who had answered the phone. She poured her heart out to Fred and he invited her on to the site to meet him. The outcome was a job as a Bluecoat for £2 per week, plus free accommodation, uniform and food. Carol was a big lady with a big personality and was simply adored by the guests. She completed the season at Brean Sands but it was not long before she graduated from Bluecoat/Entertainer to touring cabaret. I can remember, vividly, seeing her perform at Camber Sands and very conscious of the pleadings of the Centre Manager to 'plug' the chip shop and the beefburger bar during her act, she paused half way through her very funny rendition of *Big Spender* – where she sits on some poor unsuspecting guests knee and wickedly bounces up and down during the chorus – and blatantly announced the instruction she had been given to plug the fast food outlets.

"I'm not going to recommend something I've never tasted," she said – and immediately ordered the poor guest (that she was currently flattening at the time), to limp to the 'chippie' and bring back a large portion of haddock and chips.

"Who's going to pay?" muttered her scapegoat.

"Tell them – it's for Carol Lee Scott," she roared imperiously. Within minutes he was back with the order and she spent the next twenty minutes munching fish and chips (she did pass a *few* around) and eulogising at the taste. Great, I thought. Here am I paying her a fat fee for her cabaret, watching her eating our fish and chips on our stage and in front of our guests. Nice work if you can get it! Commercially, the show was a great success for the queues outside the chip shop that evening were the longest of the season.

Carol eventually devised her 'Grotbags' character and for the next twenty years, had her own programme on children's television and appeared both on TV and on the touring stage with Rod Hull and Emu. Children everywhere recognise and love her and it's nice to know that she, amongst many, started as a Pontin Bluecoat.

Amanda Reddington (GMTV), was another to make the grade, as was **Helen Chamberlain** (Sky Sports – Soccer AM). Then there was **Jimmy Mulgrew**. Never heard of him? – read on.

I was introduced to this gentleman by Ronnie Baker of the Black Abbotts, who knocked on my office door one day and ushered Jimmy in.

"Want's to be a Bluecoat...does a comedy act."

I asked him to perform but he had nothing prepared. He assured me that all would be well and I wouldn't regret giving him a start. Despite not viewing his promised talent, I liked his warmth and his open face and decided to offer him a job at our Morecambe Centre. Off he went, full of enthusiasm and all was quiet for two months. Then the phone rang.

"Hallo – its Jimmy Mulgrew here. Listen, I've got an act together and its really going well. When you're up in Morecambe next, will you stay on and see it?"

And so, as promised, I stood at the back of the Sunset Bar and awaited the arrival on stage of Mr Mulgrew. He bounded into view carrying an invisible bag (he told us that, for we couldn't see it!) and placed it gently onto the floor. From the bag, he extracted three invisible Indian Clubs (he told us that too) and proceeded to juggle. He went through the entire jugglers repertoire – one handed, flick under the leg, flick over his head, balance on the forehead – the lot! He then stunned everyone, who wasn't already stunned, by producing two more invisible clubs from the non-existent bag and repeating the routine once again – this time with an incredible five clubs! Impossible, I hear you cry – but Jimmy did it and if the clubs had not been invisible, he might even have got a standing ovation. As it was, the crowd rose as one and disappeared in the direction of the late night drinking hole to discuss what they had just witnessed.

"Well?" said Jimmy, his face full of anticipation. "What did you think?"

I replied with my fingers crossed tightly behind my back and in a low voice so that no one could overhear.

"Very good," I muttered. "It was original but it does need working on!"

A year passed and I never heard from Jimmy until, one afternoon, I received a phone call out of the blue. "Hallo," he said "It's Jimmy Mulgrew here."

I threw myself under the desk for protection, as memories of that painful evening at Morecambe came flooding back. Jimmy pressed on unabashed.

"No don't worry, I've scrapped the juggling act – I've got a new one now. I'm working in a club in Preston tonight and will you come and see me?"

My head told me emphatically to say no, but my heart and my curiosity got the better of me and I duly turned up, certain I was to witness another disastrous debacle. What transpired, however, turned out to be quite brilliant. He sloped onto the stage looking totally gormless, wearing a floppy hat and wellington boots and proceeded to tear the club apart.

"Well," he said seeking me out after the show. "What did you think?"

"Jimmy," I replied. "That was quite brilliant. You've got it, my lad, you're going to be a star."

Jimmy's face flushed with pleasure. "Thank you boss," he said. "You've no idea what those words mean to me. Oh and by the way – I've changed my name too. I'm now known as **Jimmy Cricket**!"

That night a star was born.

The season he spent with us at Morecambe proved to be double edged, for not only did he hone his timing and delivery on our unsuspecting guests, but an incident in the restaurant changed his life in another direction. Preparing for an evening show and dressed in his best stage suit, he rushed in and pleaded with the pretty waitress to give him special service that evening as he was on show twenty minutes later. She wanted to help this charming Irish Bluecoat and, as she raced to his table, tripped and the soup she was carrying, emptied itself over our hero. The girl was distraught and instead of dissolving into a furious rage and tearing the girl apart, Jimmy's heart melted and he asked her out instead. Jimmy is still asking her out today, for the two got married sometime later and raised a beautiful family of little Crickets. A lovely, gentle man is our Jim and someone that I, and many, many others are so glad that he chose to pass our way.

We interviewed and auditioned a young man with a burning ambition to be a singer. It was obvious that he had a great talent for comedy but his ambition, beyond any other, was to set the world alight with his vocal prowess and become an international star. We sent the young **Brian Conley** to our chalet/hotel Centre at Barton Hall, Torquay as a Bluecoat and as the season wore on, his flair and talent for comedy became more and more obvious – but he was still having none of it. Any young lady colleague capable of carrying a tune, was propositioned by Brian, in the nicest possible sense, to join him and form a vocal duo, but nothing appeared to work out, at least to his satisfaction. Bridie Reid, my counterpart in the Southern Area, sat with Brian for many a long hour trying to persuade him to concentrate on making people laugh and play down his singing ambitions for, as she put it 'vocalists, even good ones, are ten a penny but comedians, particularly good ones, are rare'. He had a good voice, we could not deny that, but Bridie felt that he was going in the wrong direction and everyone, including me, agreed with her.

"A few years later," she recalls. "I sat in my seat at the Victoria Palace on the opening night of the musical *Jolson* and watched as Brian, in the starring role received a standing ovation from the press and celebrity audience alike. I realised then, it was time to eat humble pie!"

His voice had made him a star, but in a way *we* were also right for he is not a bad comedian either – is he not? Brian had still not reached his full potential but already he had achieved National and International fame and it is a heart warming thought to all of us at Pontins that we played a part, in helping him reach that peak.

I recall sitting in my office in Blackpool, one Saturday afternoon in the early summer and reading the riot act to a bevy of extremely pretty young girls who sat facing me. They were the resident show dancers who were contracted to appear in the Pontin summer revue show in the Centre Theatre five evenings per week. To offset their food and accommodation costs for the full season of twenty-two weeks, they had happily agreed to work a further twelve hours a week in Bluecoat uniform doing the duties required. It was, of course, greatly beneficial to us, too, having eight slim, personable and very pretty, young ladies parading as hostesses and I was delighted to feature them, particularly on reception duty each Saturday, imagining the impression they would have on travel weary, irritable and hen-pecked husbands as they arrived with their dominant wives and screaming kids, ready to book in. As for the single lads amongst the incoming guests, well, they would surely rub their hands together and think that this was Utopia! The scenario was perfect except that the girls decided to ignore those people they were instructed to meet and greet and instead, stood around in groups chatting to each other, prompting me to convene a hurriedly arranged 'bored' meeting in my office. I went through the full gambit of what one is expected to say and suitably chastened (I hope), they rose to leave.

"Would the Head Girl please stay," I requested and a very attractive young lady detached herself from the group and resumed her seat. "What do I call you?" I asked, still trying to be the tough, gruff boss but failing miserably under her spell.

"My name is Gemma – **Gemma Craven**," she replied and I automatically went into the special mode reserved for middle-aged men in the company of lovely young ladies: A frantic pulling in of the stomach, jutting out the chin to take up slack flesh hanging below and the cursory hand movement that glides over the hair line ensuring that what is left, of what was once a hairpiece to be admired, is firmly in place and hiding the barren prairie, increasing with age. We chatted for a while and she promised to make sure the girls behaved in the future. Needless to say, I found it necessary to be at rehearsals for the Sunday show the next day and she danced with grace and elegance.

One of the other girls in the team moved over to me. "Have you hear her sing?" she whispered. "Go on – ask her to sing!"

I did – and she did and was superb.

"My God," I thought. "This girl's going to be a star!"

A short time later, my prediction came true when she starred with Richard Chamberlain in the film chosen for the Royal Film Performance, *The Slipper and the Rose*.

Her role in that production catapulted Gemma to international stardom and she never looked back. Since then she has headlined on film and stage throughout the world – a far cry from my office in Blackpool and yet again, we are enormously proud to record the blossoming of a great talent, that once wore the colours of a Pontin Bluecoat.

There were so many others too that crossed the line into stardom. The brilliant vetriloquist **Roger de Courcey** with his cheeky friend, Nookie Bear, the wonderful comedian **Mick Miller** – he of the bald head and shoulder length hair, some times compared by many to that of a pink crash helmet – who served his Bluecoat apprenticeship at Broadreeds, near Chichester. And the energetic, zany style of funny man **Stu Francis** who commenced his career in blue at the most northern of the Pontin sites, Middleton Tower, near Morecambe. Stu became a household name through his appearances on children's television, hosting many programmes for the younger viewers. His catchphrase 'Oh – I could crush a grape', was the title of his own series of shows which ran for many years. Mick, Roger and Stu still appear in the star cabaret slots at Pontins today and each still performs superbly. Always in great demand, they remain a credit to the profession they grace and to the Company that provided their grounding.

The same could be said of that cheeky chappy comedian, **Bradley Walsh** and the game show host **Andrew O'Connor**. Bradley's early ambition was to be a professional footballer – indeed he signed for Brentford Town FC – but the lure of showbusiness proved too much and he changed direction. Once again, we were able to offer him the chance to gain valuable experience, to polish his delivery and sharpen the timing so necessary in the field of comedy and he donned the blue jacket before hitting the road to the big time and fame. Andrew came to me as a budding magician. At the time, I was using a very funny comedian by the name of Ian Kent in our professional revue show. Unknown to me, Ian had inherited the skills of his father who designed and constructed stage equipment for magicians and illusionists and one day, he approached me to introduce a young up and coming performer who had asked Ian for some second hand magic props. "He's a natural," Ian enthused. "Excellent personality and so much confidence!"

I agreed with Ian's assessment and took Andrew on as a Bluecoat at Blackpool. He had hardly been at our Centre for more than a month, when he waylaid me and pleaded for me to view his own magic show being presented in the main theatre. I could not believe that he had persuaded anyone in such a short space of time, to let him present his own show and especially to allow him the Princes Theatre in which to perform. I agreed to look in, by now, utterly intrigued by the confidence he apparently had in his own ability. I was not to be disappointed. If the content of his show lacked in originality, his presentation was superb. He totally commanded the large audience with his stage 'patter' and his stage presence was awesome for someone so young and so inexperienced. Once again I felt that tingle at the back of my neck in recognition that I was watching something, or someone, special – although I could not pinpoint into which category Andrew would eventually emerge. The introduction of game shows on TV proved the vehicle that he craved and soon he proved a natural within that medium. Other skills blossomed and I was privileged to watch him, many years later, take the title role in the musical *Billy Liar* at the Edinburgh Festival. He was brilliant and so, too, are his writing skills, producing many wonderful scripts for use by the most distinguished performers both on the live stage and on TV today. Andrew, however, reached personal acclaim when he took over the hugely demanding role of *Phineus T Barnum* in the touring version of the hit musical *Barnum*. To take over the part from such luminaries as Michael Crawford and Paul Nicholas, was to attain the highest peak and justified the gut feeling I experienced when I first saw him hold an audience in the palm of his hand at Blackpool. Congratulations to both Bradley and Andrew, who continue to polish the reputation we are proud to hold for finding, nurturing and polishing the finest of embryo talents around today.

No description of those who climbed the showbusiness ladder of success from wearing the famous Bluecoat of Pontins, would be complete without mentioning the name **Shane Richie**. An extrovert, exuberant personality, full of the joy of life but without the veneer of cynicism and self-adoration that blights the lives of many so-called celebrities of lesser talent. It was obvious from the first meeting that Shane, were he to progress no further than Bluecoat, would be a spectacular success and, without hesitation, was offered the job. His first moment of individuality arrived during the week of training allowed to each new Bluecoat recruit, prior to the commencement of the main season. During that period, the new Blues are trained in First Aid, Bingo, Ballroom and Line Dancing, personal grooming and hygiene, health and safety plus much more. The whole package is started off by the 'Welcome to Pontins' meeting, chaired by yours truly and introducing the Managing Director, the Operations Director and finally Jan, who would look after the boys and girls for the remainder of the seven day course. Timing in this business is paramount and Shane proved how superb he was in that department by making an entrance that immediately placed him amongst the legendary characters of today.

Jan was in full flow with two hundred pairs of ears hanging on every word. "Punctuality is prime," she intoned. "You must be on time whatever duty you are on and, in addition, you must look the part. No weird hair cuts, no male ear-rings to be worn and no adornments or tattoos."

At that point (he swears it was not done deliberately), Shane chose the moment to join the company. He appeared in the doorway with hair dyed a bright orange and not one, but many rings attached to his ears and nose. "Sorry I'm late!" he said waving at the platform where Jan stood and promptly found himself a seat.

Give Jan full credit – she was superb! Coolly she waited for the horrified gasp to subside, then countered, "That – ladies and gentlemen – is exactly my case in point. Anyone appearing in such a manner and in such a contradiction to the rules laid down by the Company will be instantly dismissed. Thank you Shane for taking the time, effort and trouble to illustrate the point!"

Shane, in his own admission, shrank at the rebuke but being Shane apologised profusely to Jan and managed (I don't know how!) to convince her that the hair and facial adornments were only because of a stage production which he had just completed and had not yet found time to remove. A weak and unoriginal excuse no doubt, but thankfully both for him *and* us, it was decided to be believed and he was forgiven. When he next appeared, some two hours later, humanity had been restored and the theatrical mask had been removed.

As a Bluecoat, Shane was excellent and the sexual prowess for which he received much press acclaim in later years, was an exaggeration only *he* could have invented. He was larger than life but the guests loved his style and his wildly wicked sense of humour. Eventually, because of his conscientiousness to the job, he was promoted to Entertainments Manager and was posted to Little Canada on the Isle of Wight. His attitude was excellent and his work rate was unparalleled, but that cheeky, impish sense of humour prevailed. Shane tells the story of the P&O Cruise liner *Canberra* with great glee and I am sure the facts are true, if not the outcome. Word was received from Head Office that the *Canberra* was returning from the Falklands war, battered but unbowed and would be passing the Isle of Wight at 7.30am the following morning. Shane, patriotic to the last, decided to impart the news of the passing ship to the guests and invited all those interested to assemble outside the reception building at 6.30am in order to be in position by the appointed time, to cheer the vessel on its way to Southampton. Over two hundred enthusiastic holiday makers turned up at the appointed hour and Shane supplied them with Union Jacks, banners, tin whistles, toy trumpets and anything else that would either look or sound good to those hardy sailors on the way home. They marched toward a high knoll overlooking the sea and as they settled down to await the great moment, a thick sea mist settled on the area and the waiting throng could not see their hands in front of their faces – far from recognising a 45,000 ton ocean liner! Shane was determined that the event (or the ship), would not pass without due deference and he led his party of merry campers in songs of patriotic praise, listening intently for the sounds of the ships engines. All was quiet, except for the voices of those guests still buoyed with the thoughts of bringing our lads home from the war but perceptibly becoming less enthusiastic with each passing hour. It was now 9.30am and Shane was becoming the flavour of the month that no one wanted. The mist persisted, it was cold and all those who had started out with such verve had finally decided that, in more ways than one, they had missed the boat. Suddenly, seconds before mass mutiny was about to break out and the bedraggled party returned dispirited to the centre, the sound of a ships engine was clearly heard by all through the fog. Flags, banners, whistles, voices and spirits were raised and they cheered and sang and waved at the shadowy shape at sea. The passengers of the Portsmouth Car Ferry still talk today of the band of crazy people who welcomed them on the forty-five minute crossing to the island. If they were enamoured with the scenario that befell their senses – the guests involved were not and it took all of Shane's persuasive powers, plus a few bottles of vintage champagne, to quell the uprising. Shane recalls that he was sacked because of the incident but I can reveal that even if I had wanted to, it was impossible to effect. I was too busy laughing...!

Inevitably, as we had sensed, Shane made the big time. His appearances on TV became more and more, culminating in the *Shane Richie Experience*, transmitted at prime time on a Saturday evening. He signed for the lead part in the musical *Grease* at the Dominion Theatre in the West End of London and was with the show for over two years before joining the same production in Manchester. What is lovely about Shane, though, is his gratitude and loyalty to everyone at Pontins. Megastar he may now be, but Shane will always find time to judge a Talent Final or make an appearance at a major event in the Centres and will, as often as not, waive the fee. He just wants to reunite with all his old mates, once again, just for the fun of it! Whilst he was appearing in Manchester during the run of *Grease*, we visited the city as part of our National recruitment tour for Bluecoat Entertainers. We were aware, of course, that Shane was in town and hoped that we would be finished the interviewing and auditioning in time to pop into the theatre to say hello. We needn't have worried! At midday, with the room we had hired bursting to capacity with nervous hopefuls, in walked Shane with no announcement. The kids, waiting to be put through their paces, froze in mid-whatever-they-were-doing and with the awe of the pupil awaiting the master to address, hung on his every movement as he approached the microphone. "Hi guys," he said by way of introduction and proceeded to eulogise about his days with the Company and assured them that he, too, had taken the step they were about to undertake and had never regretted it. The few minutes he spent with the boys and girls did more for the Company prestige and, indeed, the morale of those listening, than we could have done in a whole day of selling our product and merely compounds the respect and admiration I have for this great guy. He is openly proud of the years he spent with Pontins and is never ashamed, or reticent, in admitting it. He is the salt of the earth and yes, sometimes he can shock both on and off stage, but we are forever honoured that he chose to learn his stagecraft at the Bluecoat academy and that, despite the trapping of stardom, he was, and still is, one of us.

A footnote to the Pontin connection for, when it became obvious that Shane needed a personal Manager as he climbed to the top of his profession, he ignored the multitude of blatant hangers on who cling to the star names like theatrical leeches and returned to his colleagues whom he worked alongside with during his Pontin days, to choose a very efficient and likeable fellow Entertainments Manager, by the name of Chris Gosling. That was many years ago and Chris, to this day, still looks after Shane's attentions, but more than that, he is a great companion for they were great mates then, and remain so today.

Having graduated from the stars who made the big time through the ranks of Bluecoat, to those who made the grade from the loftier heights of Entertainments Manager, brings to recall the young man who held the post at Camber Sands near Rye in Sussex. Despite being a very passable compere/ comedian, he never reached the heights of showbusiness stardom, but found everlasting fame in quite another direction. His name was Ian Robinson, but was known to all and sundry simply as 'Blockhead'. How he achieved that particular moniker, no one is quite sure but it had stuck and even when he fell in love and married, his wife had the misfortune of being labelled for the entirety of their time together as – 'Mrs Blockhead'! His moment of destiny arrived one evening in the early summer. The centre was, as always, full to overflowing with guests mainly from the area in and around the East End of London – wonderfully warm, down-to-earth characters who work and play hard. They enjoy a good laugh, a sing-song, a couple of pints (more if pressed) of the local ale and if one can be arranged, a good fight – and that's just the women! On this particular evening, Blockhead intended to introduce the early evening cabaret – a superb comedy/speciality act by the name of Muzzy Main (I've changed his name to protect the guilty) – before dashing downstairs to the Night Club for a quiz game he was hosting. He duly presented the artiste and dashed off to the lower floor to start his game show. Muzzy, on hearing his cue, staggered onto the stage and began mumbling incoherently into the microphone, punctuated with hysterical laughter as he listened to himself deliver extremely funny jokes that even *he* had never heard before.

At first the audience – ever trusting – assumed that what they were witnessing was a part of the act that, for the moment, they were unable to unravel but quickly they cottoned on to the fact all was not well. "Gerroff!" they yelled. "You've obviously been indulging in an excess of alcohol!" – at least that's what they inferred. The actual sentence was much shorter and ended up with the word 'missed' or 'fist' or something that was similar – or at least rhymed.

Blockhead was summoned immediately and, rather than dash on stage and drag the performer ignominiously to the safety of side stage, he diplomatically grabbed the microphone lead and slowly began to reel the babbling Muzzy in, like a deep-sea fisherman landing a shark. The audience could see what was happening by this time and began giving Blockhead their vocal support. Cheering, mixed with laughter, filled the room but Muzzy, unaware that his mike lead was getting shorter by the second, suddenly registered that the sounds of approval he could now hear from the audience must surely be for him and fought back. There followed a tug of war that neither was prepared to lose until the lead decided it had had enough and lost its grip on the microphone head, rendering it silent. Muzzy was then led off the platform to an ovation he would never have got normally and the incident appeared to be over. Muzzy poured out his bleary apologies and sank into the chair provided for him, seemingly on the way to sleep. His brain, however, refused to succumb and suddenly, as if someone had flicked a switch, he leapt to his feet and systematically began to trash the dressing room. Security was sent for, he was overpowered and rushed through the doors at the back of the room and into the reception. Once again he was becalmed and contrite, apologising to everyone and everything in view – until he caught sight of Blockhead. The switch went into overdrive, once again, and he hurled himself at the Entertainments Manager intending, if not to kill, to seriously maim. Muzzy was a big solid man but Blockhead was even bigger and after all, this was the man very able to control the guests when the disagreements broke out in the late bar, especially on a Friday night. If Henry Cooper was to be called 'Enry the Ammer' then, from this moment on, Blockhead was to be known as 'Blockhead the Belter'. He produced a right uppercut from near to the floor and it caught Muzzy right on the point where his Gillette Mach II razor couldn't reach and if sleep almost closed him down minutes before, this brush with Blockhead's fist finally did the trick. From that moment on Blockhead was 'Le God'. Guests slapped him on the back, plied him with champagne and sung his praises for the rest of the evening. They demanded a re-run of the 'cabaret' every week with a festive repeat at Christmas and not one to waste an opportunity, Blockhead actually had Christmas cards printed, showing him stripped to the waist and brandishing his right fist, this time suitably clad in a regulation sized boxing glove with the inscription 'Blockhead wishes you a belting Christmas!'

Poor Muzzy never worked for us again but Blockhead became a star overnight and later, retired to run a pub in Luton. I am sure to this day, customer will approach the bar and say to the landlord, "A pint of your best ale, sir and would you show us the fist that took out that great comedy act Muzzy Main?"

And knowing Blockhead as we do, I'll bet he'll oblige!

CHAPTER SIXTEEN

Promotion and the joys of the Showcase

We were now into the 1980's and as we moved into the new decade, Trevor yet again made his presence felt. The Company was now owned by the brewers, Bass Plc and Trevor, as Managing Director, decided that the split in the Entertainment Department, with Bridie controlling the South and me looking after the North and Pontinental, was not to his liking. He, himself, worked from the Head Office at Bournemouth and rightly felt that the person responsible for what was now an increasingly important segment of the business – namely entertainment – should be within reach and shouting distance. He decided, therefore, to move Bridie into the Pontinental division and I was to take over the entire UK operation, working of course, from the south coast. Jan, too, was to join me and this meant sadly putting our delightful thatched cottage in the village of Elswick (near Blackpool), up for sale. If this move was to bring some grief, the job prospects fully compensated and I could not help but look back at my early days at Butlins, with the ubiquitous Wally Goodman and my joining the Pontin team in 1967 thanks to David Lever – two men who held the position of Entertainment Executive with their respective companies and two men whom I held in awe and great respect. Ironically, here was I, now attaining the position held by them and if anyone had told me way back yonder that I would achieve similar status, I would have dismissed them as mentally deranged. The increase in responsibility was, too, spectacular to say the least for although I controlled the five

Northern Centres (Tower Beach, Prestatyn had been added to the list), the fourteen Pontinental sites required my presence more than my organisational skills. Now I was being handed twenty-four centres throughout the UK – all requiring top class cabaret, bands, groups, solo musicians, sports personalities, star weekends, wrestling and many more and the buck stopped with me. Jan, too, had the same increase to cover, with Entertainment Managers, Bluecoat/ Entertainers and Children's Uncle and Aunties and although we were totally confident in our ability to produce the goods, it was still a daunting task for there was no doubt that Bridie Reid was a hard act to follow. We settled in quickly and if I had had any fears before, that working and living with Jan twenty four hours a day was going to affect our marriage, I needn't have bothered. Our two desks actually faced each other and we sat close enough to hold hands across the paperwork but, such was the manic pressure of our respective jobs and the incessant ringing of the four telephones we shared, neither of us knew what the other had done during the day until we drove home that evening and discussed our various problems. The hours, too, were long and restrictive, especially for the pre-season period from January until early June and it was not unusual to work from 9.00am until 10.00pm with hardly a break for lunch or tea.

We had managed to find another delightful thatched cottage in the picturesque village of Tarrant Hinton, near Blandford Forum, in Dorset. It turned out to be a major mistake on our part for, as lovely as it was, we quickly realised the drawbacks. In the first place it was nearly an hours drive from the office – not all funny when you've been working flat out for thirteen hours. Secondly, because of its age, much of the stonework was beginning to show signs of wear and tear and we spent long hours patching the gaps as they appeared. It became so bad at one time, we thought of renaming the cottage 'Polyfilla Villa' for obvious reasons! The garden became a nightmare too, for such was its size, that on the odd weekend we managed off, we would commence weeding, digging 'et al' on the Friday evening and not finish until dusk on Sunday, exhausted, yet unable to see much difference from our labours. We were only keeping pace with nature. My one pride and joy, however, was the lawn and this I tended with loving care, watching it blossom from a wild overgrown field into the texture of a bowling green. Unbeknown to me at the time, however, was the wicked sense of humour imbedded in the local strain of moles that roamed the area. Weekend after weekend, they watched with growing glee as I toiled over the grassy carpet. Towards the completion of my labours, they probably invited their families to join them for a Sunday picnic, such was their joyous intentions. On the evening I stood back, filled with pride at my achievement, and wallowing in the anticipation of the local bowling club paying vast sums on money to experience the joys of playing their sporting prowess on my manicured verdant lawn, the moles decided the time had come to declare war. A meeting of the top military moles was convened, war was declared and, like the escape from Colditz, tunnel committees were formed and as darkness fell, digging began. The following morning, eighteen molehills decorated the surface of my pride and joy and the language that flowed from my gentle frame, was recorded and used in the training manual at the near by army barracks in Andover.

The final straw was the realisation that, such was the outlying position of the village, the morning papers, on which I revel, were delivered late in the day, long after I had left for work and the Sunday papers, which rebalance my sanity and with which I cannot live without, were not delivered at all. The outcome was that the inhabitants of the hamlet drew up a list of 'delivery boys' which meant that every sixth Sunday, I had to rise with the lark, drive two miles to the paper shop, collect the Sunday rags ordered by my neighbours and spend the next hour and a half dropping them through the letterbox whilst listening to the sound of happy snoring coming from within. Isn't it great, I thought. Head of Entertainment for a national Company, responsible for the happiness of over a million guests per year, a showbusiness icon worshipped by all the acts, revered by their agents and here I am with a bloody paper round. Life has a funny way of keeping your feet on the ground!

We soon decided to move, found a nice Georgian style house, ten minutes walk from the office, a small garden with *no* lawn and papers which arrived by breakfast! Life was worth living once again and we settled down happily to find the best entertainers available for the budget we had been allocated.

We have been asked many times in the past, how and where we find the good standard of artiste we provide year after year and, quite honestly, there is no real answer. We simply have to be prepared to look and look again, slumming it in the roughest clubs and lording it in the plushest nightspots. By the end of any given day, particularly in the run up to the main season, the phones on your desk become a molten mass of melting plastic from agents ringing with their latest discovery and insisting you give up everything to see them work and, sometimes, you fall for it!

I recall one insistent call from Liverpool agent Tony West who desperately wanted me to view a young comedian he had recently signed up. The venue was to be a small nightclub, not far from Flint in North Wales. Having worked a full day in the office (I was still working from Blackpool at this time), I really did not feel like driving that distance – about ninety miles – for what could possibly be a wasted journey but I gave in, partly because he invited me to meet him at the club around 8.00pm for a sumptuous meal before viewing his artiste. I arrived just after the appointed hour, ravenous but anticipating with pleasure, the gastronomic treat awaiting me. Tony had not yet arrived – in fact no one had yet arrived and I sat on a bar stool applauding the

With Ken Dodd and Jan at Blackpool.
It was hard enough to get him on and even harder to get him off.

Mixing with the 'Neighbours'. Singer/Songwriters Tony Hatch & Jackie Trent. It only took them 20 minutes to write the theme song for the soap opera and has made them a fortune.

The man who taught us all to 'Play in a Day' –
the legendary guitarist Bert Weedon.

Three 'star' comedians and a prize idiot!
I share the limelight with (L to R) Billy Pearce, John Inman and Jimmy Cricket.

*No – it's **not** one of the Vernons Girls! Backstage with Danny La Rue.*

I pose with Keith Chegwin and Melvin Hayes after the farce of the 'Sky Star Search'. My smile was very forced.

cleaners as they put the finishing touches to a sterling job. By 8.30pm I was chewing the beer mats and by 9.00pm I was about to phone the Samaritans, when Tony arrived full of apologies and bonhomie, but little else. Being the perfect host, he returned from the bar and placed before me a diet coke but, to add insult to injury, forgot to bring over the complementary peanuts and crisps, which even now, were being rapidly devoured by persons who had already had their dinner and were eating our of pure diabolical greed! No mention of food passed the lips of Mr West and no particle of food passed mine. Tony's 'turn' never stood a chance. All I could think of were the pains of approaching malnutrition and where I could possibly find something to eat. I don't think I smiled all evening at any of his gags – I was just too weak! Tony still never twigged at my discomfort caused by his broken promise and he waved me off into the night, convinced I would be on the phone first thing the next day with a seasonal contract and a vow of gratitude for bringing the comic to my attention. I never spoke to Tony West for over a month but when I did, I thoroughly recommended the Kentucky Fried Chicken Restaurant in Connahs Quay, for on that night, it saved my life!

The most sensible way of viewing acts is, without doubt, by way of the showcase – or tradeshow, as it is sometimes called. Most of the better agents, at some time or other, put together a full afternoon and evening of their own artistes and bands and invite the major bookers to attend. In this way you can see something in the region of twelve bands during the afternoon and sixteen acts during the evening and on paper it sounds grand but, in the hands of some of the agents, it could, and often was, disastrous – particularly in the bad old days before 'booker' power, eventually and finally, got it right. The invitation arrived on my desk the week before and lay there in full view, pompous and important. 'A Supershowcase' it announced, 'commencing at 2.30pm (sharp) and finishing (without fail) by 11.00pm.

Featuring the best artistes in the country. Don't miss it – don't be late!' At this time in my career I was known to all the bookers, including the TV moguls, as 'Mr Tradeshow' for I never missed one, attending an average of four per week and studiously recording each performer, what they wore, what they sang (if vocal) etc.

It was not uncommon for TV producers to ring me up, like some kind of information service, and say, "Danny Whitbread, please?" I would immediately produce the card giving all the details, including what he had had for breakfast and the last time he visited the men's room.

The system was excellent and I was proud of it. It was essential, therefore, that I was not going to pass up this particular show event. I always made the mistake of going into the office before heading up the motorway for the extravaganza and, when the time came to leave my desk, I was suffering once again from telephoneitis and a building headache, born through batting maiden overs to the devious spin bowling of arrogant agents and tedious performers. On the motorway itself, the rain had started but I ploughed on regardless, through the spray of twelve wheel transporters and Eddie Stobart delivery trucks, arriving at the destination totally wrecked but pleased that I would see the first band on stage at 2.30pm – ('sharp'). Of course – no one knew where the club was and I eventually found it at the bottom of a cobbled one way street, sandwiched between a disused cotton mill and a crumbling railway viaduct that had seen better days. The club was one of the better ones for it had its own car park – a rock strewn battlefield that lay flooded in the pouring rain and I eased my way in, relieved to be able to drive up to the main entrance. I entered only to find the place eerily empty, apart from a group of hairy layabout musicians, wearing the obligatory uniform borrowed from local gypsies who frequent the corporation rubbish tip. It was now half past two (sharp!) and I slowly realised that I had been taken in again. The agent arrived at 3.00pm and the show commenced at 3.45pm. Of the twelve bands promised, four just didn't turn up, three had had a fight within the last two days and broken up and two had had their equipment repossessed by the hire purchase company and obviously couldn't perform and one had only just formed – so much so, that they were still being introduced to each other when the curtain went up. The remaining two couldn't read music, so the afternoon became a wash out, both inside and outside the club.

By 5.30pm the session was over and, as if by magic, the club emptied – musicians, bar staff, the lot, even the agent who had begged my presence, waved an airy farewell as he went off to his wife and kids and – no doubt – a sumptuous supper. "See you at eight," he cried and disappeared into the rainy afternoon.

I was on my own – just me and my headache – and I contemplated a dash for freedom. Determination, however, won the day and I wandered into the centre of the metropolis, seeking a friendly face to while away the hundred and fifty minutes separating me from the recommencement of the concert. The main shop had closed for the day and the pub had not yet opened but sanctuary was at hand in the shape of a 'greasy spoon' transport café that welcomed me heartily with the beckoning smell of chips, frying bacon, grilling mushrooms and sweaty truck drivers.

Suitably replenished, I returned to the club for the 8.00pm (sharp) start and found a transformation had taken place. The car park overflowed with vehicles of all shapes and sizes spilling into the cobbled road and causing chaos. The occupants of the cars had swarmed into the club and had commandeered every seat and stool on offer and planted their size eleven pit boots on every inch of standing space capable of seeing the stage. By sheer luck, I managed to find a parking space by moving two dozen empty beer kegs and was met at the door by a shoal of gasping sardines desperate to get back into their tins for some breathing space and my heart sank. I finally found a spot in which I could just see the top of the artistes' heads and there I was when the show started (as promised) at 8.55pm sharp. Now it was the turn of the individual artistes and the opening act, instructed to do no more than eight minutes maximum, found, to his delight that he was actually going rather well. (He didn't get any applause but the arguing and fighting paused long enough for him to take heart) and he came off the stage after a full forty-five minutes. This set the scene for the other acts who decided that, if he was to be allowed extra time to perform, then so would they, with the result that, when 11.00pm finally arrived – the time in which the show was *definitely* going to end, only three acts had performed, with another thirteen still waiting. The final straw came when the concert secretary announced a thirty minute interval when 'Bingo' would be played. I had had enough! I fought my way to the exit and made for my car, only to find that I was now blocked in by around two hundred other vehicles and couldn't get out. I was distraught and about to end it all when, at long last, my luck turned. A club member, seeing my problem, came to the rescue and thanks to his prowess with a handy JCB and the key to a hidden gate which only he knew about, I was soon on my way home, vowing never to fall for the five card trick again. But like a fool I did! Of course, some were better than this but many were even worse and it gives a pretty accurate description of the pitfalls we had to endure. Shows almost never started on time, acts always overran, bookers, for whom the show was presented, were actually ignored and the shows always ran into the early hours of the following morning. Today, thank goodness, things are so much different and for the better. Bookers stopped going to the bad showcases and agents quickly stopped presenting them. That left the cream of the agents to arrange their own tradeshows in a professional manner and, although it was hard work assessing all the performers on show, it became at least a pleasure to be there. Agents like Wally Dent, Tony West (he learned his lesson),

Paul Bridson, Michael Breese-Davies (Cambrian) and Trevor George do it superbly but, arguably, the ultimate in artistes presentation is organised aptly by *The Stage* newspaper, under their *Showcall* banner.

Showcall is a publication of over a thousand pages in which performers of all the Arts take out advertising with photographs, biographies etc and, to me, and most others who book, it has become a bible. How often have I opened its pages, bereft of ideas on an act or band for a special event and found the answer in minutes. The idea was born in 1982 and was first presented in Blackpool at the Imperial Hotel. In 1984 it was decided to split the country into a North and South divide and a similar presentation was staged in Brighton. Before long they had moved the venue to Leicester, before finally finding the perfect centre at the Civic Hall, Stratford-on-Avon. The show runs for a full five days – afternoon and evening – and in total, if one was brave enough to sit through the marathon, almost two hundred acts will have been on show. Each act has a limited time – strictly adhered to – and is superbly supported by the very best technology – stage lighting, sound, musical backing and it would be remiss not to mention the doyen of comperes – surely the very best in the business – Tufty Gordon. Not only is he the chieftain of chat but also a highly accomplished musician, specialising in tenor sax and clarinet. So good is he musically that, often, I would hope for a technical hitch back stage, thus allowing Tufty to perform a solo spot as a filler. No filler to myself and many others, Tufty – it was one of the highlights of the day! It was no surprise either, to hear him deftly mingle with the backing band and add his skill to an artiste's musical arrangement. Yes – the *Showcall* showcase has become *the* big event of the year and the venue is packed to the rafters with the major bookers from home and abroad. It is my proud boast that I attended the very first one in Blackpool all those years ago and have not missed a single year to this day and that, if nothing else, takes stamina.

The one type of act I found difficult to find, particularly in the UK, was the speciality act. These performers were to be found opening a variety bill and consisted of jugglers, unicyclists, fire-eaters, plate spinners etc and although they existed, most had quit the business after the demise of the Music Hall. One further problem for those still working (and of the standard I required), was their inability to fill the time slot. I used this type of act in the early part of the evening in order that the kids, as well as the Mums and Dads, could enjoy their talents, but looked for them to fulfil a twenty-five minute show. Many, however, could do no more than eight to ten minutes, the time previously allotted during the variety years and I was unable to use them.

When agent Billy Forrest rang me one day and suggested we fly to Hamburg to visit the famous Hansa Theatre, I was interested. The Hansa Theatre specialises only in this type of act and books them from all over the world. They are contracted for one month and for us, the clever thing to do was to stay over two evenings, catching the last night of the concluding show on the first and the opening night of the new show on the second. Billy ('Cocker') Forrest was a character in every sense of the word – almost every layman's perception of what an agent should look and sound like. He wore a brown suit and a camel hair coat with a brown checked tie held in place by an ostentatious tie clip, designed to represent a spinning world globe – his company logo. He travelled everywhere in a large Mercedes-Benz car driven by his own chauffeur. I had known Billy for nearly twenty years and I never saw him wear anything other than his brown suit, camel coat and checked tie – it became is trademark, as did his nasal 'Brummie' accent and his terrible memory. He had an assistant called Jim, who thankfully was able to remember all that Bill forgot and many times Bill would telephone me and rave for twenty minutes about a new band he had discovered. He'd tell me how brilliant they were, how they were storming the audiences everywhere they played and how his phone never stopped ringing from clubs, theatres and TV magnates wanting to book them and, when I asked him what they were called, his hand would cover the mouthpiece and I could clearly hear him call out the side of his mouth, "What are they called – Jim?"

Only Billy could get away with it!

Sadly, Billy is no longer with us and with his passing went one of the last few characters left in our business. I am certain, however, that when he arrived at the Pearly Gates and St Peter said, "Come on in Billy – we've been expecting you. Step inside and we'll fit you with your wings and heavenly robes."

"Not a chance, cocker," Billy would indignantly reply. "I'll just keep wearing me brown suit, camel coat and checked tie – oh and by the way – who books the acts up here?"

Typical Billy Forrest, never one to miss an opportunity!

Anyway, here was Billy inviting me to Hamburg and I accepted. We flew during the afternoon and that evening saw us in the quaintly charming Hansa Theatre, enjoying twenty of the worlds most famous speciality acts. The show came down at 10.00pm and we decided, as most male visitors with an ample supply of natural hormones do, to visit the viewing gallery of the Reeperbahn – or at least I did! Billy wanted to retire to bed with a cup of cocoa and a copy of *The Stage*, but was finally persuaded.

Nevertheless, he continued to protest as we neared the red light district. "What if Maureen was to find out!" he moaned, referring to his wife of many years. "She'll bloody kill me!"

I am sure that no such thoughts would have entered her head but Billy was racked with conscience. We entered the street reputed to be the Harrods of naked exposure and gazed at each open window revealing young ladies of indiscriminate age, smiling and waving coyly at us, inviting us into their web of erotica. The perspiration flowed down Billy's face but his protestations had diminished somewhat, now reduced to a mumble and his eyes appeared brighter than usual.

We reached the end of the sexual shopping arcade and Billy was gasping. "Let's have a coffee!" he croaked and we went into a friendly little German café to refresh ourselves.

A near naked young lady was writhing around a metal pole as we sat down and we ordered the drinks. Within seconds, two young ladies appeared out of the darkness and sat down beside us, much to Billy's indignation and embarrassment.

"Go away," he said in fluent Brummy. "My colleague and I are here to talk business. I'm Billy Forrest." He produced his business card and thrust it into their hand. "I'm Billy Forrest – the agent!"

What reaction he expected, I do not know but the girls had never been trained for this eventuality and retreated – to be replaced by the German equivalent of the Kray twins.

"We haf a problem?" they enquired and I didn't know about them but I was beginning to think that *I* had.

Billy, once again produced his business card. "I'm Billy Forrest – this is my friend and we want to have coffee and talk business!"

"You not like our ladies?" Adolf asked and Billy repeated his statement, emphasising his name once again. "You talk business outside," shouted Fritz and with an encouraging hand on our elbows, they propelled us to the doorway and we were out on the street.

I walked quickly in an attempt to put as much space between myself and the 'heavies' but Billy stopped me short. "Jim," he wailed. "I've left me gloves on the seat – I'll have to go back and get 'em."

"Don't be a burke." I yelled. "I'll buy you another pair. If you go back they'll kill you!"

"Bugger them," said Billy. "They were a present from Maureen. If I don't go home with them in one piece – *she'll* kill me!"

He went back – brave, brave Billy – and I watched from a distance of a hundred yards as he stood explaining to the doorman, who couldn't understand English let alone Brummy, all about his gloves and Maureen and the fate that awaited him. I saw his business card change hands yet again, and suddenly he was in. A lifetime went by and I anticipated the joy erupting from the news of his disappearance from all the artistes who owed him commission when, suddenly, he reappeared supported on either side by two heavy-weights. Billy's feet were a yard off the pavement and he was cycling his imaginary bike when he was dropped onto the concrete pathway like a bag of cement. I cringed and imagined the worst but suddenly he moved, sat up and a slow smile crossed his face. He looked at me for a moment before raising a hand to reveal his precious gloves, untarnished and in one piece. He had gone into the valley of fear and lived but his marriage had been saved and all was well. I'm just surprised that Billy didn't secure the contract to provide the club with acts for the next twelve months. He must be slipping up!

Enough of tradeshows and showcases just for the moment but I will return to the subject one more time to describe a showcase that was to change my life for ever, but that was still many years away and to learn just what happened, I must ask you to be patient for just a little bit longer.

CHAPTER SEVENTEEN

The Golden Handshake

If things were going extremely well for entertainments, it was not so harmonious in the Boardroom. Trevor Hemmings did not see eye to eye with his colleagues from Bass Plc and it came as no surprise to learn he had resigned. It was a blow to everyone who knew and had worked with Trevor, for in addition to his superb man-management skills, he knew and understood the peculiarities of the holiday camp business while those who succeeded him, frankly did not. There is no doubt that they were great businessmen, wonderful financiers and brilliant retailers but the expertise required in administrating in excess of twenty Holiday Centres was something they lacked. It became a period of unease and unsettlement for the permanent staff at Bournemouth and the uncertainty of the situation hung over our heads like a cloud. When Trevor offered Jan the position within Entertainments, one of the stumbling blocks was her involvement with three acts that she had signed for personal management and she felt strongly about breaking her part of the bargain. She informed Trevor of her commitment and he agreed that she be allowed to continue to manage their careers with two provisos. One was that she would not add to her stable whilst in the employment of Pontins and the second was that if, or when, any of the three decided to leave her agency, they would not be replaced. The acts she looked after were Ray Cornel, a dancer, vocalist and choreographer, Aloma and Jones, a boy/girl duo who sang, played keyboard and harp and, of course, Jacqui Scott. All three were of the highest quality and worked a great deal on television but the time came when they felt that changes were necessary. Ray, very aware that time was not on his side, gradually moved away from the rigours of performing and began choreographing and show directing, before finally opening up his own agency which proved highly successful, particularly in providing dance troupes for the number one theatres and cruise line companies. Aloma and Jones worked in most of the top summer shows and on television and, indeed, Aloma became a major solo star on Welsh television because of her beautiful voice, harp playing and, especially, her fluent grasp of the language. In time, their stage partnership became a personal involvement and wedding bells rang only to be followed, a year later, by the birth of their first child – a daughter. This obviously curtailed their work and availability and they finally decided to open, and manage, a hotel in the Blackpool area, with great success. And so, like Agatha Christie's, *Ten Little Male Youths of Coloured Persuasion*, the acts dropped out, one by one, leaving only Jacqui Scott!

Since signing with Jan, Jacqui had gone from strength to strength. Almost immediately, she rose to national prominence by way of the BBC TV talent show *Rising Stars*, being voted by the judges as outright winner over the six-week series. In addition to being presented with a beautifully engraved crystal bowl, she was invited to appear in the Canon and Ball summer season show at the North Pier, Blackpool and was obviously delighted to accept. Success followed success and at the conclusion of the twenty-two week season in her home town, she was signed by BBC TV to appear as the star name in a late night show called *Contrasts*. In 1983, Jan secured yet another top summer show for her, namely, *The Keith Harris Show* at the ABC Theatre in Great Yarmouth. After agreement with Trevor Hemmings, Jan travelled to the East Coast resort for the opening night. As expected, the show got a great reception from a packed house and everyone was in high spirits at the opening night party. Jan had decided to mix and mingle for an hour, before diplomatically taking her leave and driving back south. Keith Harris was, at that time, signed to London Management, the Company headed by the brilliant, highly respected and greatly loved agent, Billy Marsh and the great man was there in person to give support to his Artiste, in addition to the other members of the cast. He had anticipated travelling back to London the same evening but was disappointed to find that the next train back to the Capital was the following morning and had resigned himself to an overnight stay at a local hotel – something he hated. When Jan heard of his dilemma, it seemed only natural to offer him a lift back to London, which Billy accepted gratefully. The journey to their respective homes changed the lives of both Jan an I – particularly Jan, for during the three hours they shared each others company, they talked incessantly about showbusiness, their artistes, their hopes and plans for the future and by the time they arrived at Billy's London flat, near Regents Park, there was no doubt that he was captivated by Jan – her ambitions, her dedication and her style. Sensibly, he didn't jump in straight away and offer Jan the world but said enough to tantalise her into thinking of her future away from the Pontin environment and invited her to meet him at a later date in his office in Regent Street, London.

It was only natural that Jan was flattered and excited by the course of their conversation and its outcome, but she was also deeply concerned at the implications it would have on our relationship and me. We discussed every aspect of what may or may not happen, well into the night and we finally came to the conclusion that she should meet Billy, once again, to confirm the details of what he had in mind. On the assumption that the offer was genuine and suitable to her, we would further discuss what was to be decided, but the feeling was, from both of us, that such a move could only be beneficial for Jan. The prospect of being taken under the wing and personally trained by one of the greatest agents in the business, past or present, was an opportunity that no one in their right mind could afford to refuse and for me – well, we both felt that a professional separation might not be such a bad idea with personal prospects in mind, for at the moment, we were twinned as Jim and Jan. If promotion was to follow, I had to be recognised on my own and I saw sense in the argument, for I now had the ambition to be invited onto the main Board of Directors. With the decision virtually made, Jan visited Billy, as suggested and the meeting concluded with her being offered a job, working with Billy at London Management – and so began an association and deep friendship with this lovely, delightful man that was to last until his sad death, some twelve years later.

Jan moved to a flat near her new office in London, but each weekend, travelled back to Bournemouth to share the weekend with me. To many, it could have sounded a death knell to our association, but do remember that I was away from home myself for most of the week, travelling to the centres, tradeshows, business meetings and meeting agents – so it worked. The uncertainty of the Company administration, however, niggled at the back of my mind, not helped in any way by my current salary which began, increasingly, to upset me. In the years up to then, the pleasure of doing a job that I loved rather obscured the weight of the weekly pay cheque and it never even began to present an issue. The physical act of Jan leaving the employment of the Company, however, coupled with the shock of realising that her new salary with London Management totally outstripped my annual remuneration of £12,000 per year, was a blow to the stomach, not to mention my pride and I began to re-assess my whole financial package. I was now totally responsible for the entire UK entertainment structure – the acts, bands, discos, sound equipment, lighting rigs, staging as well as recruitment and departmental policies. I controlled a budget of nearly five million pounds per annum and answered to the Managing and Operations Directors and, for the first time (maybe stupidly), I began to look at my earnings and conclude that I was simply not being paid enough! It was then that the first glimmer of a change of direction entered my head and I began to consider the possibility of opening my own agency/ management company and as that thought grew in strength – fate, for once, dealt me the most beautiful hand!

The more I thought of the idea, the better I liked it. With Jan now working in London, there now seemed no reason for me to stay with Pontins, particularly in view of the uncertainty and especially, the inadequate salary (in my opinion, at any rate). I had established good contacts in every sector of our business and I felt that, if ever I was going to make the break, now was the time. Naturally, I took Jan into my confidence, along with one or two close friends and from each direction, I received nothing but encouragement. The one question I was constantly asked by all was "Why haven't you done this before?" There was an easy answer, being simply that I didn't feel ready, lacked courage and was low in confidence – but now it was different. The confidence was in place and the courage was born out of irritation – even anger – at the way my dedication, loyalty and expertise were being abused. If I couldn't make £12,000 profit a year from commission, bearing in mind the knowledge I had of acts, bookers and potential outlets, then I didn't deserve to be in the business – far less running it! I confided, too, in my secretary Flora, an older lady, who simply loved being a part of the showbusiness scene and was immensely flattered when she asked if she could join my new Company in a similar capacity.

Her name wasn't Flora by the way – it was Marjorie and on the first day we met, she said, "Call me what you will, but not Marge – I can't stand the name!" Immediately I christened her Flora and she was tickled pink – but I am still, to this day, the only one to call her that and live! So the plan was drawn up and I worked out carefully in my mind the day I was going to reveal all to my employers. The easiest time for me to leave the Company and cause the least disruption, would be at the beginning of December (1985) and working back the six months notice I would be required to give, decided I would drop the bombshell on the 1st June. I admit to being just a little nervous as the day approached, not really knowing the reaction that I would receive. Would they, I wondered, throw their hands up in horror and offer me a huge salary increase to stay? Unlikely! Would they rant and rave and accuse me of disloyalty and leaving a ship that was certainly foundering? Possibly! Or would they pat me on the head, wish me well and escort me to the door with their best wishes ringing in my ears? Probably!

In fact, I was never to find out, for incredibly on the 30th May, two days before my announcement, a memo arrived on my desk (and the desks of everyone else who worked in the Bournemouth Head Office), requesting us to attend a meeting in the Boardroom the following day, for a major declaration by the Managing Director. We filed in at the appointed hour, fearful of what we were about to be told and the fears of most were realised. The offices at Bournemouth were to close with 90% redundancy and those remaining would have to relocate to the Bass Head Office in Banbury. The redundancy terms were, in fairness, well above the minimum rate – one would say even generous – but was little consolation to those losing their livelihood and a pall of gloom hung like a cloud as we filtered back to our desks.

The Operations Director, Mike Rumke, quickly grabbed my arm as I passed and whispered in my ear. "You've no need to worry Jim – it doesn't apply to you. Your job is safe!"

That evening, I turned the day's events over and over in my mind and came to a devious (to my mind), decision. A wonderful opportunity had landed in my lap which would enable me to finance the opening of my new Company – an opportunity which I grasped with one hand, whilst taking the extended hand of fate in the other and shaking it warmly. The following morning, I sought out Mike Rumke and informed him that, because of Jan, the house in Bournemouth and a hundred other reasons, I had decided not to make the move to Banbury. I was prepared, instead, to accept redundancy. My face was sorrowful but my heart was leaping with joy and it was agreed I would leave the company on 30th November 1985, having completed the summer wind down and setting up the Christmas and New Year programmes to come.

The six-month period went quickly and I was naturally intrigued as to who my successor would be. Speculation was rife but it came as quite a surprise when a young Jamaican singer called Winston Cockburn, whom we had used many times on the cabaret circuit, was given the job. He was a delightful man, warm, gentle and sensitive but I wondered how he would cope with the tough, uncompromising agents he would have to deal with – to say nothing of the artistes and musicians who would hone in on him, sensing a target of inexperience and ready to exploit this apparent weakness. I gave him what help I could in the comparatively short time we had together and promised him the benefit of my experience in the months following my departure – he only had to ring. In gratitude for this 'insurance cover', he told me gratefully, he would ensure that a percentage of the artistes and bands he booked would be through my new agency – Kennedy Leisure and Management. That seemed a fair response and I felt a good start had been made. Sadly, from the moment I left the Company to this day, I never heard from Winston again. I cannot begin to wonder why but, as it turned out, it proved to be his undoing for he was only to last for twenty-four months in the job – such a shame for, although his heart was in the right place, his head had difficulty in getting around the administrative and technical side of the job – it was simply too much for him! The implication of that, however, was to come later but in the meantime, I rejoiced when my redundancy payment finally arrived and I stared happily at a cheque for just under £20,000. If I had handed in my notice two days earlier than planned, or if the mass meeting had been called twenty-four hours later, I would have walked out of the job with nothing more than a P45 and a handshake from the top. Wherever you are Mr Fate and wherever you work from – I thank you with all my heart. I owe you one!

CHAPTER EIGHTEEN

Kennedy Leisure and Management

Flora and I found a suitable office in the Winton area of Bournemouth and spent the preceding days cleaning, polishing and painting everything that stood still. On the 2nd December 1985, I opened the doors of my office and sat back waiting for the phone to ring or the fax machine to start – or better still, both – but for that first morning, Flora and I sat looking at each other in silence. The world outside the window continued to exist – lorries and vans ploughed up and down the Charminster Road, trading continued in the shops and people went about their business as they always had done, but no one thought of ringing Kennedy Leisure. My world had turned upside down and by lunchtime, a tiny spark of panic, flamed by fear, began to glow ominously in my mind. A few short days ago in my ivory tower at Pontins, I had screamed my frustration at the four telephones on my desk, each ringing incessantly, each demanding immediate attention and all heaping more and more work on my already overloaded desk. Now, my one phone lay dormant, idly passing the hours in total silence, daring me to pick up the receiver just one more time to assure myself it was still connected. It gave me time to think and reflect at the giant step I had undertaken. No more the clattering of the letterbox flap as my monthly paycheque dropped onto the welcome mat. No more lying on a beach somewhere on a sunny Mediterranean Isle, basking in the baking sun, enjoying an annual vacation, safe in the knowledge that my salary was still being paid. No more taking two days off to nurture a slight cough or a runny nose, safe in the knowledge that my Bank Manager's smile would remain unabated and perhaps, worst of all, no more driving the luxury car, given to me by my loving superiors, into the local petrol station and filling the tank with the local brew and knowing that without fail, some faceless wonder in Accounts would settle the bill!

My lunchtime snack filled me with tea, an egg sandwich and a generous helping of depression. Even Flora's wild sense of humour and optimism had deserted her for the moment and we looked forward to the afternoon with foreboding. At ten minutes past two the phone rang. At first we thought it was a figment of imagination and stoically carried on endeavouring to solve the cryptic crossword in the local rag, but realisation suddenly hit that someone knew where we were and that we existed.

Flora ripped the phone from its cradle and uttered the magic words I had dreamed of for the past six months. "Good afternoon," she said in a voice borrowed from the BBC. "Kennedy Leisure, can I help you?"

I studied her face, trying to decipher the nature of the call. Bernard Delfont, perhaps, needs an act urgently for this weeks London Palladium show? Better still – the BBC? Terry Wogan's gone sick and someone is needed today – this afternoon – to front his show?

Flora replaced the phone on its spot, looked up and said "Wrong number."

I slumped into my expensive leather bound executive chair like a deflating balloon. The little man residing in my conscience tapped on my brain for attention. He of the red forked tail and the evil horns wished to speak and because no one else apparently wanted to, I figured I might as well listen. "Go on, my son," he urged. "Eat humble pie. Ring them up at Bass and say it was all a mistake. Ask for your old job back. You'll get it, you know. They love you. Tell them it was all a joke and they'll give you a huge increase in salary. Go on, my son – ring them!"

Temptation unfurled before my eyes like an ensign raised before battle and I felt my resolve weaken. "He's right," I thought. "I don't need this at my time of life. Where are all the great supporters of my cause? The hundred and one agents who promised – oh so faithfully – to repay me for past favours. The bookers, who were my colleagues, with assurances of aid in the shape of shared requirements, the artistes themselves who vowed to pass their careers into my eager hands. Where are they all?"

Convinced and totally mesmerised by the promptings of my inner malefactor, I reached for the phone to enact his bidding but my hand never made its goal. As if by magic, it rang out and Flora grabbed it. "It's for you," she said. "It's someone from Butlins."

The someone turned out to be a gentleman by the name of Keith Palmer, then the Entertainment Executive, based at Bognor Regis. "Is it true?" he enquired. "Have you really left Pontins?"

I confirmed that was indeed the case and he followed up with the invitation. "Why don't you come over to Bognor for a chat, Jim. I may have something of interest to you."

I put the phone down and looked around. The sun suddenly shone, the flowers bloomed and everyone I saw, smiled. Life was wonderful again!

Keith Palmer spelt it out and what he had to offer was right up my street. The job suggested was for me to act as Entertainment Consultant to Butlins, requiring me to visit all their centres and hotels during the summer season and compile reports, pin pointing what was wrong, what could be improved and what was good. The hours involved still left me free to build up my own business and with Flora's invaluable assistance, keep my hands on the every day running of the Company. The fee that was offered to me was one I did not expect and fully justified my dissatisfaction at the Pontin salary and my ultimate decision to move on.

"Would you accept twelve thousand pounds per annum?" Keith asked and assumed my gasp as affirmation of my acceptance.

The wheel had turned its full circle and I was back at Butlins! From that moment on, the phone, as if ashamed at its previous idleness, began to work at earning its keep and its happy ringing on a more daily basis, proved part of the turning curve.

Of all the assurances we were given by the agent fraternity, only three kept their promises. Chris Ferguson, who operated from the Bournemouth area and, seemingly unafraid of local opposition, decided that if you can't beat them, join them and he and I collaborated in making many good deals together, for which I was fully grateful. Colin Deaton, the boss man of International World of Sport, was another whose loyalty to me was most welcome. Colin was a bluff, hearty Northerner who, in addition to his sports business, successfully ran a scrap metal yard, near Chesterfield and the combination of the two had made him a millionaire. His wife Sandra had worked for me many years before as a Bluecoat (they turn up everywhere!) and had met Colin when he toured the centres giving table tennis exhibitions with the, then, current England Number One Dennis Neil. Since then, in addition to piling up the pounds, he unfortunately began to pile *on* the pounds but underneath the somewhat rough exterior and the barrel chest, beats a heart of burnished gold. If work was going, then Colin shared it with me and I will never forget, when my funds were in danger of being swallowed up by the ever increasing cost of furnishing a new enterprise, a cheque from him, amounting to five figures, arriving for no reason other than a thank you for helping him start *his* business and the hope that what was enclosed would help start mine. That is friendship and I am glad of the opportunity to say a public thank you.

CHAPTER NINETEEN

Billy Marsh – the Supreme Doyen

Then there was Billy Marsh...! By now, despite him being Jan's mentor and Boss, the three of us had become very close friends. At the age of sixty-nine, Billy, perhaps, saw in us the family he never had and we, in turn, loved him like a second father. He came with us when we took a break and travelled abroad and his wickedly endearing sense of humour kept us laughing each and every day. To say he was revered in the business was an understatement – he was more a legend. The stars he discovered and the big names he imported into this country, particularly from America, was something that will never be surpassed. Why he never received an honour from the Queen, remains one of the great mysteries of our time and one which will probably never be answered, for was there ever any person in the cut throat business of Agency and Star management more loved, more honest, conscientious, dedicated and generous than Billy Marsh? Sir Billy Marsh should have been the least of his rewards and doesn't it sound so right! If he failed to be honoured publicly, there are two accolades that exist – one in his lifetime and one after his death in 1995. The first was a special *This is Your Life* programme which saw Thames Television break a golden rule that an agent would never be the subject. The feeling was that such national publicity would serve to promote and commercialise the individual as well as, perhaps, and most likely, greatly upset the star names (many of whom worked for ITV), who were not fortunate enough to be on the books of the 'victim'. It was a question of quiet diplomacy but when, at Jan's continual insistence, Billy's name was considered – it proved no contest. The show was recorded and I was in the audience that night, so proud and sharing Billy's obvious but humble pleasure in the moment. The video I retain today is one of my most treasured possessions.

When Billy died in 1995, another great honour was bestowed in the shape of a plaque, placed, with his ashes, beneath the stage of the London Palladium. If you are ever fortunate enough to be backstage at the world famous Theatre, you will find that the only way to transverse the stage from one side to the other, without actually treading the hallowed boards, is by a passageway underneath and there, on the left side, is the plaque bearing Billy's name – 'the Doyen of all Agents'. When one considers the many hundreds of wonderful performers and star names who have graced the portals of this 'Theatre of Dreams', surely the greatest honour the showplace can pay to any one person – especially an agent and manager – is to rest his ashes and his earthly spirit within their surrounds. He is the only one ever to be given this honour and it is such a joy, in view of the multitude of household names he presented on the stage above his remains, including over thirty years of being totally involved with the *Royal Variety Show*, to think that from now on, every wonderful production seen at the theatre will be heard and judged by the spirit of Billy. And should you spot a faint whiff of cigarette smoke, wistfully wending its way through the shaft of spotlights, ring not for the Fire Brigade for it will, in all probability, be Billy giving the cast his legendary seal of approval – and one which I am sure they will cherish. One day, I am sure, a book will be written on the life of this widely acknowledged personage and should this be the case, I will be the first to purchase. I urge you to be the second!

Without stealing its glory, let me underline only a fraction of the names he found and propelled to stardom. Norman

Wisdom, then an unknown, whose appearance on the *This is Your Life* show saw him flop to the ground, face down, to kiss Billy's feet. Frankie Vaughan, who Billy first saw in Leeds, was brought to London, given a change of name (Frank Ableson didn't sound right) and, on the day when Judy Garland was taken ill and could not appear on *Sunday Night at the Palladium*, was given the vacant spot on the bill. The unknown singer, with the film star looks and the wonderfully warm and sexy voice, became a star overnight and stayed a star for the rest of his life. Bruce Forsyth, an unknown comic in a small summer revue in Babbacombe, Devon was seen by Billy, signed immediately and within a year took over the compering duties on *Sunday Night at the Palladium* and he, too, never looked back. Harry Worth, the bumbling character who started his career as a mediocre ventriloquist but, with Billy's help and guidance, converted into one of the best loved stage and television comedians of his day. Arguably the greatest of them all, however, was Eric Morecambe and Ernie Wise. They were not 'discovered' by Billy but he was there when they decided that a change of agent was necessary. They had climbed the ladder of success with some speed but, on reaching the upper rungs, had faltered. Their career was going nowhere, particularly after a disastrous series for ATV and it looked inevitable that the slide into obscurity was about to begin. It took them all of five minutes to decide that Billy Marsh was the man to arrest the decline in their fortunes and they shook hands on the deal. Significantly, no contract between the two parties was ever signed and, such was the honesty, sincerity and loyalty the three shared with each other, one handshake was enough. The bond was never broken by either and with the supreme skill that made Billy such a 'tour de force', he piloted Eric and Ernie into the recognition of being probably the funniest, and best loved, comedians this county has ever produced.

One of the showbusiness greats. The much respected and greatly loved – Billy Marsh.

It is fitting to record that Billy's unerring eye for talent did not cease within that circle of potential showbusiness greats for, in Jan, he ensured that his Company – now named Billy Marsh Associates – would continue after his death. In 1995, she took over the reins of the Organisation and such was the grooming she received from the Master, the stable of artistes she inherited is still with the Company today. Jan has added many more household names to her ever growing list of clients and the great reputation she is forging in the business of providing entertainment, is one that Billy would undoubtedly be more than just a little proud. Of all the star names he discovered and managed she is, arguably, his best ever signing – and no one, in their right mind, would disagree.

CHAPTER TWENTY

The Sandcastle

Kennedy Leisure, as it was now known (the 'and Management' had somehow been dropped), continued to prosper and, although the abbreviation of the name was easier to say, especially when answering the phone, I refused to make the shortened version official because someone, who had flown on the Dutch airline KLM, had sent me a tie with the three initials combining to make a subtle design and each time I wore it, I convinced people it was my new company logo. Such was its success, I requested my friend to collect beer mats, ashtrays and anything else with the letters KLM on to spread around the office. It pays to advertise!

Perhaps one of the biggest contracts to come my way was, again, wrapped up and presented to me by Billy Marsh, early in 1986. A massive leisure centre to be called The Sandcastle was being planned to sit opposite the Pleasure Beach in Blackpool and, typical of all things in the resort, was to be bigger and better than anything yet seen. Its centrepiece was a magnificent heated swimming pool with sliding chutes of all shapes and sizes plus a wave machine that operated every thirty minutes to the great joy of those in the water. In addition a Night Club/Theatre was being built and the Company involved with the construction – Leisure Services Ltd, based in St Annes – were tasked with, not just the assembling of the centre, but the operating too, including the entertainment. This was an area in which their Managing Director, Steve Paxton had little knowledge and when feelers were put out to find the best agent in the county, all the answers pointed to Billy Marsh. As it happened, he discovered he already knew Billy from a previous meeting and when the two met to discuss the project, they greeted each other like old friends. Steve outlined what he had in mind but Billy held his hand up in admission that this was not his field but quickly followed his decliner with the words that would reach national fame in future years, through a TV advertisement.

"I can't – but I know a man who can!"

Within minutes I was being summoned by phone to meet with Steve Paxton and within twenty-four hours, I was on my way to St Annes and a visit to The Sandcastle. With Billy's recommendation and the many years of experience I had endured doing exactly this type of presentation, I felt I had a very good chance and so it proved. I signed a three-year contract to control the full package of entertainment including, not just the provision of musicians and artistes, but to produce a programme of events running twelve hours a day, seven days a week.

The General Manager of the Centre was a flamboyant character by the name of Michael Prendergast, who wore a bow tie like a badge of authority and drove, periodically, an enormous American Lincoln car that was undoubtedly only built for the wide open spaces of Arizona and not for the narrow streets of Blackpool. Nevertheless, despite his extrovert exterior, he and I saw eye to eye on the functioning of the entertainment and we decided, until the Centre discovered its own personality and we, in turn, discovered the leisure tastes of those who would frequent the room, to present for the first summer, at any rate, a different style of evening entertainment each day. We would carefully monitor the popularity of each event with a view to the future and I set about planning a Country'n'Western Night, a Big Band Bash, Celebrity Night, Game Show Extravaganza, Caribbean Evening, Ballroom Dancing and a Quiz Show and Talent Night with cash prizes. The budget was my main concern especially as I had persuaded Michael and particularly Stephen, that not only would the retractable roof have to remain closed during the evening performances (they were totally convinced that the sunshine pouring through the open roof each evening would save them the cost of a 'follow-spot'), but the glass would have to be blacked out. The cost of that and the resultant spotlight was deducted from my overall budget and made life just that little bit more difficult. So much so, in fact, that I took an unforgivable risk in booking one of my two big bands that were to alternate throughout the summer. One was to be the Terry Reaney Big Band – sixteen local musicians led by TR himself, one of Britain's top trumpet players and soon to join the wonderful Syd Lawrence Orchestra. The other was a problem, due to the limitation on the budget still available and each time I felt I had found the right outfit, cash (or the lack of it), reared its ugly head. I was becoming just a bit desperate, when an audio tape dropped on my desk sent by a man by the name of Ian Darrington, representing a big band called The Wigan Youth Jazz Orchestra.

Time, by now, was of the essence and when I played the tape, I was more than impressed. How easy and how sensible it would have been to have booked the band for just the one evening with a view to offering the rest of the season, if successful – but my brain was suffering from a storm not forecast by the met office and on the strength of the one tape, I actually booked them for the entire summer. What a way for me to hand in my notice, I thought, cursing my stupidity and this was compounded on the first evening they were due to appear, when I met their hired coach as it pulled up by the stage entrance. The door of the vehicle slowly opened to reveal what I can only describe as a bunch of school kids on a day trip to the seaside.

"I should have twigged it," I groaned. "Of course – a *youth* orchestra! How could I have been so crazy?"

I knew that Stephen and Michael, plus a few hundred more Blackpool holidaymakers, were booked in to see the

CHAPTER TWENTY ONE

Las Vegas, Tom Jones and Bill Cosby!

Meanwhile, back in Bournemouth, the bills were being paid and the Bank Manager stopped slamming the door in my face when I entered his building and began acknowledging my presence by waving airily in my direction and muttering, "Morning Mr...eh...Mr...uhm...eh – how's the shop doing?"

It wasn't quite accurate or, indeed, what I hoped for but it was, at least an improvement. At the end of 1986, I decided to venture into the promotion business and after protracted negotiation with the Bournemouth International Centre, I booked the hall for one evening during the Christmas season and presented The Squadronnaires Orchestra with special guest star, Anne Shelton. Like The Sandcastle, it didn't go good yet it didn't go bad and I was able to pay the musicians and the guest star with a couple of bob to spare. What was the biggest buzz for me to date, however was seeing the giant posters that blitzed the town with photographs hugely enlarged of the two stars, headed by the caption 'Kennedy Leisure and Management presents...!" Fame at last! In retrospect, however, I wish now that my first venture into promotions had been a sad and dismal failure for, with fingers burned and smarting with pain, I might well have thought twice before attempting a second bite at the cherry – one which cost me an enormous amount of money, a great amount of sleep and could have resulted in losing everything I had worked for. That frightening chapter of my life was still eighteen months away, however, and I will tell you what happened in due course.

Once again Billy proved my benefactor as the summer season of 1987 approached. He rang me up one day and simply asked, "Which Harris do you want – Rolf or Keith?"

I did not have a clue what he was going on about but, suspecting some sort of joke, I replied, "Neither – I'll have both!"

Billy's distinctive laugh came over the phone. "Okay," he said. "You can have them. I've just negotiated an excellent deal with Butlins for Rolf Harris to appear at Bognor during the summer and Keith Harris and Orville to appear at Minehead for the same period. Frankly – I'm too busy to do the paperwork and the setting up, so you can have the bookings – if you want them."

Want them? Billy had done all the hard work for nothing and was now handing me the deal, which meant I could take the commission from each artiste, amounting to something in the region of £20,000 over the next six months. I could not, and still cannot, believe the kindness and generosity of this man. Another phone call from Billy that same week, with a different invitation brought another excited response from me. Billy had, for many, many years, been a great friend of a man called Charles Mather. Charles had emigrated to the USA and opened a highly successful theatrical agency in Las Vegas, Nevada and, in doing so, had accumulated a personal fortune. Running in Los Angeles, at that time, was a show called *The Magic Castle* and the Americans had taken the concept to their hearts. It featured many of the USA's top illusionists and magicians and it was presented with a medieval theme. Such was its amazing popularity that Charles decided to introduce a similar show into London, using British performers. It was to carry the same show title and, topping the bill, was the Scottish born, international illusionist – Johnny Hart. It was beautifully recreated and no expense had been spared with the costumes and stage sets but, for reasons that no one could fathom, it failed to take off. Charles poured good money after bad into the production but still the public stayed away and finally, he had to admit defeat and the show closed. He returned to the USA beaten into submission, but it was not all bad news for, during the run of the show, he met and fell in love with a lovely English 'rose' and the invitation Billy extended to me was to attend the wedding – all expenses paid by Charles and his bride to be, along with Billy, of course, and Jan. Billy, still the businessman, was doubly excited for, with another Royal Variety show on the horizon, he saw the opportunity to visit Tom Jones, who was appearing on a long contract at the MGM Grand in Las Vegas and offer him an appearance at the Royal event. Jan, being Jan, decided too, that if we were to represent England at an American wedding, we should arrive in style, so Billy and I were duly measured for grey morning suits, complete with coat tails, waistcoat and top hat. The wedding was arranged for the Saturday evening and we were to fly home the following Wednesday lunchtime, leaving us three open evenings to visit the Tom Jones show. We did not allow for Charles Mather's organisational skills and when we finally caught our breath after the excitement of the journey and the wedding itself (the top hats etc proved a masterstroke and we were photographed more than the bride and groom!), Charles gave us an itinerary of functions we were to attend – all highly important and mostly arranged with our visit in mind. There was no way we would offend our host and Billy resigned himself to missing the chance to negotiate with Tom Jones. His brain, however, refused to malfunction and it sent out a wave of sheer brilliance. "Jim?" Billy asked. "If I paid your hotel bill for another three days and we can change your flight, would you have a word with Tom? When you've seen him, ring me in London. I have to get back but you could stay...couldn't you?"

It was a difficult decision to make and I hesitated for a full second and a half. "Well," I replied. "It will be such a hardship but I'll make the effort."

Billy was delighted and I was ecstatic.

Charles made contact with the MGM Grand and on the Thursday evening, saluted and pampered by the Maitre D' and everyone else in sight, I took my seat in Tom's private box and watched the great man perform brilliantly, much to my patriotic pride, the great delight of the American audience and the shareholders and management of Victoria's Secret, the fashionable and very chic emporium whose line in frilly knickers were widely thrown with gay abandon, especially by the women in the audience. The invitation to visit the inner sanctum at the conclusion of the show was duly met and I was seated in a private room, just off his main dressing area which reverberated to the shouts, screams and raucous laughter of a somewhat hysterical American contingent of well-wishers who invaded his quarter, but ever the diplomat, Tom finally succeeded in ushering the last of the congratulatory mass through the door without offence. He poured us both a long cold drink and we sat and talked as if we had been close mates all our lives.

He was delightful and was genuinely thrilled to be asked to appear in the Royal show. "It is such a great honour," he told me and I could see he meant it.

Sadly, the invitation was not fulfilled, for the MGM Grand refused to release him for the five days it would require for him to travel, rehearse and perform (understandably, in view of the enormous business Tom was creating). If Tom was disappointed, I too, suffered, for the prospect of booking a major superstar for a Royal Variety show would look impressive in my future CV. However it was not to be but the Las Vegas story did not end there.

The following day, Charles asked me to attend an opening night at the Las Vegas Hilton, to view a singer he had just signed to his agency. "If you like him," he enthused, "you could recommend him to Billy for the Royal show or, if not, perhaps you can find him work in England. He's brilliant Jim – I promise you."

I must admit, I recognised agent talk but, nevertheless, I was not going to turn down such an occasion as a Las Vegas opening 'do' – so I accepted. The seats were good and like opening nights in London, a glittering event. The singer Charles had so strongly promoted appeared, did well, but frankly was no better than a hundred others currently and desperately looking for work in Britain.

"What did you think?" said Charles enthusiastically. "Wasn't he brilliant! Can you use him?"

I was non-committal, not wishing to offend Charles in any way but anxious not to say too much that would give him the wrong vibes.

"I'll go back stage and see him," said Charles, still carried away by his protégés performance. "You join me when the show's finished."

So I sat and waited for the opening night Star to appear. I had never heard of him – an older, black man who was so laid back, he actually appeared on stage in carpet slippers, whilst relaxing in an easy chair. Whether I knew him or not, the audience certainly did and they screamed and hollered as he began to talk. I was totally mesmerised by his performance. He was not just brilliant, he was sensational! I rolled on the floor, accompanied by the rest of the audience, captivated by his wonderfully original material and marvelling at his timing and delivery. He got, and deserved, a standing ovation and the spectators were still chuckling as they filed out, recalling gags he had used and filing them into memory to retell at future parties. I made my way backstage and made the usual complimentary, (but empty) remarks to Charles's singer and was about to take my leave when the Star of the show walked in, hiding behind the biggest and fattest cigar I have ever seen. He sat down and we chatted – me telling him how fantastic he had been and he wanting to know all about England and London (he didn't seem to be so much bothered about Bournemouth, Blackpool or *The Sandcastle*). For the second time in successive evenings, I had met and spoken to two major stars and, on each occasion, had found them modest and unassuming. We shook hands, I wished him luck for I felt he had quite a future in our business and he left.

"He's brilliant," I said turning to Charles. "I'm going to ring Billy in the morning and tell him – if he wants to chance an unknown comedian for the Royal show, I've found him! By the way – what was his name?"

Charles looked at me for ten seconds as if I'd gone stark raving mad. "His name?" he said "...Bill Cosby!"

I rang Billy and to his great credit, he was prepared to take my recommendation – supported, I might add, by Charles – but his initial feeler to the comedian was disposed of at birth, for Bill Cosby, obviously humbled at the mere suggestion, decided not to entertain the thought. His reasoning was that, although now fast approaching super stardom in the States, he was relatively unknown at that time in the UK and to appear in such a prestigious show as the Royal and perhaps fail, would put his career back for many years to come. He did, of course, become a big star in Britain, but that was later and so my attempt to project an act into the annual Royal show ended in failure. I will admit, however, that the joy of meeting these icons of our business, seeing them work and the delight in discovering that they are warm, friendly, human beings, makes the disappointment of not fulfilling my objective, seem of little consequence. And so it should be!

Meanwhile – back at The Sandcastle, everything was going well for our second summer season and now we had the bit between our teeth. We threw caution to the winds and decided to present a full-blown summer revue show starring Keith Harris and Orville and Frank Ifield. The show would be produced and directed by Keith himself, who was proving not only to be a superb artiste in his own right but a highly inventive and imaginative show organiser. He worked day and night to transform the somewhat austere room into a warm and attractive auditorium and we were confident that the show had everything for the family. The inclusion of Frank Ifield on the bill was a bonus, too, for he still had a multitude of fans from the residents and visitors to Blackpool and the bookings reflected the quality of the show. We never totally sold out at any time during the summer but the ticket sales were healthy enough to give us encouragement, particularly as the whole country was beginning to feel the grip of a world recession and money was tight. People were beginning to pull their belts in and the immediate future, particularly in the world of showbusiness, was pessimistic. I thanked God and Billy for The Sandcastle, for had it not been for the revenue gained from the commissions we received, life would have been difficult indeed. Like any other businesses of similar type, we suffered from the changes instigated by the clubs, pubs and hotels that were our bread and butter in supplying artistes and musicians. Because of the economic crisis, customers who frequented these establishments five or six evenings a week, were now attending only one or two and some not at all, with the result that the outlets began by cutting their weekly entertainment programmes. It was fast becoming an unhealthy situation and one which worried me a great deal. The worry was compounded when I was asked to attend a meeting at Bognor Regis with the Butlin hierarchy and was informed that sadly, Keith Palmer had left and the decision had been made to dispense with the services of the entertainment consultant (me!). This was quite a blow to my cash flow, especially on the 'in' tray but at least I was grateful for the two years work I had been given. Nothing lasts forever in this world – one door shuts and another one opens – and all the other unhelpful metaphors spun around my mind but the bare fact of the matter was that I had lost £12,000 a year from my turnover and that was a blow!

Jan was taking to working with Billy like a duck takes to water and loving it! She had now taken over the personal management of Paul Nicholas from *Just Good Friends* fame and was quickly making an excellent reputation for herself within the business. She booked Jacqui Scott on to the *Friday Night is Music Night* show, relayed live from the Golders Green Hippodrome on the BBC Radio 2 programme. We decided to make an evening of it by seeing the show and relaxing after its conclusion in a delightful Italian restaurant, situated almost opposite the stage door. Taking part in the broadcast that evening was the BBC Concert Orchestra, conducted by Michael Reed, Jacqui Scott and the brilliant Michael Ball. It was, as always, a joy to see and listen to and the programme is never long enough. With Jan and I in the audience, were old friends Tony Hatch and Jackie Trent and we duly trooped across the road at the finish for a glass of vino and a plate of pasta. Shortly, we were joined by Jacqui, Michael Ball, Michael Reed and another long standing friend, pianist Bobby Crush. It did not take long for someone to spot the piano hidden in a corner and before long, we were all grouped around its frame enjoying a star studded sing song which would have cost a veritable five figure fortune had it been booked it as a cabaret attraction. Michael Ball, at that moment starring in Andrew Lloyd-Webber's *Aspects of Love* and currently enjoying a huge hit with *Love Changes Everything,* Tony Hatch responsible for more hit songs than I care to remember – songs like *Don't Sit in the Subway, Downtown* and of course, in collaboration with his wife Jackie Trent, written the signature tune for the hit show *Neighbours.*

"It took twenty minutes to write," he said, "and it made us fortune."

The same Jackie Trent, whose recording of *Where You Are Now, My Love,* stayed at number one in the charts for a total of eleven weeks in 1965, Bobby Crush who never made the charts, but who has topped variety and revue shows all over the country, Michael Reed, himself a beautiful pianist and who has conducted some of the greatest orchestras around the world, Jacqui, who was at that time appearing in the musical *Chess* at the Prince Edward Theatre in London's West End and of course, Jan and I. I looked on in wonderment as these showbusiness greats sang song after song, queued up to play the pianoforte and laughed at the sheer pleasure of it all. What a thrill, too, for the unsuspecting diners who turned up expecting a simple meal and pleasant company and instead, were party to a theatrical 'who's who' of stage performers, letting their hair down and giving them the show of a lifetime. Each vocal and musical rendition was met with tumultuous applause and it could, and should, have gone on, long into the night – adding, I suspect, greatly to the takings behind the bar, but it was not to be. Had any of the gathered galaxy burst into Neapolitan rhapsody or operatic area, I am sure the Italian owner would have waived his advertised programme and wallowed in the nostalgic recollection of his homeland but, sadly, no one had the inclination to render their version of *Come Back to Sorrento* and he dramatically stepped into the ring of household names in full voice and held up his hand, like a policeman stopping the traffic in the centre of Rome. "You pleasa stoppa dis music," he cried. "You no more sing – it ees nowa de time for the deesco!"

At that, the recorded music blared out from the speakers, the coloured lights flashed, the Italian owner smiled from ear to ear and we all left. The poor man will probably never know the show of the shows he turned away – maybe one day I'll tell him!

CHAPTER TWENTY TWO

Back in the Hot Seat

The phone call came out of the blue – totally unexpected and one of those moments when your life jumps the tracks and veers wildly in another direction.

"Mr Kennedy?" the voice enquired and I affirmed. Something inside told me that this was no ordinary call. Maybe it was the plumy voice of the caller or perhaps, just sheer instinct, but something important was about to happen. I could feel my heart beating as I waited for her to say more. She obliged. "I have Mr Hemmings for you."

Trevor Hemmings? For me? Why would Trevor want me?

Trevor's familiar voice came on the phone. "Hi Jim," he said. "What are you doing, right now – this minute?"

He always came straight to the point – no messing!

"Right now?" I asked.

"Right now!" he continued, sounding irritated. "Have you heard – I've bought back Pontins from Bass. I want you to come and see me. Soon!"

A man of few words was our Trevor but the news of his move back into the hot seat of Pontins sent my mind racing and unaccountably, I filled with an excitement I found difficult, at first, to understand. I had a good business, I reasoned. I was my own boss and within reason, I could come and go as I pleased. So why should I feel a tingle at this news and invitation to meet the big boss? I knew, and I had known all along. I was not, and never would be, an agent. I was not comfortable selling and managing artistes. I was a square peg in a round hole and I felt it. My strength was in buying. I was a very good booker and could find the best acts at the most reasonable prices and I could work a budget to within a farthing. I looked back on the two years running my own Company with some pride – but where would I have been without Billy Marsh? No Sandcastle, no Superstars working for Butlins and paying me commission and no many other tit-bits he continually put my way. I was a success and a failure. I was never cut out to sell for a living and I hated it. I wanted out – I wanted my position in Pontins back – I wanted to be the buyer and wield the power that goes with the territory! I felt the excitement grow! "I'll be with you tomorrow at ten o'clock," I said and it was done.

Flora looked at me quizzically for a second and she knew what was in my heart. "Good luck," she told me. "It's what you want. It's what you're best at and it will make you happy!"

With that in mind, I went home to iron my best shirt, look out some clean underwear and polish my shoes. I wanted to look my best for the visit to Banbury and my confrontation with the great white chief. It would be a big day in my life and I wanted to be ready for it.

I sat outside Trevor's door at 9.55am and, as usual, he was delayed. His phone rang incessantly and people of all shapes and sizes hurried to and from his office, some wearing frowns of worry and others wearing smiles – probably with relief. It was a typical day in the life of this human dynamo. He never changes, I thought and settled down for what I anticipated to be a long wait but I was pleasantly surprised. At 10.20am, I was called into his office and we sat facing each other, like the western gladiators at the OK Corral – each waiting for the other to make the first move.

Finally he spoke. "How's your business?" he enquired. "How much do you make a year?"

So down to earth – so straight to the point! I told him an excessive figure, but not too much so. He never flinched but then, why should he, for his annual turnover was a million times greater than mine.

"Would you like your old job back?" he asked.

"No thank you," I declined, shaking my head. "Not in that position and certainly not at that salary!"

And so it continued – thrust and parry, attack and counterattack. Perhaps, in the end, Trevor felt he was not gaining as much ground as he had hoped for and he suddenly changed direction and now he was firing from the hip. "Okay," he said. "Lay out your terms. What is it you want?"

In for a penny, in for a pound, I thought. "A Directorship in the Company and a commensurate salary." I named a figure that was probably too high and this time, he did react.

"Can't do it," he said. "I'm only able to appoint six Directors and at this time, the Board is complete." He paused for a moment. "Wait there, I have an idea," and he was gone.

I waited for a full half hour and my patience was beginning to wear a bit thin. I began to believe that his idea was to get out of my sight as quickly as possible and to have me removed by the white coated gentlemen of the strait jacket persuasion, when, as quickly as he had departed, he reappeared, again to the point. "Right," he began. "This is the offer. We'll pay you the salary you have requested and you will continue to fulfil the role of Managing Director, retaining your company Kennedy Leisure. KLM will become a Limited Company and two hundred shares will be issued at ten pounds each. I will purchase one hundred and eighty and you will purchase the remaining twenty. You will be responsible for the entire Pontin entertainment output within a given budget and you will answer to me. What do you say?"

He underlined further conditions and terms that were relevant and sat back waiting for my answer. Before I could give it, he added a beauty. "Oh and by the way, you will have to move to Chorley in Lancashire for that's where Head Office will be."

That was a drawback, for I had grown to love the gentleness, the elegance and the climate of Bournemouth but a sacrifice had to be made, for the rest of the package was brilliant. With regards to Jan it, in effect, made little difference for, such was her pressure of work in London, she was required to be available most weekends for meetings with the media etc. and I travelled up to her flat in the Capital most Fridays, returning to Bournemouth on the Sunday. The only alteration to the system would be that I would arrive into Euston station from the North instead of Waterloo station from the South. So we shook on the deal and all I could think of for the first initial period was – I was back! A devious but delicious thought suddenly raised its grinning head and, realising the implication of what it would entail, I joined in the merriment. What would all the agents be thinking as the news leaked out? I chuckled to myself. I could visualise the mass panic within the ranks as the announcement of my return was finalised; "We turned our backs on him," they would wail. "We thought he was gone for good and no more use to our bank balances – and now he's back. Our business is doomed! No more work from Pontins. He'll hate us and cut us off without a thank you note! Woe is us – a thousand times woe!"

The thought kept me laughing all the way back to Bournemouth and the following morning, the switch had been thrown. Word had spread and the vultures, who had lain dormant for the past two years, reappeared unabashed and shameless, their wings spread and their eyes glistening brightly at the thought of the rich pickings on possible offer. The agents were back! Each offered an apology and excuse, a reason for not ringing sooner 'but you know how it is mate?'

Suddenly, I was the flavour of the month and invitations for lunch/dinner flooded in. My food account at Marks &

Spencer's was hit by famine, as my purchases dropped dramatically, causing the shares in M&S to plummet and perhaps being partly responsible for the traumatic period they are undergoing today. I would be a complete hypocrite if I did not admit to enjoying every last revengeful moment of my re-incarnation and, although I have always wakened each morning with a glow of pleasant anticipation looking forward to the day ahead, the sense of well being now had an extra zest. I was back and I was glad!

I found a flat overlooking the sea on the northern cliffs of Blackpool and settled into my office at Sagar House, Eccleston, near Chorley the new head office of Pontins. Sharing the quarters was the ever faithful Flora who decided to uproot and travel north with me – a gesture that was so much appreciated by me and typical of the lady – and a young man by the name of Bob Summers who had worked under the recently departed Winston Cockburn. Winston, he told me, had suffered greatly from his own inexperience and during the first year of his command had booked artistes certainly good enough, but totally wrong for the Pontin guests and many complaints had been received from disgruntled customers. His choice of performers was roundly criticized and in year two, he hedged his bets and insured himself of being accused of the same errors of judgement by heavily overbooking the circuit with professional entertainers of all shapes and sizes. Comics, singers, magicians and jugglers turned up for lunchtime cabaret spots by the carload, whilst similar numbers and types appeared for the evening performances. It was overkill with a vengeance and, as he was drastically overspent in his budget, something had to be done. Trevor made contact with me, the deal as described was arranged and Winston was asked to leave. I cannot imagine a happier man in England than Winston, when he left the office for the last time to return to the environment in which he was most happy and appreciated – the stage. His wonderful voice and his gently relaxed demeanour was a joy to behold and wherever he is now, I wish him well and hope he is happy singing again and bringing pleasure to others.

My first task was the hateful one of cutting the budget and deciding which artistes had to go and, for the first few weeks, I toured the centres, viewing the overabundance of acts and weighing up the implications to be faced when contracts had to be broken. It was a horrible assignment but one that I had to face up to and I tried to do it with as little pain as possible.

Life has a disturbing habit of mixing cocktails laced with joy and sadness, pleasure and pain, and if served too much of one, will quickly compensate with a portion of the other. Such was my experience, for after going through the happy experience of returning to the job I enjoyed and loved best, with a vastly improved financial package, the news I had feared for the past few months came in a phone call to inform me that my dear Dad had passed away. I took no solace from the fact that he was eighty-six years of age when his call came, for he was my Dad and simply could not be replaced and, although we lived hundreds of miles apart, there were weekly phone calls and many happy visits to Edinburgh, always carefully planned to coincide with Hearts playing a home game so that we would attend the match, enjoy the atmosphere and each others company, whatever the result. Apart from the passion for his (and mine) favourite football team, he loved to play the violin and played it well enough to be the lead violinist in a local orchestra specialising in Scottish music. I think back on the wonderful Hogmanays we enjoyed so much as a family, with Dad playing the violin, my Mother, a stalwart of the Southern Light Opera Company, singing her heart out, Sister Kath, already mentioned at the beginning of this book, a highly talented and skilful pianist, brother Ian, a television cameraman previously with BBC TV, now under the banner of his own Company, touring the world filming documentaries of superb quality – but then a highly rated drummer, Uncle Bob, a tenor, who should have turned professional, being good enough, and me – the one with the least talent but, strangely, the one who made more out of showbusiness that the rest put together. Wonderful evenings, now gone.

I thank God for allowing Dad time to make a journey weeks before he became too ill to travel, to our beautiful thatched cottage in Tarrant Hinton (before the mole invasion) and I will never, never forget his words to me on a beautiful sunlit evening, when we stood together enjoying the splendour and joy of nature wearing its very finest cloak. He recalled his advice to me many years before, when I contemplated entering into the world of showbusiness and admitted his great fear for my future in such a fickle and unforgiving business.

He gazed now at the trappings of what I had achieved – the car, the beautiful picturesque cottage and the delightful garden surrounded by peaceful and gentle countryside and placed a hand on my shoulder. "I am so proud of you," he said. "So, so proud!"

That was all he said. He was not an emotional man and maybe, because of that, the words he spoke have remained with me to this day and even recalling it now, brings a lump to my throat. A wonderful characteristic Dad possessed, was his delicious sense of humour – a dry wit delivered with lightening speed and delivery that would dissolve us into paroxysms of laughter. His face would remain straight but his eyes would twinkle and that somehow, made it all the funnier. He made us promise that his funeral was not to be one of gloom, doom and sorrow but one to be enjoyed with laughter and jollity. Easier said than done, so Dad decided from his heavenly position on high, to take a hand.

On the morning of the cremation, we awaited the arrival of the hearse which would pull up outside the front of our bungalow at 81 March Road on the outskirts of Edinburgh.

We would board one of the limousines following and convoy to the crematorium. March Road at that time was a quiet, residential thoroughfare that lay undisturbed by the increased traffic horrors of central Edinburgh and any vehicle that dared to venture into its embrace would have to endure the closest of scrutiny from the local residents, hiding behind closed net curtains. The hearse was due to arrive at 10.00am and at 9.30am we heard the sound of a vehicle pulling up outside the front gate. Early, we thought and didn't rush out. Within seconds, we were subjected to the most frightening racket as two men attacked the road and pavement directly outside the house with pneumatic drills. We rushed out and waved at them to stop. They waved back and continued drilling. Finally we managed to penetrate their cacophony and they ground to a halt and at least had the decency to apologise, when they learned of the circumstances.

"That's Dad's doing," we said and everyone agreed and smiles faintly began to appear.

We sat in the small church with the coffin in view at the front. Mum sat on the front row with Kath beside her for company and comfort. Ian and I sat two rows behind and, as the service droned on, I suddenly noticed Mum's shoulders begin to shake and my heart went out to her. She had been superb up to then, in control and coping, but the emotion of the moment had finally eaten into her soul and sorrow had overtaken her. Or had it? I looked hard at my beautiful Mother and looked again. She wasn't crying – she was *laughing*! I could not believe it, was it hysteria? Had her mind gone – or worse?

She explained, when the service finished and we were in the car heading for the superb George Hotel, Edinburgh for a slap up meal – (something else Dad had insisted on). "I wore a brand new coat for the occasion," Mum said. "I took it carefully from the wardrobe and put it on. It didn't feel right but I put it down to it being new and unworn. During the service, I was suddenly aware of someone tapping me on the shoulder. I looked around but there was no one there, nor was there anyone in touching distance. I felt myself go cold but I decided it was simply my imagination. It happened again – Tap! Tap! Tap! And once more there was no one near. By now, I was rigid with fear and convinced it was Bill (my dad) trying to make contact. Once again – Tap! Tap! Tap! I muttered 'What is it Bill – are you all right?' Kath heard me say the words and I told her that Bill had made contact with me to let me know he was fine and not to worry. Kath, being the disbeliever, told me not to be so silly but I insisted. 'Show me where you're being tapped,' Kath asked and I did. Slowly Kath put her hand inside my lovely new coat and slowly withdrew the coat hanger, which I had failed to remove. We both went into fits of hysterical laughter."

"That's Dad again," I said and we all agreed.

The lady who met us at the hotel was expecting a gloomy, sad party to arrive and was surprised as we tumbled from the cars, still laughing. She showed us into the private room laid aside for us and we sat down to enjoy our meal. The soup arrived, steaming hot and we were just about to begin, when the fire alarm bell suddenly boomed out forcing us to abandon the gastronomic treats spread before us. We stood outside the hotel in the pouring rain, whilst fire engines arrived to search the premises – unsuccessfully as it turned out.

"Dad again," we yelled and by now we knew he was there with us enjoying the joke.

One more event during the evening brought it all home. That afternoon Hearts were playing an away fixture at Kilmarnock and Ian and I were pleased to note that the highlights of the match were to be shown on STV at 10.00pm. Because of the day's events, we didn't know the score, so we switched on in hope. The game was an unmitigated bore. Neither side appeared as if they wanted to win and the match was petering out into a goal-less draw. With seconds to go, the ball was pumped into the

Kilmarnock goalmouth and rolled towards their goalkeeper. He rushed from his goal and aimed a kick at the ball that would have sent it soaring over the main Grandstand and into the car park – if he had connected! Just as his boot swung downwards, the ball hit a divot, looped over the despairing goalie's size eleven boot and trundled into the unguarded net. There was no time to restart the game and Hearts had won by the only goal. Ian and I leapt to our feet. "That's our Dad!" we screamed.

We had seen enough and I was totally convinced that he was there, unable to make contact but allowed for that one day to give us signs that he was well and surviving. Sadly, my Mum was to rejoin him four years later but, each time I need comforting, or find myself with worries I want to share, or even worse, have a major decision to make, I find myself speaking to them from the privacy and quietness of my bed when the lights are out and darkness spreads it's cloak and, although they never answer, I am sure that they are listening and helping as they always have done. Of that I am certain and the sure knowledge that they are watching over me, gives me great faith, comfort and peace of mind for this day and for the days yet to come. Mum and Dad, I love you and miss you both!

Back at the Fun Factory, things were beginning to return to a semblance of sanity. I had managed to reduce the overspend by a reasonable amount and the acts that had been dispensed with for financial reasons, had had the blow softened by the promise of a full summer season the following year. The new Managing Director of Pontins (Trevor was now Chairman) was Graham Parr – son of the, then, Chief Constable of Lancashire, Stanley Parr – and one of my ex-Bluecoats at Blackpool whilst I was still Entertainments Manager there. Like many other students, he viewed his time with us as one to let off steam and played the role to extreme. He loved the company of pretty girls and was always the first to offer his bawdy congratulations to the weekly winner of the 'Miss Pontin' competition. He drove a battered old car and I remember clearly, the first three letters of his registration number – XTC – aptly chosen, for I am sure the emotion was experienced many times in the back seat of his 'passion wagon'. To say he enjoyed a drink, too, was an understatement and many a time, although he didn't realise it, I viewed his inebriated body being dragged (head first with the heels of his shoes trailing twin furrows in the expensive carpet), by his supportive mates out of one door of the bar, whilst I entered from the other. He walked a very fine line in those days and was extremely lucky to have lasted the course. Nevertheless, maturity blossomed and he eventually joined the Company on a full time basis and such was his transformation, he progressed through the ranks to Centre Manager and finally to Managing Director.

CHAPTER TWENTY THREE

Ken Dodd – The Bookers Dream

Kennedy Leisure, by decree of statute, had to be governed by a Board of Directors and Graham was appointed Chairman with myself, as Managing Director. Two other Directors made up the Board – Jeff Mallinson and accountant Robert Downie. We met on a monthly basis and any innovations, proposals or ideas from me had to be brought up, discussed and sanctioned (or otherwise) by committee. All very democratic and businesslike!

To push the sales for the traditionally slow month of June, I proposed contracting a star name to augment the existing cabaret and this was agreed with enthusiasm. One name I felt would have the greatest impact as an attraction was the squire of Knotty Ash, King of the Diddy Men – Ken Dodd. I rang Ken at home (you had to deal with him direct) and he liked the idea. We agreed that he would work on the four Northern centres, starting on the Monday at Southport and finishing at Blackpool on the Thursday. The fee was agreed and I promised him the contract by return. I was delighted with the result and contacted our marketing department with the information. Within days, the National Press carried our advertisement and, such was the pulling power of this comic genius, the bookings poured in and within two weeks from the first advert, we gleefully began turning customers away. We were sold out! I sat back glowing with self congratulatory smugness at my suggestion to book Ken and when two weeks went by, followed by three and then four, with no sign of the contract being returned, I began to feel just a bit jumpy. Another two weeks and still no sign of the signed document and by now, it was turning into panic.

I rang the great man but only conversed with his answer-phone. "Ken – Jim Kennedy! Starting to get a bit worried. Perhaps you don't want to sign your name for me. Okay – I'll accept that but will you just give me a ring and confirm you'll be with us? Cheers!"

Nothing! Two more calls to Ken and, each time, my voice was getting progressively higher as panic gave way to fear and fear to terror. How in God's name was I going to explain to approximately five thousand people who had booked their holiday on the promise of seeing the great Ken Dodd, that he would now not be appearing due to me having lost him? How would they react? Would they laugh and pat me on the back and say 'Never mind old son – Have a drink!', or more likely, tear me limb from limb, carry the pieces in a cardboard box to the Centre Manager, dump me on his desk and demand full reimbursement, with compensation and damages.

By now I was a babbling wreck and every time the phone rang on my desk – which was often – I grabbed it and yelled down the mouthpiece, "Hello – Ken, is that you?" and it wasn't – until the Saturday afternoon, before the Monday opening.

By now, everything I ate or drank was Valium based. Valium sprinkled on my morning cornflakes, Valium cutlets for lunch and T-bone Valium steaks (with chips) for dinner.

Through my tranquillised state, I heard the familiar voice of Ken Dodd. "Jim lad," he intoned. "What's all the panic about? What's all the fuss? I've been away on holiday and just got back. Course I'll be there – I don't need a contract, my word is my bond."

If he had been standing in front of me at that time, I would have kissed him – protruding teeth and all (*his* not mine!). Lovely, warm, honest, old fashioned Ken Dodd. I was saved!

Came the Monday, I made my way to Southport to greet my Star and welcome him to the fold. The ballroom, converted to a theatre for the evening, was bursting at the seams and the air was electric. The buzz of excitement rose by the minute and at 9.15pm, fifteen minutes before curtain up, I went backstage to say hello.

I was met by a white faced Entertainments Manager who told me in a voice trembling with the same affliction I had been suffering with for the past few weeks. "He's not arrived! He's not turned up! He does know he's on at 9.30pm?"

I tried to assure him all would be well but that lump in my stomach had reappeared and was beginning to hurt once again. 9.20pm came and went, 9.25pm and still no sign of Doddy. 9.28pm and the stage door opened and in he walked, cool and calm and totally unruffled. "Hi Jim," he said as if we had just met casually in the street. "What's the house like?" He took off his outer coat, smiled a benign smile in my direction and walked on stage to the sort of reception usually reserved for royalty and Gods!

Two and three-quarter hours later, he finally decided to leave the audience wanting more and we pulled the curtain. I shook his hand in awe, what is there to say? The man had driven us mere mortals to distraction and yet he had appeared, as promised and entertained his public for almost two and three quarter hours. He had fooled, sung his hit songs, gagged without a swearword or a rude gesture and had made his audience weep tears of laughter for all that time. The man is a genius and a complete one-off. He will never be repeated or replaced. He is unique in the annals of showbusiness and whatever his shortcomings, you can only forgive the man and love him. The fact that he continued the week at each of the other centres in the same way he had begun, arriving within seconds of curtain up then lifting the audience to the greatest of heights, was of little significance. By now, we knew what to expect from him and relaxed just a little bit more. Since that time we have used Ken Dodd on numerous occasions and he has never failed us once. The crowds adore him and he, them. They are his kind of people and the only trouble we have now is getting him off the stage. Ken is not cheap but he gives his employers the greatest possible value and that is all we ask. The fact that the poor booker is carried off for rehabilitation at the conclusion of the deal is inconsequential. We are both slaves to the master, in this case the customers and if we don't like it then there is no place in showbusiness for either of us to hide. The role of booker, or indeed impresario, is one the audience never considers as anything other than a licence to print money. It is a strange concept – and to see the words 'so and so' Productions Presents... over a theatre entrance, featuring a well known star or stars, paints a mental picture of a well heeled and clearly affluent person visiting his fawning bank manager each morning and depositing a bag bulging with banknotes of every denomination. Far be it from the truth, and after regaling you with the pressures and worries in booking a big name star, let me take you one step further and recall the one and only time I was tempted to promote a major show using my Company's hard earned cash balance. It is the one period of my life in which amnesia would be welcome and to recall the period, even today, brings pain to the memory.

The Keith Harris Show had completed the season at The Sandcastle with much acclaim and the figures, if not spectacular, were reasonable. The country had been dragged through a world recession but John Major was confidently prophesying that the worst had passed and by the spring of the following year, boom time would be with us once again. I listened and foolishly believed! Looking at the figures of the season just finished and anticipating an upsurge of holidaymakers with more money in their pockets to spend, I proposed that Kennedy Leisure finance the following years Summer Show and The Sandcastle, with financial worries removed, were delighted to accept. So, too, were my Board of Directors for they had faith in my expertise and, when I informed them that we only had to fill the theatre/club by one quarter to break even and any more than that, would take us into healthy profit, they rubbed their hands together in anticipation. The show, on paper was a winner. Headlined by the original Bucks Fizz (who had never appeared in Blackpool previously) and supported by zany comedian Stu Francis, Mike Terry the 'camp' pianist (who played in the style of Winifred Atwell) and family favourite Charlie Cairoli, son of the famous clown of the same name, everyone who read the bill said the same – "Great show, can't fail!"

By the start of the summer the Country had, in fact, moved from the previous year's recession – and got worse! It was at its depth and Blackpool was empty. I knew that the first few weeks were going to show a loss and for that period, I didn't worry too much, but when the figures refused to rise as we went into August, I began to feel a sickness in the pit of my stomach. Each week I was paying out wages totalling £12,000 and each week, I was banking takings of £3,000/£4,000. In anyone's language, I was losing a fortune! I tried everything to attract an audience – two tickets for the price of one, competitions on the local radio and TV stations with tickets for prizes, giving away prizes during the show itself – but nothing worked. My Board were asking leading questions and demanding answers and I could only be honest with them. I called a meeting with the cast and invited their Managements to attend and we kicked around every possible idea or suggestion to save the season but without really coming up with anything feasible.

I guess, deep down, I desperately hoped that one, two or more would stand up and say, "we understand the problem and have agreed that you can cut our wages," or even better still, "we've decided that you're losing too much money and if you want to pull the show out from today we'll back you up!" – but no one did and I can't blame them. In their position, I would have done nothing either and why should they? Their wages were safe and guaranteed. I was the only one to suffer and suffer I did, like never before. I would awake at around 5.00am every morning, and pace the floor, my brain whirring madly, trying to find a solution to end the nightmare I was living through. I lost weight (some would say – about time!), I began to hate going to work and I honestly feared for my job. Each monthly Board meeting, I attended like a condemned man awaiting execution and each time I read out the monthly figures with the losses escalating with frightening speed, I awaited the sight of Graham Parr, placing the black cloth on his head and pronouncing the death penalty. In all, we lost a total of £90,000 that summer and at the conclusion of the disastrous period, the Board met to review the considerable damage to its profits and to my reputation. I thank God that the meeting was conducted with sympathy and compassion for what I had grossly underachieved and the motion was minuted that no blame was to be attached to any one individual and that any further recrimination for the decision to undertake the summer season at The Sandcastle, would be collectively and jointly proportioned. Having escaped from the worst period of my life, bloodied, battered and mentally scarred, I vowed I would never risk my, or any Company's money again and to this day, I never have. I would ask – nay plead – to each and every member of the public visiting a poorly attended theatre or concert hall in the future, to look just a little deeper. It is *not* a shame for the artistes working hard to arouse a small audience. Spare a thought for the person whose money is upfront, ensuring that everyone bar himself, gets paid. It is the path to hell and I know for I've been there!

CHAPTER TWENTY FOUR

Lorna Luft, Liza Minnelli, and Frank Sinatra (Nearly)

My weekend journeys to London were tiresome, to say the least, although Jan fitted in as many trips to Blackpool as she possibly could, to help me cope. There was double reason, however, for her to journey North for her Mum, Dad and Brother lived in the resort and it was good that she was able to see them also. One of the great bonuses of being in the Capital with someone in Jan's position, was the invitation to attend opening nights and Gala performances. We were fortunate enough to be part of the star studded audiences attending premieres of most of the major musical shows of the time – *Phantom of the Opera, Miss Saigon, Aspects of Love, Buddy,* plus Royal Variety Shows and Tribute Concerts. I was as thrilled as Jan was when she rang to say that she had taken on the UK management for the American singer Lorna Luft, daughter of the legendary Judy Garland and a few weeks later, I went with Jan to the London Palladium one Sunday evening to see the lady appear in concert with the dancer, Wayne Sleep. Jan had to be at the theatre two hours before curtain up, as she had some business to discuss with the Star and ever eager, with a promise to keep quiet, I went with her. Lorna turned out to be, as with many others, a normal, natural, down-to-earth human being. Her hair was in rollers and the make up was still in the pot. To complete the picture of domesticity, her three-year-old daughter was crawling happily around the floor. The two business heads were locked in combat and I was knee deep in a Sunday paper, when there was a knock on the dressing-room door.

"Someone to see you, Miss Luft," a female voice called out.

"Go away," yelled Lorna. "I'm busy at the moment. Have them call back after the show."

The voice came again, insistent. "Someone to see you ma'am, won't go away – says it's urgent – won't give a name. I think you should see them!"

By now Lorna was irritable and with an exasperated sigh, she wrenched open the door ready to give someone, or somebody, a piece of her mind. Standing before her with a grin that spread from ear to ear was the very recognisable face of her half-sister – the brilliant actress and musical star of films and theatre – Liza Minnelli. Each screamed and locked into each other arms, hugging and kissing whilst I looked on in wonderment, thinking all the time I was dreaming. I was introduced by one famous lady to another, glad that no photograph had been taken in view of the silly, it-isn't-happening-to-me smile on my face. The door closed behind her as she entered and my abiding memory of the moment was of Jan and Lorna continuing to sort out their business problems whilst Liza Minnelli – Superstar – lay on the floor playing with her three year old niece, like any other loving and caring Auntie. It wasn't to end there, for two more members of her party were admitted a few minutes later – her Father and ex-husband of Judy Garland, Syd Luft and dancer Lionel Blair. By now, the show was about to commence and the stage manager had discreetly waited until the lights had been dimmed for the opening, before taking us through the pass door into the auditorium and the house seats which were being held for us. If he thought that would fool the assembled audience, he had another think coming, for the 'jungle drums' had done their work and, as soon as Liza Minnelli came into view – albeit in semi-darkness – the audience rose as one and cheered her all the way. The show itself was superb, but one moment lives in the memories of all who saw it. The lights dimmed and died, with the exception of one overhead spotlight which cast a circle of light on a solitary stool – central stage. The stool was occupied by Lorna Luft and, for a brief second, she sat frozen in time, waiting for the last sound from the audience to die away. The music slowly surrounded her with the opening bars of *Somewhere Over the Rainbow* and as her voice picked up its cue and soared into the first line of the song, a gasp of disbelief came from a thousand or more throats. The sound was uncanny, incredible and in a sense eerie. We were witnessing a theatrical miracle – like watching, and listening, to the reincarnation of someone long gone. The voice, so reminiscent of her revered Mother, the mannerisms, the posture and the total command was there for all to see and wonder at. She stood on the very spot Judy Garland had stood on many years before and time simply fell away. It was an emotion I have never experienced before or since. I looked along the row of seats beside me and Liza had tears pouring down her face. Syd Luft pressed a white linen handkerchief to his eyes and his whole body shook as he sobbed uncontrollably. All others, too, caught up with the sheer drama of the moment, cried unashamedly. The last note of the song died and for a full five seconds there was total silence. Lorna sat still with her head bowed and, quite suddenly, the explosion erupted. Everyone was on their feet, shouting, screaming, cheering and I knew without doubt I had experienced one of the magical moments in theatre history – one that happens so rarely and when it does, is such a privilege to have been there. A moment I will never, never forget.

One moment I thought I would never forget, but did, because it failed to happen, came a few weeks later and once again, was instigated by the same lady – Lorna Luft. Of all the heroes in my life, the one who stands head and shoulders above all others, the one I'd like to share a desert island with and the man I would give up my life to meet, is Frank Sinatra. The news that he was to appear at the Royal Albert Hall in London, for what was billed as, and what turned out to be, his final, final concert tour of the UK, was greeted by great excitement by myself but only pleasant anticipation from Jan, who was not his greatest fan, but nevertheless, loved a theatrical event. Tickets were purchased and I eagerly awaited the big night, conscious of the sad fact that his voice was no longer the resonant instrument it once was but nevertheless, eager just to see the man, the legend, in person.

On the day of the concert, when about to leave Jan's flat in St Johns Wood, she asked a question that hit me like a sledgehammer, took my legs away and sent me spinning into space. "Would you like to meet Frank Sinatra?" she said.

I tried to answer but I could not find the breath. She guessed, however, from the apoplectic look on my face that my answer was affirmative and she explained further. "Frank Sinatra is Lorna's Godfather and she is there as his guest. I told her of your lifelong love affair with the man and she will arrange for you to meet him during the interval."

I didn't take a cab to the Royal Albert Hall – I floated on air – the only way to travel during London's rush hour. We picked up our tickets from the box office and found we were on the first shelf to the left of centre. From our lofty height, we scanned the VIP's seated at floor level and there on the front row was Lorna and Wayne Sleep. Using frantic tic-tac signal that would have made any bookie envious, we finally attracted their attention and using the same code of signal, Lorna relayed the reminder to meet us at the interval. It was going to be one of the great moments of my life and I am never ashamed to admit that, for all the star names I have either met or worked with in my life, I still get the thrill and the buzz any fan would experience. I hope I never lose that feeling of excitement for, if I do, much of the fun will go out of my job. But this monumental meeting planned to bring Frank Sinatra and me face to face with his hand touching mine and he saying to me, "Hi Jim – how's tricks? Course I've heard of you! How's Pontins? Maybe I can work for you someday!" would be something special. The great thrill of my life!

The show began and the whole of the first half was taken up by the incredible Cleo Laine and husband Johnny Dankworth and his Orchestra. It was good, it was jazzy and it was supremely professional but it was merely a background. I was hardly aware of the music, as good as it was, for my mind was fully occupied with the thought of the engagement to come. Frank and me! The first half finally dragged to a close and as the house lights rose we made our way along the labyrinth of corridors and rooms that surrounds the main auditorium, looking for the one passageway that led down to the backstage area and Frank Sinatra!

We eventually found the magic entrance and were about to descend to the joy awaiting below, when 'man mountain' materialised from the gloom, held out a hand with fingers like overgrown bananas and growled, "Sorry folks – you can't come in here."

There was no way through. He measured at least six foot, not up and down, but side to side. In the perpendicular direction he grossed six feet and a half and weighed, I guessed, around eighteen stone. Not one to argue with – but I did! "It's okay," I stuttered. "We're meeting Lorna Luft downstairs and she's arranged for me to meet Frank Sinatra!"

The smile lit up his mouth but left the rest of his face cold. "Show me your pass," he growled.

I growled back, "Haven't got one."

He completed the growling contest by repeating his opening gambit. "Well then – you can't come in here."

I thought for one moment about grabbing him by his evening jacket lapels, lifting him off his feet and smashing him against the wall and uttering the words, "Listen you punk – no one messes with a friend of Frank Sinatra," and watching him grovel as I passed him by, but I'm not really the one to cause a scene and I really didn't want to hurt him, so I refrained. If I had been on my own, of course, I might have been tempted but I was with Jan and, knowing she doesn't like violence, decided not to embarrass her. So we retreated into the bar for a quick diet coke to steady my frayed nerves.

"Don't worry," consoled Jan. "He's probably just arrived and psyching himself up for his performance. It would be better for him to meet you *after* the show."

It made sense and, feeling reassured, we retook our seats to await the second half and the great man himself.

Frantic hand signals fluttered from the distant figure of Lorna in the stalls. "Where were you?" we interpreted.

I tried to convey what had happened but didn't know the tic-tac for 'Neanderthal' and had to give up. Frank Sinatra entered the stage, a shadow of what he had once been. His body language reflected his age and lifestyle and his voice was dry and weary. Surrounding him, from one edge of the platform to the other was bank upon bank of fold back speakers, interspersed with giant television monitors, feeding him the words of the songs, his memory had long since rejected. It was a sad, sad sight and yet, through it all, the man still had an aura, a presence – a super star quality that he would never ever lose and the fans rose to him. He was on stage for over an hour and as the audience screamed and hollered and pleaded for more, he left the platform for a brief moment that seemed forever. Slowly he re-appeared, in response to the tumultuous ovation from the crowd, manipulated the steep incline to centre stage with difficulty and stopped. The noise of the audience died in anticipation of another familiar Sinatra melody but Frank slowly looked around, drinking in the scene, the baying fans on their feet, the orchestra, the atmosphere and it was painfully, but sadly, obvious that the realisation had struck home that this was for the very, very last time. It was a moment of nostalgia, of sadness and of deep emotion. Sinatra was saying his final farewell. The moment was frozen forever in the minds of those who saw it and, as if he decided that he had seen enough, he turned his back on the audience and, still walking slowly, disappeared from view. The last glimpse they had of the phenomenon that was Sinatra, was a weary wave of the hand that emerged from behind his back and if I hadn't known better, I would have sworn that this hardened, tough, hell-raising singer, who had fought his way from the slums of Hoboken in New York to the highest paid, best loved singer in the world, was crying! We leapt from our seats and fighting the tide of spectators wending their way to the exits, rushed back to the passageway in which we had been so cruelly stopped before. The gorilla had gone but in his place was a young man, smartly evening suited and wearing a smile of indifferent patience.

He listened to our pleas with some compassion and gave us a ray of hope. "If you'd just like to stand there for a few seconds longer, I'll be able to let you pass."

My heart leapt and the excitement caught fire again. I was conscious that other people, too, were being stopped but so wrapped up was I with the impending introduction that I never gave it a thought. Within seconds I had the answer. There was a commotion from the passageway and suddenly he appeared. Sinatra was standing in front of me, so close I could have touched him, kissed him or even shaken his hand.

"Hi Frank," I said. "I'm Jim Kennedy."

But he never heard me. He had gone. In a flash and out of my life forever. My dream was shattered and all because of ape-man. Whoever he was, I will never forgive him. His name has now been removed from my Christmas card list.

"Where were you?" Lorna asked when we finally caught up. "It was all set up for you to meet him."

I never replied – I was gutted. It seems that the pre-show period was the only time he will see anyone for, at the end of his performance, he walks straight off the stage, out the theatre into a fast waiting car and is gone. Tonight was no exception and in a way, I feel so sorry for him. He'll never know what he missed!

Jan, I, Lorna, Wayne Sleep and Lorna's musical director, retired to Joe Allens, London's popular restaurant frequented by those who populate the showbusiness profession and the thought crossed my mind that maybe Ol' Blue Eyes would be there, full of apologies for the disappointment that he had caused me. It was a long shot but it didn't happen and I really didn't expect it to. These things only happen in films and this was real life. Sadly, unfortunately and cruelly! Never mind, I consoled myself – I nearly met him and that's more than most of his fans can say. I'll have to live with that and, with his recent passing, that's all I can do.

CHAPTER TWENTY FIVE

Celebrity Stars – Past and Present

With the traumas of The Sandcastle beginning to fade into a distant memory, I set about presenting a conveyor belt of top quality artistes and bands in front of the Pontin guests with some success and the reputation I had had so badly damaged by the ill fated promotion, was happily well on the mend. The work place was a happy one and I enjoyed, so much, being a part of it. Sadly, the same could not be said of my personal life and it was becoming very obvious to both Jan and me, that our separate life styles was not contributing to a happy marriage. More and more, I was making the five hundred mile round trip to London, to be met by a note explaining that she had been called to a meeting or had to see a client or maybe both. Her work was expanding and her career was the love of her life. We both tried so hard to make it work but it was becoming more and more difficult. No one was to blame. It was simply a case of two people, dedicated to their careers, highly motivated, both successful which fate had decided to keep apart. Thoughts of a split in our marriage was put on hold when, sadly, Billy suffered a massive stroke. He should, by rights, have died at that time for he was in a coma for four days, long enough for him not to recover. But Jan never left his bedside during that awful time and I am convinced (and she will no doubt deny it), her love and dedication pulled him through. He was confined to a wheelchair and was unable to speak coherently, but she continued to look after him, attending to his needs and nursing him to a quality of life he deserved so much, but never expected. I helped whenever I could, if only to give Jan a break, but she was the one who gave back to Billy his pride and dignity in the last years of his life and it is important that her dedication be recorded. God gave Jan the opportunity to return to Billy all the love and help he had unselfishly bestowed on us and she took it with both hands. Billy passed away peacefully at the age of seventy-eight and is sadly missed by everyone who knew him.

My relationship with Jan had changed from husband and wife to that of brother and sister and the thoughts, which had been suppressed, finally came into the open in the early part of 1993. We decided that it would be best for us both if the marriage be annulled, so that each of us would be free to pursue a personal and private life without the restraints of marriage bonds and, in December of the same year, the decree became absolute. We both reacted to the split in similar ways – throwing ourselves into our work with renewed vigour and enthusiasm.

Things were building up well within Kennedy Leisure and I now employed a staff of five for, not only did we control the entertainment for the Pontin Group but had also built up a large list of clients from the major hotels in the Lancashire area. At that time, I was delighted to receive an invitation from Reg Grundy Productions on behalf of Sky Television to appear as a judge on the final of *Sky Star Search*, compered by Keith Chegwin. My fellow judges were Melvyn Hayes, the comedy actor from *It 'Aint 'Alf Hot Mum*, Suzi Quatro and Joe Ferrari, the head of a recording studio in London. The show was recorded at the London Weekend Television Studios for transmission the following evening and, in addition to picking an overall winner, I agreed to donate booking engagements at the Pontin centres to the value of £1,000 to an act of my own choice. Similarly, Joe Ferrari had the same brief to choose an act and present them with studio time and a recording session to a similar value. The show went well and Keith Chegwin and I enjoyed a 'chat' on air and I felt it would serve as good publicity, not only for myself and my Company, but also for Pontins. The final act appeared and we went into a commercial break, before recording the final segment of the show in which the winners were announced. During the break the judges and the shows' Producer, Peter Grattan, met for a quick consultation to agree on the prize-winners and I was asked to nominate my choice to receive the Pontin prize. There was no doubt in my mind and I nominated an excellent young vocalist from Wales, by the name of Richard Beavis.

"Impossible," said the Producer. "He's been awarded the overall prize. Pick someone else!"

I began to feel anger come to the boil. "I was asked to make a choice and that is who I want," I said and the smile on my face had become icy.

"Have the juggler," came the reply. "He'll do very well at Pontins."

That did it for me! I exploded and we were still furiously arguing when I heard the Director yell, "On air in five seconds!"

I returned to my seat, my mind in turmoil. What would happen now? I wondered, and waited for Keith Chegwin to make the formal announcements. Poor Cheggers! As soon as the voices became heated and raised, he fled the room and never reappeared until the show recommenced. He announced the overall winner – Richard Beavis – and came to the winner of the Pontin engagement. To my total disgust and absolute fury, the juggler was announced as my choice and I had to walk onto the stage and present him with his envelope which contained absolutely nothing – merely a symbolic token for the purpose of the occasion. I make no apology for not remembering his name but he was not the act I wanted, or even needed, for the circuit and because of the fiasco I was forced to be a part of, I had to accept the outcome. In front of the TV cameras, I gritted my teeth, smiled, but could not prevent my body language giving my feeling away. I felt cheated and used and, what's more, my integrity had been demeaned in full view of the public and I was not very happy! I had no axe to grind with the juggler himself and, in fairness to him, having been put in the position of accepting the inevitable, I honoured the engagements promised and surprisingly, he did very well. Melvyn Hayes, a gentle and likeable man, was upset at the atmosphere created by the turn of events and headed me off as I made for the main door, to persuade me, for the sake of diplomacy to at least show my face in the Green Room, the hospitality suite set aside for performers and guests, before, during and after a show. I acceded to his promptings but only stayed for thirty minutes and made my excuses to leave – still mumbling furiously under my breath and threatening everyone connected with the programme with legal action. Of course I never did and contented myself by filing the whole dreadful experience to a folder marked 'Lessons To Be Learned'. The whole event, in my opinion, was run in a slipshod and unprofessional manner, without contracts and it appeared (to me at any rate), that the rules were being changed at will to suit the purposes of the programme. Sky Television have, thankfully, now come of age and operate as a highly polished and professional Company but, had they not made the transformation to what they are today, they would not have survived. I'm glad they did.

We continued our policy of booking star names, past and present, much to the delight of our regular guests and we started offering celebrity weekends, particularly during the winter months. When deciding the type of artiste best suited for the Camber Sands Centre, near Rye, Sussex the two names who sprang to mind were Jimmy Jones, the brilliant Cockney Comedian who would pack them in, such was the size of his massive following, and Chas'N'Dave who had fans all over Britain. We built a series of 'knees up' weekends featuring these two acts and as anticipated, sold out on all. The Centre Manager, at the time, was an ex-army

Officer (Major) David Fairs with the type of accent that could cut glass, not really the perfect choice for the East End Families who frequented the site. On the opening weekend, Chas'N'Dave were the star performers and the ballroom was bursting at the seams, awaiting their appearance. The lights dimmed and on they came to a huge and noisy welcome. Their opening number caught the mood and hands clapped to the rhythm of their infectious music, whilst voices sang out to the familiar words. Everything was set for a wonderful evening in their company when, with an audible 'pop', the power died plunging the room into darkness. No light, no sounds – nothing. At first there was good-natured comments shouted out amidst laughter but, as time went on, and the power remained dormant, the mood perceptibly changed. The boys had returned to the dressing room and they could, I am sure, hear the slow hand clapping from the auditorium. It was, however, beyond the control of the centre, for the power cut covered the whole of the County. Suddenly to a great cheer from the audience, the light and sound were restored and Chas'N'Dave returned to the stage to resume the show. At exactly the same moment as before, on the same beat and on the same line of song – 'pop' – off went the lights and the sound and we were again plunged in to darkness. Once more a long delay but again, they came back on. Chas'N'Dave had hardly started when – you've guessed it – the dreaded 'pop' and darkness fell for the third time. This time, seconds before murder was about to break out, the lighting and sound was restored and this time, for good. The crowd settled back, finally, to enjoy the musical talents of Chas'N'Dave and that caused the biggest problem of all. Chas'N'Dave had gone – given up on ever seeing lights and hearing sound again, they'd hopped it and were well on their way back to London – and sanity. Now David Fairs had not been an army officer for nothing – he was brave and fearless and he walked onto the stage and said into the microphone that was now working perfectly, "I say – you chaps!" – a roar of derision – "We've had some jolly bad luck..."

The crowd advanced towards the stage like the Zulu warriors marching on Michael Caine – and David fled! All night long, gangs of irate East End families hunted the hapless manager, seeking revenge, restitution and reimbursement, but he was never discovered. Of course the guests *were* refunded the entire cost of their holiday and Chas'N'Dave did apologise, although each party blamed the other, and peace (plus the sound/lights) was restored when we invited them back and they absolutely tore the place apart. David Fairs, though, suffered from a nervous blockage from that day on and one only had to say the words 'Chas'N'Dave' to him and he transformed before your every eyes into a gibbering wreck, foaming at the mouth and diving for cover. He was eventually transferred to the position of General Manager at our luxurious (and peaceful) hotel in the Lake District where he resides today. Highly successful, highly appreciated by the guests and at ease with the world.

Until recently, one of our most popular weeks enjoyed, particularly by our older guests, was the 'Bless 'em All' event. As the name suggests, it re-created the days of two World Wars but it was mainly the second confrontation that took centre stage. Military bands, marching displays, armoury exhibitions and anything else that fitted the category was booked, whilst the restaurant was renamed the NAAFI and anyone entering had to have his ration book stamped (we did issue them free of charge at reception). As always, I had to provide the entertainment and, as the years progressed, it became increasingly difficult to find the big names from that era, for they had either given up performing to make way for younger and more agile artistes or had packed their kit bags and marched off to join the heavenly ENSA concert party in the sky. I tried desperately hard to entice Vera Lyn to our reunion but even she was limiting her performances and I was never successful in persuading her. One lady I did manage to persuade, however, was the wonderful Anne Shelton. Amongst the many name big bands she had worked with, was the legendary Glenn Miller Orchestra, in addition to recording a string of hits during the forties and fifties. The tremendous buzz of excitement amongst the guests when her name was announced was joy to my ears. She was a true professional, in every sense of the word. Not only was she on time for her band call, but she was gracious with everyone she met and was prepared to meet, greet and mingle with anyone who wished to share her time. She brought with her, her own accompanist, the brilliant Ronnie Price and when she walked on stage to a tumultuous reception, every person in that room knew, before a note was played, that we were in the presence of a 'star' in the true sense of the word. I have to be honest (and I would love to be otherwise) and admit that the voice that had thrilled a Nation, not to mention the Armed Forces fighting a war in foreign fields, was not as it had been. It had lost some of its quality and the notes she now sang were slightly off key. Standing at the back of the auditorium, I cringed and feared the worst – but I needn't have worried. The lady was big enough to acknowledge the very fact that things had changed and instead of blindly battling her way through the songs of the period, she chose ones with which the audience could join in. Join in they did and when they felt that they had had enough, Anne talked and talked and talked, recounting the war years, her time with the big bands and regaled us with wonderful stories of her life and loves. She was on stage for a full hour and a half and when she finally took her bow, there was not a man or woman in the room who was not on their feet, paying tribute to a lovely lady who had turned adversity into a triumph, such was the presence she commanded. The overpowering recollection of that memorable evening was not just in viewing one of the showbusiness 'greats' of our generation, nor was it in experiencing the talent of yesteryear but simply, the giving of her love to an audience ever willing to receive it. It poured over the footlights like some tidal wave and embraced everyone in its path. I went back stage to congratulate her and although drained from her efforts, she looked radiant and it was obvious that the joy of entertaining and the buzz she got from it, was still as strong as it always had been. I was, as were many millions of others, saddened to hear of her death not long afterwards and if there is any way for my written words to be conveyed to her, I would like her to be reassured of the enormous pleasure she gave to her adoring public throughout the time she graced this earth – but I suspect she knows that already.

Another artiste who left an abiding memory in the same venue for the same event, was Teddy Johnson. Teddy had sprung to prominence as an exciting new vocalist but it was with his lovely wife, Pearl Carr, that the two found National and International fame. They were not, by any stretch of the imagination, an act from the war years and for that reason, I had not booked them. I heard, however, that Teddy had undertaken a National Tour in which he paid tribute to the late, great Bing Crosby and, although unable to see the show for myself, had received glowing reports from those who had. I had no reason to think otherwise, for I knew Teddy to be a supreme professional and a superb singer. I rang to invite him to present the 'Bing Crosby' tribute at our Osmington centre, near Weymouth, and he was delighted to do so. We quickly agreed a fee and such was the warmth of the man, never having met or even spoken with him before, I felt that I had known him all my life. I made a mental note of the date he was to appear and was there to meet him when he arrived. Pearl Carr, like any dutiful wife, came along with her support and we chatted away like long lost friends. At the given hour, Teddy was introduced and for the next sixty minutes, he mesmerised the full room with his uncanny rendition of all the Crosby melodies. He finally came to the end of his presentation and, as expected, the enraptured audience rose to their feet in acclaim. He came off but the crowd continued to cheer and applaud. Suddenly the call for 'more' was beginning to wane and a new call was beginning to take its place. "Where's Pearl?" they yelled and Pearl joined Teddy on the floor, to the delight of those demanding her appearance. Now they wanted even more. "Give us *Sing Little Birdie*!" referring to their top twenty hit of 1959 and they did.

For the next hour Pearl Carr and Teddy Johnson sang their hearts out and the audience lifted the roof off. It was nights like these that made my job such a joy, for in the process, I was meeting and talking with many of my showbusiness heroes of the past and present and many of them became close friends.

To finish this section of recall, bringing back warm memories of the big names of the past, may I pay tribute to the man known as 'Mr Moonlight', the great and (sadly) late, Frankie Vaughan.

Our Sandbay centre, close to Weston-Super-Mare in Somerset, is one set aside for our more senior guests and is full for eleven months of the year. The grounds are flat, so there are no hills and few steps to negotiate and three meals a day, served in a delightful restaurant, with the entertainment geared for the older generation, make it a highly popular site for those in the fuller age group. For one month however – June – it flags and to arrest this trend, we decided to present a star name for each of the four weeks during the period. I contracted Max Bygraves for one, then singer Vince Hill, Little & Large for the third and finally Frankie Vaughan. The first three named performers did, as we expected, huge business and as they say 'brought the house down', but on the final week, I was privileged to witness, arguably, one of the greatest receptions I have ever seen (or heard) an artiste receive from a Pontin audience. Frankie Vaughan and his lovely wife Stella, expected early evening, arrived just as the guests had settled down to lunch. There was a mini-panic for his accommodation was

*Chas 'N' Dave smile happily – **before** meeting the problems of Camber.*

The script is fine but I still can't get my fingers around 3-2-1. With Ted Rogers at Bexhill -on-Sea.

Britains King of Rock'n'Roll. The 'Bad Boy' himself – Marty Wilde.

I swap roles (for the moment) with the lovable, gentle but wonderfully funnyman – Jimmy Cricket.

Blowing up a storm with Don D. Williams and his lovely wife Doreen Savage. I rate Don as being one of the best acts I ever booked.

The 'Comic Heritage' Luncheon at The Raddison Edwardian Hotel in London. Front row (L to R) Jon Culshaw, Tom O'Connor, Bert Weedon, Ernest Maxin and Vince Powell.
Back row (R to L) Gareth Marks, Paddy O'Neil, me, Gordon Peters and Wyn Calvin.

With Tom Jones in Las Vegas in an attempt to arrange an appearance in the Royal Variety Show. Tom was willing but the MGM Grand said – No!

My favourite photograph of Maggie – known to millions as 'The Girl With The Glasses' from her years on TV's 'Oh Boy' and 'Top of the Pops'

Maggie and I tie the knot – 17th April 1999.

The legendary Vernons Girls – Penny Lightfoot, Maggie Stredder and Sheila Parker.

not completely ready. Frankie was charm itself. "Do not worry one bit," he reassured us. "Stella and I will find somewhere close at hand, have lunch and rejoin you in an hour."

The General Manager, however out of courtesy and not expecting his offer to be accepted, invited the couple to join him at his table for the meal and to his surprise (and mine), they agreed. We walked, totally unannounced into the restaurant area and the effect was electric. Spoons dripping to overflowing with tomato soup, froze half way to open and expectant mouths, knives buttering bread rolls stayed submerged in the spread and those already chomping on the lamb cutlets, stopped suddenly in mid-chew. Knives and forks clattered back onto the tables and the whole dining room rose to their feet cheering and clapping as quickly and as loudly as their limitations would allow. I have never seen or heard anything to match this acclaim in my life and both Frank and Stella looked overcome. From that moment on, there was an air of frantic excitement throughout the centre with the realisation that the great man had actually arrived – it was for real and he was here. The same reaction greeted the Star as he took the stage and there is little need for me to describe his performance or the reaction of the crowd at its conclusion. It was sheer magic but for me and, I guess, the majority of those present, the greatest part of the evening had yet to come. Frankie had every right to bid us farewell and disappear into the night, for he faced a long journey (two and a half hours) back to London. Instead, he appeared from the dressing room, having changed from his stage attire and, for the next hour and a half, met with his fans, signed autographs, posed for photographs and generally mixed and mingled with all who wished to say hallo. It was a lovely and endearing gesture by a man who genuinely cares for, and appreciates, his followers. He was the perfect ambassador for the business we are in and his death shortly after, robbed us of one of Britain's finest and humblest of stars.

It seems we had hardly got used to working under the Trevor Hemmings banner than it was all change once again. This time the buyer was Scottish and Newcastle Breweries and Trevor was appointed to the S & N Board as Director of the Leisure Division which included, not just the Pontin Empire but also that of Centre Parcs. Drastic changes were imminent but before they were put in place, I was contacted by a gentleman by the name of Nigel Fortnum from the Newcastle office of S & N to ask for help in providing star entertainment for the annual charity ball held in the Mayfair Ballroom, Newcastle. Nigel was on the committee who ran the event and with my connections, thought I could help. I was happy to oblige and spent many hours on the road, travelling between the Northwest of England and Newcastle to attend meetings and organising star names for the special evening. The main charity was one called The Yellow Brick Road Foundation, which specialised in sending terminally ill young children to Disneyland in Florida and, in addition to the profit from ticket sales, we ran an auction half way through the evening, offering superb prizes donated by local and national businesses. Along with Nigel, I landed the job of compering and directing the evenings entertainment from start to finish and I must admit, it proved a task that drained me totally, but well worthwhile. Each year – I was involved for three consecutive years – tickets sold like hot cakes and, in many cases, Companies bought full tables of approx twelve persons for their staff. The evening always commenced with drinks as the guests arrived, followed by a sumptuous five course meal before dancing to a live Big Band, cabaret, the auction, more cabaret and a disco to finish off in style. A very full and comprehensive programme for the nine hundred guests which filled the room. I used Big Bands of the calibre of the Jack Hawkins Showband, Les Howard and The Northern Dance Orchestra and The Eric Delaney Big Band whilst the cabarets included The Drifters, Rockin' Berries, Little & Large, Roy Castle, The Nolan Sisters and Bob Monkhouse. The later they went on, of course, the more difficult it became to succeed, for 'vino' was always king on these nights and one could judge, almost to the litre, the amount of alcohol that was being consumed by the increase in the level of chatter. Nevertheless, all succeeded by virtue of the sheer force of their personalities, experience and stage presence. The biggest hit of all, however, was from a young lady, relatively unknown in national terms but reasonably famous around the clubs of Lancashire and Yorkshire. Her name was Maxine Barrie and she was the very first outright winner of the *Stars in Their Eyes* TV show. Her voice, her looks, her style and her demeanour were a carbon copy, in every sense, of the brilliant Shirley Bassey and I decided to put it to the ultimate test. She was not advertised in the programme and it was arranged that she should make her appearance, prior to the evening's auction. I assured her that I would not reveal her identity until *after* she had performed and she was happy to go along with the subterfuge. I walked onto the cabaret floor and had difficulty quietening down the audience sufficiently, but regardless of their apparent disinterest, managed to convey that I was about to bring on stage a young lady, who, because of contractual reasons, could not be named. Nevertheless – "Please welcome our special surprise guest for this evening – the wonderful Miss X." A polite smattering of applause greeted the introduction before they turned away to continue the evenings main pastime – talking, drinking, eating, drinking and or course, drinking and drinking! That was until Maxine made her entrance! I passed her as she moved to the microphone and at a range of eighteen inches, I would have sworn it was the Tiger Bay Songstress in person. If the effect on me was electric, the effect on the audience was stunning. As if a switch had been pulled, the noise suddenly stopped and heads swivelled to catch a glimpse of this figure on stage. Shirley – sorry, Maxine – started to sing and eyes opened in wonderment all over the room. Waiters, waitresses and bar staff froze, totally hypnotised by what they were watching and listening to. Maxine stayed on the floor for nearly half and hour and introducing each of her 'Bassey' hits, convinced the public even more, that this was the genuine article. Dammit! – even her speaking voice was spot on! She left the floor to a standing ovation and to my shame, I broke my promise to her, by refraining from revealing her true identity. I was determined to keep the 'hoax' alive and to this day, I am certain that the majority of those present are still convinced that the 'Miss X' they saw and heard on the night of the charity ball in Newcastle, was the sensational Miss Shirley Bassey. As a footnote to what I have described, Maxine very kindly stayed on the floor to start off the auction and whether it was her presence or merely the fact that we had caught the *glitterati* amongst the audience in a particularly generous mood, we broke the record for the highest amount raised in one hour – a total of £66,000. It may have been naughty and, if they had found out they had been conned, some may have been a trifle cross, but it paid the way for a lot of children in the last few years of their tragically short lives to enjoy a little extra happiness and, put like that – who would dare to complain! Out of the great respect I have for Maxine Barrie, both as a lady and as a performer, I must point out that she does not make a living impersonating other singers of international fame. She is a highly talented singer in her own right and, unless specifically requested to, avoids any of the songs relating to Bassey. She also had a great, wicked sense of humour and that, along with her uncanny impression, allowed us to perpetrate such a naughty deception which I am sure took the evening by the scruff of the neck and indirectly allowed us to raise such a phenomenal amount of cash for the charity involved. Thanks Maxine!

CHAPTER TWENTY SIX

Country'n'Western Hoedown

As previously mentioned, Kennedy Leisure now had five staff, excluding myself, on its payroll. We had managed to overcome the traumatic six months of The Sandcastle summer show loss and the bank balance was, once again, beginning to show a healthy glow. Once again, I was no longer in dread of the monthly Board meeting, for good things were happening and it was pleasant to report them along with the increasing profits. I was, therefore, unprepared for the bombshell Graham Parr dropped on me, by informing that the new parent company – Scottish and Newcastle – were decidedly unhappy that a Company (referring to Kennedy Leisure), was working under the Pontin umbrella and that such a practice was to be discontinued as quickly as possible. The proposal was that I would integrate back into the Pontin fold as Entertainments Executive, my former position, but would retain my present salary. The two secretaries would join the main pool of girls serving the Senior Management and would effectively be paid by Pontins, (by this time Flora had retired officially and returned to Poole in Dorset to be with her family). Her place had been filled by Janet Neve, a highly efficient and totally loyal secretary and personal assistant. Bob Summers, ex-Bluecoat and Entertainments Manager, would remain as Assistant Ents Executive and Cameron Scott, brother of Jacqui, responsible for the OP side of the business (OP – other than Pontins) would be made redundant. Such a plan was not at all to my liking but it appeared I had little choice for, in holding only one tenth of the shares issued, I was heavily outvoted. I voiced strong objections to the redundancy proposal for Scott. It never is fair to effectively close the career of any employee, hard working or not and, in Cameron's case, he was certainly doing an excellent job, opening new outlets and paying his way. I persuaded the Board to listen to a counter-plan which I hoped they (and Scott), would accept. My idea was that, with the closing down of Kennedy Leisure, the contacts we had built up with the major hotels and nightclubs around the area would be defunct and to offer this business for Scott to continue, would not only keep faith with them as their suppliers but would virtually give him a business that would initially earn him a gross profit of almost £20,000 a year. Thankfully, each accepted my proposal and I am delighted to say that Cameron Scott never looked back from that day onward and has built his business into the thriving Company it is today.

That left only the question of my shares and if S & N were going to discontinue KLM as a trading company, they could not do so without purchasing them at a value to be agreed. I instructed my accountant to argue the case and after a series of protracted arguments, finally received a cheque for £34,000. Not a bad return on the initial £200 I had paid four years ago! So now, I was back where I had left off six years ago but with a much-increased salary and in many ways, I was not sorry. I repeat again that I was never cut out to be a business tycoon, juggling with finances and wearing pin strip suits, a bowler hat and rolled up umbrella. I am simply a down to earth guy who loves showbusiness, the people in it and the people who put it together and made it work. That is my strength, my passion and my knowledge and I was back doing it. Fate had made sure of that, once again!

Of all the special events that fill our calendar, the most popular, without doubt, is the Country'n'Western festivals held over six weeks throughout the year and in three carefully selected centres – Hemsby (two weeks), Brean

Sands (one week followed by a further two at a later date) and Prestatyn Sands (one week over the New Year period). As one would expect, the weeks are packed with the greatest country bands, artistes and musical exponents of the Country scene we can lay our hands on. The music invades your senses from morning to night and if the performers are the stars, the ambience of the event is created by the guests themselves. It must be a branch of *Fantasy Island* for the thousands of aficionados who frequent the centre, for they are transported to another age and another continent to act out their dreams. The dress code is anything relating to the wild and woolly west, including the standard cowboy with Stetson, leather chaps and gun belts with guns, which cost thousands of pounds. Indians, too, with headdresses costing four figure sums, roam the centre. One self styled Red Indian, who shunned his first class apartment, spent the entire week in the centre of the ballroom floor, living in a tepee, continually smoking his pipe of peace. It doesn't end there, for joining in the fun are members of the Confederate Army in full dress uniform, accompanied by their ladies in crinoline gowns. Each morning at 7.30am, and again in the evening, they parade in full uniform, through the centre, marching like guardsmen and perform the ceremony of firing the cannon to welcome and say farewell to the day. My first experience of this was after being placed in an apartment adjacent to the cannon by the General Manager, with a perverted sense of humour. Perhaps he had a grudge against me for some unpaid bar bill but at 7.33am, at the sound of the cannon shot, I slowly scraped myself off the ceiling, changed my pyjamas and spent the rest of the day poking my deafened ears with cotton buds, trying to bring my hearing back to normal.

Everything happens during the seven days of the event. Gun fights at the OK Corral, real life marriages in full Country outfits, Fast Draw competitions using real guns attached to an electric timing device, Rodeo with mechanical bulls and hangings on the sports field. The first time I saw this macabre moment, I was horrified before realising that the victim, strung up for some minor offence (cheating at the Country-style bingo session?), was hoisted high onto the gallows, not by his neck as it appeared, but by a cleverly concealed harness around his shoulders. Still it all looked ghoulishly effective and was further transposed into the realm of fantasy when, after the deed had been done and the stricken body was left to dangle in the seaside breeze, young children approached the strangled malefactor, pointed a camera in his direction with the request "Give us a smile mate?"

The music is, however, what they come for and we featured every solo singer, duo, trio and band available to us throughout the UK and beyond, to satisfy the fans. It was disconcerting at first to realise that the music covered by the Country label was split into so many different categories and styles, each with their own fans who will accept nothing else.

At one time square dancing was all the rage for those who like to strut their stuff, but gradually it became obvious that something new was required and I found it, courtesy of an American couple by the name of Dick and Geneva Mateuse. They convinced me that American Line Dancing would take off the same way in England as it had done in America. I took them on and became the first to recognise and feature this new phenomenon in the UK.

The whole event was a delight to attend – even if I had to swap my traditional suit for the more acceptable check shirt and jeans. The guests, whole families included, live out their fantasies in an atmosphere of harmless fun and sheer enjoyment, even if some of it can be a trifle frightening for the unwary newcomer. I recall an incident that truly happened to our great amusement, at Hemsby, near Great Yarmouth. Hemsby had a sister camp called Seacroft and the two are separated only by the main road. On this occasion, Seacroft was host to a Religious Festival, whilst Hemsby reverberated to the frantic sound of fun and gun fire. An elderly couple arrived outside the Hemsby main gate and slowly drove their Morris 1000, laden inside and out with suitcases of all shapes and sizes, down the main thoroughfare to the Reception. All around them was mayhem! Indian arrows bounced off their car, bullets whined above their heads, bodies hung suspended from gallows and desperados smashed furniture over each others heads. They approached the counter, stepping over bodies lying prostrate on the carpet, whilst the sounds of wailing steel guitars flowed from the ballroom. "Excuse me," they enquired, their faces anxiously looking for confirmation. "Is this the Assembly of the Church of God?" The receptionist's reply was unprintable!

One of our biggest problems in putting the Festivals together was finding new names to add to the list of perennial favourites like West Virginia, Campbells Country, The Indians and Memphis Roots and, to some degree, I relied on the expertise of agents like Mike Storey, Tony Gallant and a few others. Most of all, however, I needed the assistance of a member of the Special Events team – Bob Chapple. Bob was a Bristolian with an accent as thick as your arm and a verbosity that was International class. On his frequent visits to Head Office, word spread like wildfire that he was in the vicinity and all down the main corridor, doors that never closed, slammed shut and the occupants cowered beneath desks in fear of having to face a verbal torrent that would effectively close down their day. A few colleagues, with more good manners than good sense, would wait patiently as Bob moved into top gear, praying for him to pause for breath in order that they could interrupt and make their excuse to depart – but it never came! He was a talking phenomenon. Bob was the man who ran the Festivals and was able to handle any problems that arose during the period. I have witnessed irate guests approach Bob, belching fire and ready to gun down anyone who moved, with a complaint that, to them, meant the end of the world. By the time Bob finished his solution in his own inimitable style, the guests had completely forgotten what the original disagreement was about and they left him, bewitched, bothered and totally bewildered. In addition to being well known for his continuing dispersal of verbal diarrhoea, he was also known for his white, western style Stetson hat which he wore morning, noon and night. I am sure that he slept in it, showered in it and possibly even loved in it. There are rumours abounding that when his off-springs were born, they each wore genetically formed white Stetson hats in miniature – which would be quite understandable – but I hasten to add, it is only a rumour! Bob adored Country music and all through the winter months, visited the best of the Country clubs around the UK, searching for new acts to present during the Festivals. During the events themselves, he presented talent shows for up and coming Country performers and many of today's well-known names came through by this method. He was, in effect, the Hughie Green of Country Music.

One evening, when my guard was down and I wasn't quick enough to dodge his presence, I found myself embroiled in the usual one way conversation which inevitably followed such a meeting and he brought up the subject of new artistes to be brought in. He was concerned that, although we were still finding an influx of talented newcomers to present, the more established top of the bill acts required a shake up in order to keep the Festivals fresh.

"You know what we should do?" he asked and without waiting for my reply (naturally), he told me. "Go to Nashville, USA and bring back some of the big American stars. That would wow 'em!"

I laughed at the absurdity of the idea. It was a joke – wasn't it? The more I thought about the idea, however, the more I liked it. It made sense and although I could already visualise the rude answer I would receive from Graham Parr, I vowed to attempt the well-nigh-impossible task of asking the Company to pay for Bob and I to visit Music City USA. To my stunned surprise and our great delight, we received their blessing and within a week we were on our way. It wasn't that we were in any great hurry to travel, it was simply a fear that the Company would suddenly come to its senses and change its mind. So, off we trundled to Manchester International Airport for the long haul flight across the Atlantic Ocean to Atlanta and the short onward domestic flight to Nashville.

Bob as always was conspicuous by his western headgear and if I thought he would step out of character and quietly sit out the flight in comparative silence, I had another think coming. No sooner had we levelled out at 38,000 feet and the seat belt signs had been extinguished, he was up and out of his seat, rummaging in the overhead locker. To my horror, he opened one of his two flight bags to reveal an enormous stack of advertising broadsheets entirely devoted to our Country Festivals and off he went 'working the aisles', handing out the brochures and telling those who wanted to listen – and those who didn't – all the joys to be had, should they wish to spend a Country'n'Western holiday with us. It was too much to bear – those poor people! Many tried to escape by fleeing to the toilets at the rear of the plane but had to return to their seats after a frantic plea from the pilot who found it a real problem trying to bring the nose of the plane down and the tail back up. I think he called it weight displacement! Frustrated by that futile escape route, the passengers fell on the mercies of the cabin crew, pleading for the loan of any parachutes on board to escape the verbal outpourings of this madman in the white Stetson hat. To the relief of all, however, weariness overcame his intentions and he eventually returned to his seat and fell fast asleep. His teeth, however, unable to stop as quickly as the brain beneath the hat, chattered on unabated for at least another hour before they, too, finally and slowly, ground to a halt and silenced reigned. The sigh of relief from my fellow travellers lifted the plane into the sky above by another 1,000 feet at the very least.

We landed in Atlanta and queued to go through immigration. It was here I saw the other side of Bob, for within seconds, he had charmed these huge stern faced guardians and I was quickly propelled to the front of the line. "You're goin' t' Nashville?" drawled the uniformed monster. "Hey – give ma love t' Elvis – y' hear?" He laughed a full throaty laugh as if it was the funniest joke of the decade.

"Bloody idiot," I thought. "Elvis has been dead for years." But I laughed with him and he stamped my passport and we entered the USA.

It was raining hard when we eventually arrived in Nashville and it was still raining the next day when we awoke. The image I had of the Capital of Country Music was certainly not one of misty, grey drizzle and puddled streets. We got enough of that at home! Nevertheless, we set out to explore, filling in time for, at 2.00pm we had a very important appointment with a lady who was probably the most influential person in American Country Music – The Executive Director of the Country Music Association – Jo Walker.

She was not what I expected her to be. Somewhere in my mind, I envisaged a homespun lady of mature years wearing flat shoes and a gingham apron, but instead, we were confronted by a pretty girl in her early thirties, dressed for the times. There was no doubt, however, in the power of her position for she carried an air of authority and quiet efficiency that didn't need spelling out. She was completely bowled over by these two Brits who had travelled all that distance to view the Country acts that abounded the area and she wasted no time in opening doors for us to enter – doors that would have been impossible to shift without her help. Our first port of call was the Country Music Hall of Fame, situated in Music Square East – and it was plain for us to see that this was one of her pride and joys. Strolling through the

Hall of Fame with her was like receiving an accurate short course in the history of Country music. Each year, top Country stars are honoured on a Nationally televised awards show and a bronze plaque bearing their name is erected in the Hall of Fame Museum. In addition, stage costumes worn by the legendary performers are on view plus artefacts, like Patsy Clines' compact found near the wreckage of the light plane in which she died, are there for all to see. The most fascinating item on show, for me at any rate, was the solid gold Cadillac owned by Elvis Presley – an indication of how the Superstar lived. It must have been worth well into a six figure sum and beat the hell out of the company car I was given to drive around in.

Such is the popularity of the project that a new, bigger hall was constructed, costing $37 million dollars whilst another even bigger and better one, opened in the spring of 2001. I tell you – there's gold in them thar guitars! The following morning Jo arranged for us to appear on the Channel 5 TV breakfast show and, as usual, Bob did all the talking, but it was good publicity for us and for forty-eight hours at least, we found reflected fame. Of course we had to visit the famous Conway Twittys Record Shop on Demonbreun, the centre of the music area and found it far from being just a store selling records – more a shrine to the Country singer that bears it's name. It is now owned by the legendary George Jones, a Country superstar and ex-husband of Tammy Wynette. A few yards away, selling similar merchandise is The Ernest Tubb's Record Shop and both would appear do remarkable business. Much of our time was meeting, again with Jo's help, some of the better agents that frequent the city and we compiled lists of those performers willing to make the trip to the UK and the prices expected. It was the stars however that we had really come to see and that problem was put to rest when we received an offer to visit the backstage area during the following evenings show at the Grand Ole Opry – one that we weren't going to refuse.

The Grand Ole Opry has been the shrine of Country music since its conception on November 28th 1925. The show, a live broadcast each Saturday, became hugely popular with the fans and as the demand for tickets grew, it was taken out of the original studio and moved into a succession of venues, each larger than the one before. By now, the radio production was playing to a studio audience, averaging three thousand per show and the move to the Ryman Auditorium in 1943 was a welcomed necessity. The Ryman, built in 1892 had perfect acoustics and became the Opry's most famous home. Some of the great and legendary performers who graced it's stage were Hank Williams, Patsy Cline, Ernest Tubb, Earl Scruggs & Lester Flatt, Bill Monroe, Roy Acuff and many other household names of the past. By now, the show was being transmitted live to the whole nation, courtesy of NBC Radio and still those wishing to view it continued to rise and, to accommodate their needs, a new four thousand four hundred seater Grand Ole Opry House was built – opening in 1974. It was to this purpose built theatre that we made our way. Since relocating to its new quarters, television joined the party and for thirty minutes each Saturday evening, millions of Americans still sit down to watch and enjoy the show, courtesy of TNN Television. The show is entertainment, pageantry, comedy and Country music all rolled into one. It is simply part of America's folklore! Standing on the stage of this gigantic auditorium is awesome. We were allowed the privilege before the doors opened so the seats were empty and we could only imagine the ambience generated by the huge audience, when full. Incredible!

The show began and backstage, we were accepted by performers and stage crew alike, with the utmost kindness. Nothing was too much trouble and it was such a pleasure to meet stars such as Roy Acuff, one of the early greats of Country music, Bill Monroe (and the 'Blugrass Boys') another legendary veteran and, particularly, top of the bill,

Waylon Jennings. I found him to be a warm, friendly and open character and listened, fascinated as he relayed stories of his early days in the business. I was totally astounded to learn that he was the bass player for a short time, with Buddy Holly's band, The Crickets and was part of the outfit who was playing with the Rock'n'Roller on his fateful final tour. If fate played a minor role in my life, it played a massive one for Jennings. Travel, apparently, throughout the tour, was by a hired bus and the cold weather, plus the cramped seating arrangements, made the journeys between engagements almost unbearable. The show was entitled The Winter Dance Party Tour and whoever the genius was who organised the run, he was seriously geographically unenlightened, for the journeys criss-crossed the US Midwest like a chicken with no head. After a particularly cold and hazardous overnight trip, the show arrived at Clear Lake, Iowa for that evening's performance and was due in Fargo, North Dakota the following day. Buddy had had enough and managed to hire a small four seater plane to fly them on, giving him a chance to enjoy a much needed rest and catch up with his laundry. He invited his lead guitarist and Waylon to fill the other two seats, whilst the pilot occupied the fourth. Waylon was delighted to accept and when the show was over, began loading his equipment onto the car that was to take them to the airstrip. He was interrupted by the Big Bopper, who pleaded for him to give up the cherished seat on the plane, arguing that he was close to a nervous breakdown and worn out by trying to squeeze his large frame into the restricted area on the bus. Waylon felt sorry for him and relented. At the same time Ricky Valens was pleading with Buddy's lead guitarist to give up his seat but did not have such a good argument or the persuasive power to succeed. Nevertheless, it was decided to toss a coin and Valens leapt with joy when he called correctly. Just after midnight on the morning of February 3rd 1959 the plane took off and had travelled only eight miles of the journey before crashing into a snow covered field, killing all those on board. Waylon, naturally, was totally and utterly devastated and in his own words, 'took him twenty years to come to terms with the death of his friend and mentor – Buddy Holly. His story shocked us but was not to spoil the evening. It did, however, throw further insight into the rigours of serving the public, especially for those on tour. The glamour of this business is confined to the moments on stage or in front of the camera, and rightly so, for without it, the paying public would turn their backs. Away from the glitter of the costumes and the glare of the lights, it is a business of uncomfortable travel, food consumed in some motorway service station and cheap 'digs' to keep the expenses down. The same today, as it was then. It is true that the superstars who travel, do so in style and that is their prerogative, but very seldom does one person make a show. There are supporting acts, musicians, company managers and stage crew to consider and for them, it is a hard, relentless and unforgiving business.

We left Nashville with some fond memories and some new friends to enjoy. Our mission had been accomplished and we flew back to the UK excited at the thought of presenting to the Country fans in Britain, a wonderful package show featuring some of the all time Greats previously mentioned – Roy Acuff, Bill Monroe, Minnie Pearl and Hank Williams II (son of the great man but a big draw in his own right). We would have loved to have brought over the really big names but, as always, cost was the stumbling block. Not just the performing fee but the additional extras like airfares, insurance etc. Prohibitive! We put our suggestions to the 'men in suits' and surprisingly, they agreed to cover the extra expenses. Sadly, however, the plan never came to fruition. Problems arose from the Artistes themselves and, in some minds, the thought of going on the road again, rather than spending time with their grandchildren, began to lose its appeal, despite their initial enthusiasm – and so the whole exercise came to a rather untidy conclusion. It disappointed both Bob and I but we consoled ourselves with memories of a unique trip to Music City USA, and for that we were extremely grateful. The fact that I had survived seven days in the constant company of Bob Chapple brought a new respect for me from all and sundry and that, too, was a great bonus. Sadly Bob is no longer with us but I can hear him on quiet days, still chattering away, his wings fluttering – still wearing his white Stetson hat! He was a character and there are so few of them left. He will be, and is, greatly missed. The Festivals are not the same without him!

CHAPTER TWENTY SEVEN

Musicians! – and a Big Shake-up

With Scottish and Newcastle Breweries firmly at the helm, major changes were anticipated and, as always, one looks at ones own position and wonders. I could not see any reason for them to alter my status within the Company for I felt I was still doing a good job to my own satisfaction. Yet, as we moved into the mind-nineties, my brief was subject to scrutiny and within the next two years, the whole structure of my job was to change, to my dismay and dissatisfaction.

The first of the major alterations came quickly when Managing Director, Graham Parr departed, closely followed by Operation Director Jeff Mallinson. When Financial Director Robert Downie decided also to leave – it meant that the whole of the former Kennedy Leisure Board, excluding myself, had gone. It was a sobering thought and again, I wondered if I was to be next. I guess that two things saved me, more than any other. The first was my obvious knowledge of the job itself. I knew my business pretty well by now and, in turn, was well known and (I hoped) well respected. In fact, because of my long years with the Company, and I suppose (reluctantly) my advancing years, I was referred to, by all and sundry, as 'The Godfather' – a pseudonym I accepted as a great compliment. The other reason was the very fact that I was in the entertainment business. From the Company's point of view, it was relatively simple to find another Finance Director or a Marketing whiz kid or even someone with a vast knowledge of operational skills – but entertainment? In the minds of the suited gentry, it is a business run by eccentrics, a business managed by dim-witted extroverts – *not* to be taken seriously. Any group of individuals who wear red noses and laugh for a living is not for real and any department who appears to be totally enjoying themselves and daring to smile in the process, is not considered part of the cause – but an intruder! Maybe I puzzled them for I didn't conform to the pattern they perceived and in their uncertainty, for the time being at any rate, they left me alone. There had never been any doubt in the past that I had accepted the responsibility for booking all the acts, bands and Bluecoat/entertainers since taking over the control of the UK in the early eighties and the only time an artiste tried to by-pass the system, was in the days shortly before Fred Pontin relinquished his power. He was a singer, or so he told me, and at my request, sent me an audio tape recorded by him, I imagined, in his back bedroom. If the quality of the tape was bad, the quality of his voice was a thousand times worse and if I had so desired, I could have sued him under the Trades Description Act. I sent him a kind but firm letter apologising that I was unable to use him and thought that would be the end of the matter. It wasn't to be for, somehow, he got hold of Fred's private phone number and rang him. Fred correctly told him to contact me and put the phone down. The artiste rang again and received the same answer. This went on for days on end with Fred getting more and more impatient and annoyed by the second. Finally he had had enough. "Come to my office tomorrow morning," he yelled, "and bring your diary with you."

The artiste duly turned up and was ushered into Fred's lair, full of anticipation for a lucrative booking. "Right – here's a date for you," said Fred. "I want you to entertain the guests at my Pakefield Centre on Tuesday 3rd of May." He paused for a second, "...2003!"

The artiste scribbled the date in his book, obviously not thinking, and thanking Fred profusely, backed out of the room. It was only when the door shut behind him that the penny dropped. He was consumed with rage at being conned in this way and he furiously banged on Fred's door. "Come," was the invitation and he burst back into Fred's office. "Excuse me," he shouted angrily, bravely, ready to have a go but Fred, the master of the game, took no prisoners. "You've got a date," he roared. "What more do you want?"

In the face of such an onslaught the artiste stood no chance. His anger dissolved in a second and he looked at Fred, panic beginning to rise. "Sorry to bother you, Mr Pontin," he stammered. "But what time's the Band call?"

Now you will have to decide whether that story is true or not – some say it is and others not – but it made me laugh when I heard it and I hope it's done the same for you.

Finding good resident bands for the season was one of the more difficult parts of my job and many times, more than I care to remember, I have listened to a superb band auditioning and been prepared to offer them work before discovering, incredibly, that none of them could read music. This is an essential part of the work involved, for not only do they have to play for dancing, but have to back the visiting cabaret and touring shows each evening. Normally an hour is put by for the band calls and it is expected by myself and the artistes, that the allotted time is long enough for them to fully master the acts requirements. One other problem, which thankfully doesn't happen so often, is the band, expert musicians all, who prepare their evenings programme of dancing, put their music in order and play the numbers one after the other as planned. I have no problem with that, but when they start the second evening, playing the same music in the same order as the previous one, then the third and the fourth, I, along with the guests and especially the Centre Manager, get very cross indeed. We had such an outfit at one of our Southern centres and, as good as they were musically, you could spot guests adjusting their watches, depending on which number was being played. The opening of their set was always a quick step and was always *The Lady is a Tramp*, followed by a waltz and a slow foxtrot (this *was* a long time ago!). To finish the evening they played a lovely arrangement of the waltz *Moon River* and as the last bars of the music faded away, the guest knew it was time to pack their belongings and go to bed. The manager suffered it for five nights and on the day of the sixth rang me, very annoyed and demanding I dismiss the band immediately. I jumped into my car and headed for the Centre but somewhere between Head Office and the site, word leaked out that I was on my way and the Band Leader was ready for me. "Hallo Jim," he said. "What a surprise seeing you here! We're just about to start playing. Why don't you come in and listen to us?" He smirked as he said it and I followed him into the ballroom, packed as usual with dancers, all dressed up a ready for *Lady is a Tramp*. I stood with the General Manager and on the dot of 8.00pm the band leader bade everyone 'welcome', came the downbeat and the band swung into *S' Wonderful*. There was chaos! Dancers tripped over each other's feet, some fell into the passageway and others frantically held their timepieces to their ears checking to see if they had stopped or not.

"The bastard," shouted the General Manager. "He's done this on purpose 'cos he knows you're here."

The Manager, however, was to have the last laugh for when the band commenced to play the second number of the evening, their unfortunate choice of tune was *Moon River*. There was a startled hush around the room as the band began to play, the melody sunk into the subconscious minds of the guests and in seconds they were wishing each other a 'goodnight' and leaving for their chalets to go to bed. It's probably the first and only time in history the guests were tucked up and sound asleep by eight thirty in the evening. I had the band removed and peace was restored!

If you are somewhat doubtful over the authenticity of the last two recalls (and who can blame you?) I assure you that the next recount is totally true and actually happened. I know for I was there!

When auditioning a band or group for the full summer season it was always policy to arrange the hearing at the actual centre requiring their services. My reasoning, I felt, made good sense as it eliminated a number of potential problems likely to surface when the chosen musicians arrived for the commencement of their contract. The first was allowing them to see the room in which they would be asked to perform. Secondly, they were able to view their allotted accommodation and thirdly, they would meet both the Entertainment and General Manager, an important factor. Occasionally, however, it is impossible to make such arrangements and such was the case when I heard that the superb Jack Hawkins Orchestra could be available for the forthcoming summer season. I required a band at our Centre in Southport but was unable to arrange for them to travel as they were contracted at the time to play each evening at the Orchid Ballroom, Purley near London. Once again, I dragged my weary car into action and drove to the venue to hear the band 'in situ'. As I expected, they were excellent – just what I required – and with Jack Hawkins being a fellow Scot, we talked half the night away before sealing the deal. Next morning I rang the Southport General Manager, Don Green, with the news and he was delighted. Don was a big man physically – he had once been bodyguard to Prince Charles – and he didn't suffer fools gladly, but I felt that both he and Jack would get on well enough to ensure a successful season. So it proved! The Jack Hawkins Orchestra stayed at Southport for five successive seasons and contributed greatly to, arguably, the greatest period in the centre's history. Don Green would hear no wrong of Jack or his Orchestra and vice versa – the perfect relationship! Eventually, however, all good things came to an end and the band moved back south.

Eighteen months later, I heard the sad news that Don Green had died and once I had the details of the funeral, I rang Jack, for I knew he would like to pay his last respects. The service and cremation were to be held in Doncaster, but unfazed, Jack vowed to be there. And so he was! He drove up with fellow musician Andy arriving just after 2.00pm (the service scheduled to commence on the hour). The doors of the small church had already closed but Jack and Andy managed to slip into a back pew and for the next forty-five minutes, they bowed their head in prayer, sang the hymns with gusto befitting musicians and listened to tributes from all and sundry.

Finally the Vicar rose to his feet for the final blessing. He bade the congregation stand and as they did so he spoke the words, "God, our Father, I now commit the body of your loving servant George Michael Wilson..." Jack and Andy heard no more. "Flamin' 'ell Andy," Jack muttered to his mate. "We're at the wrong bloody funeral!"

And so they were. Because of an administrative error from the Crematorium, the services that day were running thirty minutes late and whoever George Michael Wilson was, he, fortunate man that he was (or had been), received the best possible send off from two of the finest musicians in the country – at no extra cost. I can hear Don Green laughing to this day!

Two major appointments were made within the Company that were to change the face of the organisation for ever. The first was to appoint a new Managing Director and the chosen man was Stephen Haupt, a tall good-looking, elegant man in his early forties. He had left a comfortable post with Chef and Brewer, the pub and restaurant chain, but had had no experience whatsoever of holiday centres. Any fears we had in this direction were soon dispelled for the man proved to be near genius by the speed in which he learned and digested the intricacies of this unique business. He was a great leader, as hard as teak but with a warm, humorous and humane manner, which endeared him to the staff. The other appointment made by Stephen, shortly after his arrival, was that of Operations Manager and the man he selected for that unenviable task was Jez King. He was younger than Stephen by almost ten years but was cast from the same mould. He had the rare combination of a brilliant brain and a capacity for working impossibly long hours and led by example. It is fair to say that I learned more from these two men, particularly Jez King, in the art of business administration and organisational skills during the five years I worked under their command than I had for the rest of my career put together. Nevertheless, it was a decision made by one or other (or maybe even both) of these brilliant business exponents that conceived the, hereto, unconsidered thought in my mind that retirement was an option. My birth certificate insolently displayed to the curious that I had already passed the magical sixty years of age milestone, but maybe because I mixed and worked with most people more than half that total, I neither felt, nor hoped, I looked my age. I still loved the work I was doing and faced the future with anticipation. To be with the people who live and work in the offbeat world of showbusiness, is both a privilege and a pleasure and the respect I was held in by the stars, the lesser-knowns and the newcomers of my profession was a source of great pride to me. Sadly my connection with that particular part of the business was to be taken from me and it left a great void in my life that was never to be filled. My knowledge of the acts, the bands, the groups and particularly the requirements of the people I was tasked to provide entertainment for, was my strength and my motivation and to be deprived of this outlet, both surprised and hurt me. Perhaps the powers-that-be, realising that both technically and legally, I could walk from the job in the very near future and disappear into the sunset, clasping my hard won pension to my bosom, influenced them to look ahead. I would like to think that was the case.

Whatever the reason, however, I sensed that moves were in hand to off-load the booking of all the entertainment to an outside agency, with Studio One of Coventry in prime position. In fairness, I was offered new objectives and was tasked with the job of replacing the antiquated lighting and sound systems throughout the estate, plus looking at those who had good staging equipment and those who didn't. Jez made money available to me and I enjoyed the challenge but not with the same job satisfaction and sense of fulfilment I had experienced previously. Studio One was finally awarded the contract to provide the Centre's entertainment requirements and I handed over the entire project to their Managing Director, Lee Clark. Lee had been, himself, an artiste of the highest quality and had been used extensively by myself on the circuit, so he was no stranger to me. We enjoyed an excellent relationship and worked well together but it was small consolation for me to view, from a distance, the duties I had loved so much, being undertaken by someone else and out of my control. For that reason, I began to think seriously of my future and with some sadness ringed a date on the calendar – the 6th December 1999 (my sixty fifth Birthday) – as being the day I would finally sever my link with the business I had so much enjoyed – since I rose from my haystack, yawned and wandered off stage to the sound of applause, over fifty years ago. I had little to look forward to – a bachelor pad in Blackpool and a life watching *Match of the Day*, *Coronation Street* and televised cricket from Lords, plus the weekly trip to Sainsbury's to purchase the frozen chips, bottles of pop and the odd lamb chop for Sunday lunch. Oh – the joy of it! Fate, however, had one final card to play and fittingly it was Lee Clark who, unknowingly, dealt it!

It was normal, in the past, for me to offer the Artistes I had selected, a full weeks work, touring the Centres during the summer season, appearing on the different sites each evening and repeating each successive week until the end of the engagement. Most were delighted to accept six nights per week with one evening off, but the odd few opted for seven (these were either the workaholics, the very short of money or the plain greedy sods!). It was up to me, therefore, to arrange a travelling schedule for them which made sense and in most cases, I got it right. The one weakness, in the system, was the *type* of act chosen to appear and sometimes I upset Entertainments Managers by sending them a singer who specialised in modern ballads and pop songs, especially when their site catered for the more senior guests. My perennial argument was that, by contracting the artistes for six or seven nights per week throughout the season, I was able to drive a very hard bargain and as money had (and still has) a very bad habit of talking very loudly, it was accepted without question. As time went on and work for the performers became more and more difficult to obtain – especially long summer seasons – the artistes started filling their date books with one-night-a-week engagements and building on that. The good ones would still end up with six nights a week but it was often scattered and certainly not for the same company. This certainly changed the pattern of our booking and made it easier to cater for the requirements of individual centres rather than providing in bulk. With this in mind, Lee Clark of Studio One decided to let the Entertainments Managers come on board and have a major say in the type and style of artistes appearing in their centres and, naturally, they leapt at the opportunity. I must say, I had no quarrel with this system for anything that would improve the quality of entertainment provided, could only be good for the Company and would help in keeping us all in work. Lee decided to take over the concert room of a larger hotel near Kenilworth in the Midlands for three days, inviting all the Entertainments Managers to attend, plus any other Senior Staff members who were interested. During the daytime, he bombarded them with a succession of duo's, groups and bands of all shapes and sizes and in the evening he presented cabaret acts chosen as being suitable, in terms of quality, for the centres. By way of a bonus, he concluded the proceedings each night by presenting a top-of-the-bill act to round the show off – a move appreciated by the audience and even more appreciated by me.

CHAPTER TWENTY EIGHT

The Vernons Girls – and Maggie!

The reason for my delight was the opportunity to re-unite with the legendary Vernons Girls – in particular Maggie Stredder – who were to close the show on the middle of the three nights. I had used the girls a number of times in the past and it was always a great joy for me to watch this highly professional trio work the audience with their fun songs, sixties tributes and zany sense of humour. They continually 'sent themselves up' and the audience loved them. Off stage too, they were so much fun to be with and the laughter flowed continually. Looking back on our 'after show' get-togethers I realise now, not so much then, that Maggie and I shared an attraction for each other and whenever a group of us formed, it was always she that I manoeuvred to be with, to chat to and to enjoy her wonderful company. At that time also, I was not foot-loose and fancy-free and played the role of gentleman as she played, equally well, the roll of lady. We spoke, once or twice, on the phone with our business hats on and the calls always left me with a warm, happy feeling. It was with some excitement, therefore, that I waited for the girls to arrive in the early evening of that very special day. One minute they were no where to be found and the next minute they were there – three of my very favourite ladies – Sheila Parker, Penny Lightfoot and Maggie – and I felt a tingle of excitement as I walked towards them. I could not believe the emotion I was experiencing, like a sixteen year old on his first date and I told myself to act my age, but the feeling refused to see sense and even had the nerve to intensify as Maggie rose to greet me with a hug of delight. That she was pleased to see me was obvious and the chemistry between us was now becoming almost tangible. The audience as always rose to the girls but – for once – I hardly noticed their performance. I only had eyes for the girl in the middle, the girl with the glasses – the girl who was to become my wife and I knew, at that moment, that someone very special had come into my life. We sat after the show with me trying to appear casual but wishing that the evening would never end. Mixed thoughts were spinning through my head by now, alternating between the hope that such a liaison was possible, the charge of electricity I felt in her company was being reciprocated, the ghastly thought that her hugs and touches were simply that of courtesy and that she had someone else in her life, to which she was devoted to. Still in this state of doubtful apprehension, I walked her to the door and she was gone – to where and to whom, I wondered? She stayed in my thoughts for the remainder of that week and I longed to ring her. One minute I would and should and the next, I couldn't. Finally on the Friday, I telephoned her home and was met by her automated voice on the answerphone. I left a message asking her to return my call, trying hard to convince her it was a business matter but at the same time implying that my need to speak was of a much more personal nature. At 4.00pm on the Saturday afternoon, she returned my call and from that second on, I knew without any shadow of doubt, I was falling in love and the very fact that we finished the call long after 7.00pm, confirmed the fact to me that she felt the same way. I was sure then, as I am today, that our meeting together was the final ace in the pack that fate had planned and its timing was impeccable.

From that day on, we rang each other each and every day and there wasn't one phone call that lasted any less than three hours. ET's glowing finger united us both and the advertising catch phrase 'phone home' became the focal point of our daily existence. Incredibly it was to be another three months before we actually met again but when we did, the courtship we had endured telephonically, was as meaningful and secure as if we had met face to face each day. The frustration of not being with her induced me to 'manufacture' a business meeting in London near her home in Surbiton and at its conclusion, I made the short journey to meet her, spending a wonderful evening together in a local Italian restaurant, eating sparsely but talking profusely. We held hands like teenagers and kissed the same way. I could not believe it was happening to me and I suspect her feelings were similar. In the autumn of your life there is no time, nor room for subterfuge, kidology or pretence. On both sides it was a case of what you see, you get – and the more I saw, I wanted! Maggie is gentle, sensitive, generous and loving, with a glorious sense of humour that fills our time together with laughter. She is such a joy to be with and when she agreed to share a holiday with me in the USA later that year – October to be exact – I felt that the outcome had already been scripted. We arranged to be away for the traditional two weeks and for the first half of the holiday, we cemented the growing certainty that being together was the most important thing in our lives. I suppose, in some ways, the holiday was to be the final piece of the jig-saw puzzle, the 'passing out' parade, the ultimate test of our commitment to each other, for it was the longest period of time we had spent together. If there were to be any skeletons in the cupboard, now was the time to discover. There were no skeletons to be found and early in the second week when we had enjoyed our usual physically sapping routine of lying on a sunbed on the beach, engrossed in the latest John Grisham thriller, we returned to the room for a long cooling drink of Florida orange juice and an all-American sandwich (whatever that was), before stretching out on the bed and drifting into a sun fuelled sleep. I woke an hour later, feeling warm and lazy and as I stretched, our hands touched. It was electric and at that moment a strange phenomenon occurred that, to this day, I cannot explain. I heard a voice that sounded so like mine, speaking words that I wanted to say but would never have had the nerve. "Maggie," the voice whispered. "Will you marry me?"

There was a silence for at least ten seconds – Maggie, slowly digesting the momentous implication of the question I had just asked and me, desperately wondering where the voice had come from, but gloriously thrilled that some ethereal spirit, frustrated at my reticence to take the opportunity that was now so glaringly obvious, took the matter into its own hands and did it for me. "Yes," said Maggie, simply.

That evening, we visited the best jewellers in the biggest shopping mall and bought the most beautiful engagement ring. We flew back to England five days later without the aid of a plane, anxious, but looking forward so much, to telling everyone the news – especially Maggie's grown up son Paul and daughter Anna. They were as thrilled as we were and they welcomed me into the family with open, loving arms. The apple of our eyes, however, was undoubtedly Anna's six-year-old daughter, Charlotte and the obvious joy on her face when receiving her new prospective Granddad, was something I will always treasure.

We were married on the 17th April 1999 at the Surbiton Methodist Church and such was the care lavished on us by the heavenly powers above that a rainstorm, which started at noon, was whisked away at 2.30pm – thirty minutes before curtain up – revealing glorious sunshine, only to return with a vengeance at 5.30pm, by which time we were well into the reception. It was the most wonderful day of days with Maggie looking radiant in a beautiful red outfit. The service was a joyous one and the icing on the (wedding?) cake was listening to the glorious, unaccompanied voice of Mike Redway singing *Lark on the Clear Air*. The acoustics of the church lent itself to the beautiful lyrics of the melody and it was without doubt, a moment to remember. So, too, was the reception with Mike again in full song, Maggie and the Girls chipping in with their style of music, Kay Garner vocalising in a more Jazzy style, 60's icon Vince Eager topping the show and all linked together by the great musical sounds of the Mac Poole trio. A wonderful, exciting, unforgettable day and at the end of it all, I knew that I had scooped the greatest prize of my life and for that, I could not be more, or everlastingly, grateful. The knowledge that I had now wrapped the love of a beautiful woman and her adorable family around me convinced me, finally, that this was Fate's way of telling me that my days of being involved with Pontin entertainments were numbered and I should take the decision to accept retirement at the end of the year. It would be the end of an era for both the Company and myself but, happily, the beginning of a new one with my lovely wife.

What of Maggie, however? What was her background and when I tell you, you will realise, as I have done, that her journey through showbusiness far exceeds anything I have ever achieved. To see her home, such is her modesty, you would never guess the remarkable life she has enjoyed in this great business of ours. The only reference to her profession is a framed poster advertising the Cliff Richard 30th anniversary Concert at Wembley in which she appeared with the Vernons Girls and a beautifully framed inscribed poster relating to the 'Solid Gold Rock'n'Roll show' in which they also appeared with Joe Brown and the Bruvvers, Marty Wilde and the Wildcats, Eden Kane and John Leyton. The framed poster was presented to her after her appearance at the London Palladium. The rest of her life's work is hidden in drawers and shelves, hidden from most eyes. Let me enlighten you with a short précis of what she has achieved in the business of making entertainment and surely – one day – a fuller and more in depth description will be published and she will receive the acclaim she so richly deserves.

CHAPTER TWENTY NINE

Maggie Stredder

Maggie was born in Birkenhead, over the water from Liverpool, a long time ago. She swears it was only forty-five years last January but the fact that her birth certificate is chipped on a Tablet of Stone tells us it could be a little longer! Oddly enough, in view of the career she was to follow, neither her Mum nor Dad were particularly musical but Maggie knew from an early age that she had been blessed with a special talent and from the age of nine started piano lessons. This not only enabled her to play well, but also, of equal importance, taught her to read music on sight – an ability that was to pave the way for a long and distinguished vocal career. Shortly after mastering the piano, she decided that she wanted to add singing lessons to her curriculum but her Mother, on a limited budget whilst supporting her daughters ambitions, had to inform her that if she wanted to extend her musical knowledge, she would 'have to pay for it herself'. This Maggie did, but not until she had left school and taken a job in the Treasury Department of Birkenhead Borough Council.

Early in 1957, an advert appeared in the Liverpool Echo that was to totally change her life forever. The headline was 'Can you sing?' and continued... 'Female singers wanted for well-known singing group to work in London. Auditions to be held in Liverpool. Write giving experience.' Maggie replied and within a few days received a reply, inviting her to be at the Bluecoat chambers in Liverpool for an audition. She attended as requested and was offered a job with the

Vernons Girls, a television and recording, sixteen piece song and dance group, sponsored by the world famous football Pools Company that gave them their name. She, of course, accepted and thus entered the glittering world of professional showbusiness.

She was soon to find out that it was not all a world of glamour – discipline and hard training also played a major part in her new life. The girls were governed by the strictest of house rules – a factor that was instrumental in her Mum and Dad finally giving their permission for Maggie to go – and each day, along with the other girls in the group, she attended classes in deportment, make-up, stage craft and fashion. Out of the classroom, particularly when working in London, they were heavily chaperoned with a rod of iron, befitting the pristine image the public had of the girls at that time and since.

Within the first few weeks of joining, the Vernons Girls were contracted to do two shows on a series called the *Six-Five Special*. Regulars on that production were Pete Murray, Josephine Douglas, (boxer) Freddie Mills with music from Don Lang and his Frantic Five. On the very first programme of the new series, a handsome but pimply faced and very nervous singer made his television debut, and from that raw beginning emerged one of the great pop vocalists of the era – Adam Faith! More TV work was to follow for the girls in the shape of a new show called *New Look*, which featured fellow regulars Bruce Forsyth, Des O'Connor, Roy Castle, Joe Baker and Jack Douglas plus dancers Joyce and Lionel Blair – all newcomers to the visual media. It was in no way similar to the Rock'n'Roll format for the *Six-Five Special*, relying instead in the more genteel presentation for song, dance and comedy. It scored high in the ratings, however, and helped make all those who appeared in it (including the Vernons Girls) television stars of the present and indeed the future. If the girls were to achieve fame throughout the country as a vocal/dance group, a decision made by TV Producer, Jack

Good was to turn Maggie into a well-known and perceived personality in her own right.

Early in 1958 the Vernons were contracted to a new conceptional 'pop' programme to be called *Oh Boy!* and during their first meeting with Good, he outlined to the girls a draft of the projected programme, stressing his great hope that what was about to be transmitted, would be a sensation in the field of popular music.

The girls were obviously excited and as he made to take his leave, he pointed his finger at Maggie and said, "And you – don't take your glasses off!"

She was distraught at this instruction, imagining instant relegation to the back row and ultimate dismissal! A few tears were shed in private, for it appeared to her that her career was over, but being too scared to argue, she did as requested. The impact was instant! Within weeks she became instantly recognisable to millions of viewers as the 'girls with the glasses' and received sack-loads of fan mail, made personal appearances and appeared on chat shows as a star. The *Oh Boy!* show, like its predecessors, spawned many of the great names of the late fifties and early sixties including – from the regulars – Marty Wilde and the Wildcats, Lord Rockinghams XI, Neville Taylor and the Cutters, Cuddly Duddly, The Dallas Boys and comperes Jimmy Henney and Tony Hall– and from the guests – Vince Eager, Englebert Humperdinck (then Gerry Dorsey), Shirley Bassey, Billy Fury, Conway Twitty, Jerry Keller, Johnny Cash, Brenda Lee, Gene Vincent and a young man the programme claims to have discovered and placed on the path of everlasting fame – Cliff Richard! It was a wonderful period to be involved in the pop music business and Maggie, along with the majority of most others, was so proud and grateful to have been a part of it.

In time, however, the winds of change blew and Maggie decided to break away from the confines of a larger group to form a vocal/dance duo with friend Jean Ryder. They called themselves The Two-Tones and immediately left on a tour of the American Air Force Bases in Germany, thus giving themselves an ideal platform to learn the intricacies of vocal harmonising on a much smaller scale. The move proved highly successful and on their return to the UK, were offered, and accepted, a summer season headlined by Max Bygraves. Maggie formed a warm friendship with the star entertainer, which remains to this day. In 1962, however, Jean left the act to get married (her new husband was the songwriter who penned many of the great hits recorded by Helen Shapiro, including *Walking Back to Happiness* and Maggie was on her own. She linked up with great mate Lionel Blair and for many months, worked with him in cabaret. When he was given a recording contract, he invited Maggie to join him in the studio to perform backing vocals and, in doing so, she met Nigel Brooks who, with his well-known group of singers, was also in on the session. Nigel was extremely impressed with Maggie's vocal prowess and after enquiring if she read music, (a requisite for backing groups of this calibre), he invited her to join him and she accepted. At the same time, however, she decided to form a second duo, this time with a beautiful girl by the name of Gloria George and they called themselves The Ladybirds (recording a vocal number with the title *Ladybird, Ladybird*). Within weeks of the duo being reformed, they accepted an invitation to appear with Val Doonican on his TV special and, once again, the 'Girl in Glasses' was back on the box! A short time after their television success, Maggie decided to add another voice to the act – increasing the range and achieving a much fuller sound – and recruited her good fried, Barbara Moore. From that moment on, the trio took off and never looked back. They appeared in almost every light entertainment show on TV – there were many – and with every star name of the day – Les Dawson, The Two Ronnies, Morecambe & Wise, Little & Large, Glen Campbell,

'Children in Need', Tommy Cooper, Shirley Bassey, 'The Generation Game', Paul Daniels and many more. By this time, Barbara Moore had left the group and been replaced by Marion Davies and still the work poured in. Listen to all the hit records, too, of that golden era and the backing vocals you will hear supporting the recording artistes, is that of The Ladybirds. Star names like Dusty Springfield, Tom Jones, The Walker Brothers, The Beatles, Wings, Lulu, Rolf Harris, Rod Stewart, Cliff Richard, Demis Roussos, Frankie Vaughan, Bing Crosby, Fred Astaire and others, too numerous to mention. They also recorded with Benny Hill and worked with him for over twenty years on his TV specials. In that time, Maggie and Benny became great friends, ended only by his untimely death in 1992. She was never out of work, both with The Ladybirds and on her own, providing vocal backing on a multitude of TV adverts for such well know brands as Heinz, Esso Petrol, Pepsodent Toothpaste, Murray Mints and Opal Fruits. Each day saw her either in the TV or recording studios, and the 'girl with the glasses' was continually heard and seen by the television and record buying public. Amongst the prestigious and high profile presentations which littered her bulging date book were events like the *Eurovision Song Contest*, once with Sandie Shaw in Vienna, (which she won with *Puppet on a String*), and again with Olivia Newton John in Brighton, (won by Abba with *Waterloo*), *Seaside Special* for the BBC and an incredible *Ten* Royal Command Performances.

Finally (and I've merely skimmed the achievements of this remarkable lady), The Ladybirds have shared the spotlight with every recording star who climbed into the hit parade during a period of nineteen years on the evergreen Top of the Pops – a feat that will never, ever be equalled. Today unbelievably – and thankfully, for otherwise we may never have met – she is still in constant work, still in demand and still receiving standing ovations. She spends time giving a highly amusing but informative talks on her life to interested (and there are many) clubs, and still tours the country – with singing colleagues Sheila Parker and Penny Lightfoot – as the Vernons Girls. Once every eighteen months, they undertake an arduous tour of some seventy engagements (concluding, always at the London Palladium), along with pop luminaries, Marty Wilde and the Wildcats, Joe Brown and the Bruvvers, Eden Kane, John Leyton, plus the Rock'n'Roll backing band Rockin' Horse, and significantly, the theatres are always packed.

Since her momentous decision to turn professional way back in 1957, Maggie has been at the forefront of the very best in light entertainment for the past forty-three years – an amazing record! During the period, so much more was attained but space prohibits my recording each and every achievement. Nevertheless, what I have described will, I am sure, confirm my statement, made earlier, that her life in showbusiness has been remarkable and one day, if I can persuade her, the full, unabridged story will be told. I promise you – it will be well worth reading!

---

*Since completing this book, I finally **did** persuade her and the publication of her autobiography 'Maggie Stredder – The Girl with the Glasses' is now available from Showbiz Publications.*

CHAPTER THIRTY

The End of an Era

Back, however, to my tale, which in terms of showbusiness accomplishment, was rapidly declining. Just before Christmas 1998 at a 'one to one' meeting with Jez King, I made my formal announcement to retire in December 1999 – giving a full twelve months notice. I doubt very much if it surprised him, for his move to transfer the booking of artistes, bands etc to Studio One in Coventry was, I suspect, in anticipation of my retirement, but if truth be known, did much to enforce it. Nevertheless, he was very understanding and sympathetic and we spent time discussing the impact on the business and how we would counteract it. To have finally made the decision and gone public with it was a great weight off my mind, but nevertheless, it was a feeling of much apprehension and not a little fear, to look ahead, knowing that the end was now not a possibility, but a certainty. It was still twelve months in the future and, as such, an age away, but the time flew by with incredible speed. There was no doubt I was now being classed by the 'men in the suits' as a spare part and, in some ways, I could not blame them. What else could they do? Having wielded the power for so many long years and attained a reputation in the business of which I was extremely proud, it felt hollow and empty to go through the motions of day to day existence without the enjoyable pressure of working to a time and budget constriction. Now it was the turn of someone else and although I didn't like it, I had no choice but to accept it. I guess I am no different to any other in a similar position, but to know that does not make the feeling of uselessness any easier to take – a feeling which is very much a mental state.

I worked harder than ever during these final few months and got to the stage where I knew every cobble on the country's motorway system. When recently asked where my office was now situated, I could not help but answer "Somewhere on the M6!" – it was as good, or as bad, as that. On one day's journey during my summer tour, judging the centre's Bluecoat shows, I travelled from Blackpool to Wall Park in Devon, judged the show and took to the road, once again, heading for Camber Sands near Rye, Sussex – a total of six hundred and sixty three miles. Not bad for an old 'un!

The summer season came to a close and the countdown began in earnest. I hoped sincerely that when the day came, I would be allowed to slip out the back door and disappear into the sunset but Janet, my secretary and PA, let slip that something was planned. Nothing grand, she told me, but a few old mates meeting at the Blackpool centre for a glass of vino and a jolly. The date was given to me as Wednesday November 24th 1999 and I promised to be there – under duress! I pressed for details but none were forthcoming – it was a tightly closed shop and even on the morning of the bash, when I finally collared Janet and threatened her with physical damage, the only information I could extract was that they were expecting the numbers attending to lie between thirty and forty – still too many for me to cope with but acceptable nevertheless. So there it was – a few friends, a glass or two of diet coke and maybe, the presentation of a carriage clock to remind me how time flies when you're having fun. Despite the laid back, almost secretive air that surrounded the event, I dreaded the forthcoming 'celebration' knowing that at sometime during the evening, I would be forced on stage to make some sort of response. Belying the fact that I have lived a great deal of my life in the public's view – on many occasion acting as compere – I have never been totally relaxed having to talk for a living. I am told that I do it well but I cannot hide from the fact that, although my outward demeanour is one of calm and confidence, inwardly, I am the keeper of a home for demented butterflies that reside in my stomach and, such is the pain they instil in my gut, I constantly wish to be somewhere else, a million miles away. The one bright spot of the day was the unexpected bonus of having Maggie with me, to hold my hand and stop it shaking. She was knee deep in her nation-wide tour of the UK with the *Solid Gold Rock'n'Roll Show* and it was odds on that she would be on the other side of the country, singing for her supper. To my joy (and hers too) we discovered that not only did she have the Wednesday off but the previous evening the show was in Southport – only forty-five miles away. It was all set then for our night out and I crossed my fingers and wished for a speedy deliverance from what was to come. If only I had been blessed with the gift of foresight, I would have made the short journey to near-by Manchester Airport and fled the country!

The heavy rainsqualls whipped off the Irish Sea driven by the fierce westerly gale that has a permanent home in Blackpool. November is not the ideal month in the resort to spot the holidaymaker and with the residents in possession of the good sense to stay at home, the promenade was deserted. I drove slowly along the wide thoroughfare, Maggie beside me, whilst the windscreen wipers fought a losing battle with the elements. I pulled up at the barrier, stretched, imposingly across the main gate of the Pontin Centre and I wondered, again for the millionth time in my career, whether the thick pole had been erected to keep those people out who wanted to come in – or to keep in those people who wanted to get out? I expected to be greeted by a member of the security squad who religiously asked me each time I approached – despite my thirty-two years with the company – "May I see your ID card?" and when produced, and assuring him that I was not an industrial spy from Butlins, Haven or Warners, always followed up with the line that forever set my teeth on edge, (prompting a rude answer). "Do you know where to go, sir?" He knew me so well and I knew him, but it was a game we had to play. The wind was taken from my sails, however, when a familiar figure loomed out of the driving rain. The general Manager, David Roberts, bode us welcome and raised the portcullis, beckoning us to follow his vehicle and we convoyed to the Princes Theatre. I climbed the few steps to the main entrance and I will never forget the sight as the doors swung open revealing, not the forty or fifty pals I had expected, but what looked like hundreds of thousands (it was actually nearer three hundred). What followed was a blur. People came to me with hands outstretched, hugging me and I kissed every face in sight – which scared off a few of the male Bluecoats who 'dressed' the occasion. My old adversary, Graham Henry, was in charge of the microphone and despite the fact that he, more than any other Entertainments Manager was responsible for my rapidly reclining hairline, insisted that he compered the event – which he did brilliantly – as always. I recall through the haze, being dragged onto the stage and found myself the (unwilling) subject of a *This is Your Life* replication, linked together by Jez King. Like the real life subjects, I was completely overwhelmed when the curtains rolled back to reveal my dear sister Kath, who had travelled from Edinburgh to be part of the evening. The guest appearances rolled on – Shane Richie, who had journeyed from London to pay his tribute, Chris Gosling – his companion, road manager and ex-Entertainment Manager, the lovely Kenny Baker – who starred as R2 D2 in the film *Star Wars* and who I used with his partner Jacky, when they performed as the Mini Tones, Mike Lancaster – one of my favourite funny men, hypnotist, Van Elliot – also an ex-Entertainments Manager and Frank Chislett, leader of the Amazing Bavarian Stompers. There was also an embarrassing tribute relayed over the sound system from that great guy – Les Dennis. To top it all off – I was dragged into an excruciatingly painful version of The Blues Brothers by Entertainments Managers Sean Aldrige and Simon Bunting and I prayed (thankfully answered!), that no video cameras were in use. In fact, one had been commissioned but at the vital moment went on the blink, which only goes to prove that if you pray hard enough, sometimes it really can work!

More was to follow and when the lovely Gerry Johnson, who was primed to take over some of my duties in the future and was no mean singer, emerged in the spotlight to sing *I (we) Will Always Love You*, tears were not far away. I was feeling so proud that I had suppressed the ultimate emotion but was forced to give in when, again, I was dragged onto the stage and led by Entertainments Manager Carol Hartwell, was surrounded by twelve of her lovely warm, bright and dedicated Bluecoats with whom, along with all the others, I have shared so much joy working with over these many, many years. Together they sang with all their hearts, the Tina Turner hit *Simply the Best* and as I looked down at their faces, glowing with the meaning of the words they were emitting – at that precise moment I realised, finally, it was all over!

Emotion overtook me and as Maggie joined me on the platform and the whole room rose to its feet – the tears finally flowed. Memories of the wonderful years flooded my mind – of the stars I had met and the big names I had made. The happy times filled with laughter and the not-so-happy moments when there was tears. I looked again at the kids circled around my feet and I felt so much love for them, so much gratitude for the life I had been blessed with, involving them and the wonderful world of showbusiness. I looked out into the audience filled with friends, distant past and present, and I embraced them. It was a moment to treasure – the memory of a lifetime. I was filled with great sadness and immense joy and in looking back to the hazy years of long, long ago and recalling my long journey through showbusiness, I could not help but reflect that my life had become 'One Good Turn' and now, I can only wait for the encore! Maybe – one day – I'll tell you about it.

FINIS